OXFORD WORLD'S CLASSICS

GUIDE TO THE LAKES

WILLIAM WORDSWORTH was born on 7 April 1770 at Cockermouth in the north of England's Lake District. After education at Hawkshead Grammar School and St John's College, Cambridge, he lived an unsettled life in France, London, and the West Country, meeting radical thinkers and in his writings identifying himself with their cause. *Lyrical Ballads*, a joint enterprise with Coleridge, was published anonymously in September 1798, after which Wordsworth started to write his autobiographical poem, *The Prelude*. In December 1799 he returned to settle in the Lake District, initially at Dove Cottage in Grasmere and subsequently at Rydal Mount. With his *Guide to the Lakes* (1810–35) and many poems set in the local landscape, Wordsworth came to be recognized as the poet of the Lake District. In 1843, Wordsworth was appointed Poet Laureate, and died seven years later on 23 April 1850.

SAEKO YOSHIKAWA is Professor of English at Kobe City University of Foreign Studies, Japan. Her publications include *William Wordsworth and the Invention of Tourism, 1820–1900* (Ashgate, 2014) and *William Wordsworth and Modern Travel: Railways, Motorcars and the Lake District, 1830–1940* (Liverpool University Press, 2020). She has also published a collection of Edward Thomas's poems translated into Japanese.

OXFORD WORLD'S CLASSICS

For over 100 years Oxford World's Classics have brought readers closer to the world's great literature. Now with over 700 titles—from the 4,000-year-old myths of Mesopotamia to the twentieth century's greatest novels—the series makes available lesser-known as well as celebrated writing.

The pocket-sized hardbacks of the early years contained introductions by Virginia Woolf, T. S. Eliot, Graham Greene, and other literary figures which enriched the experience of reading. Today the series is recognized for its fine scholarship and reliability in texts that span world literature, drama and poetry, religion, philosophy, and politics. Each edition includes perceptive commentary and essential background information to meet the changing needs of readers.

OXFORD WORLD'S CLASSICS

WILLIAM WORDSWORTH

Guide to the Lakes

Edited with an Introduction and Notes by
SAEKO YOSHIKAWA

OXFORD
UNIVERSITY PRESS

OXFORD
UNIVERSITY PRESS

Great Clarendon Street, Oxford, OX2 6DP,
United Kingdom

Oxford University Press is a department of the University of Oxford.
It furthers the University's objective of excellence in research, scholarship,
and education by publishing worldwide. Oxford is a registered trade mark of
Oxford University Press in the UK and in certain other countries

Editorial material © Saeko Yoshikawa 2022

The moral rights of the author have been asserted

First published as an Oxford World's Classics paperback 2022

Impression: 1

Published in the United States of America by Oxford University Press
198 Madison Avenue, New York, NY 10016, United States of America

British Library Cataloguing in Publication Data

Data available

Library of Congress Control Number: 2022943951

ISBN 978-0-19-884809-7

Printed and bound in the UK by
Clays Ltd, Elcograf S.p.A.

Links to third party websites are provided by Oxford in good faith and
for information only. Oxford disclaims any responsibility for the materials
contained in any third party website referenced in this work.

CONTENTS

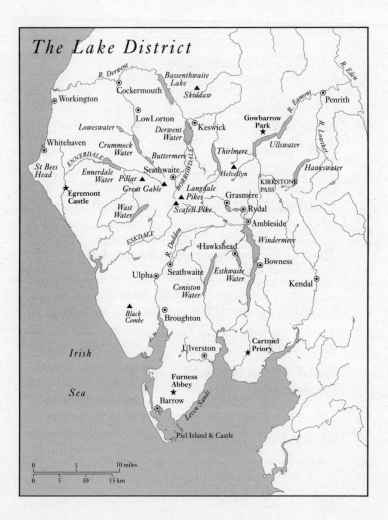

The Lake District

R. Derwent

Workington

Cockermouth

Bassenthwaite Lake

Skiddaw

LowLorton

Gowbarrow Park

R. Eamont

Penrith

R. Eden

Loweswater

Derwent Water

Keswick

Ullswater

R. Lowther

Whitehaven

Crummock Water

Buttermere

Thirlmere

Haweswater

St Bees Head

ENNERDALE

Ennerdale Water

Pillar

Great Gable

BORROWDALE

Helvellyn

KIRKSTONE PASS

Egremont Castle

Seathwaite

Langdale Pikes

Grasmere

Scafell Pike

Rydal

Wast Water

Ambleside

ESKDALE

R. Duddon

Hawkshead

Windermere

Ulpha

Seathwaite

Esthwaite Water

Bowness

Coniston Water

Kendal

Black Combe

Broughton

Irish Sea

Ulverston

Cartmel Priory

Furness Abbey

Barrow

Leven Sands

Piel Island & Castle

0   5   10 miles

0   5   10   15 km

ABBREVIATIONS

Full bibliographical information is given in the Select Bibliography.

Barker	Juliet Barker, *Wordsworth: A Life*.
CEY	Mark Reed, *Wordsworth: The Chronology of the Early Years, 1770–1799*.
CL	*Letters of Samuel Taylor Coleridge*, 6 vols.
CMY	Mark Reed, *Wordsworth: The Chronology of the Middle Years, 1800–1815*.
EdS	William Wordsworth, *Guide to the Lakes*, ed. Ernest De Selincourt.
IF	*Fenwick Notes of William Wordsworth*, ed. Jared Curtis (1993).
Journals	Dorothy Wordsworth, *Journals*, ed. Ernest De Selincourt, 2 vols.
LEY	*Letters of William and Dorothy Wordsworth: The Early Years, 1787–1805*.
Lindop	Grevel Lindop, *A Literary Guide to the Lake District* (2015).
LLY	*Letters of William and Dorothy Wordsworth: The Later Years, 1821–1853*, 4 vols.
LMY	*Letters of William and Dorothy Wordsworth: The Middle Years, 1806–1820*, 2 vols.
LSN	*Letters of William and Dorothy Wordsworth: A Supplement of New Letters*.
McCracken	David McCracken, *Wordsworth and the Lake District*.
Moorman	*William Wordsworth: A Biography*.
Poems	*Poems of William Wordsworth . . . Reading Texts from the Cornell Wordsworth*, 3 vols.
PrW	*Prose Works of William Wordsworth*, ed. W. J. B. Owen and J. W. Smyser, 3 vols.
PW	*Poetical Works of Wordsworth*, ed. Ernest De Selincourt, rev. Helen Darbishire, 5 vols.
RCDE	Nicholas Mason et al. (eds), *William Wordsworth's Guide to the Lakes: A Romantic Circles Digital Edition*.
Reed	Mark Reed, *A Bibliography of William Wordsworth, 1787–1930*, 2 vols.

LIST OF ILLUSTRATIONS

All of these images are taken from Joseph Wilkinson's *Select Views in Cumberland, Westmoreland, and Lancashire* (1810), and reproduced by the kind permission of the Wordsworth Trust, Dove Cottage, Grasmere. The captions follow Wilkinson's List of 'Contents'.

INTRODUCTION

WHAT we now call Wordsworth's *Guide to the Lakes* is in fact the fifth, 1835 edition of the book, the final version written by the poet. It has four preceding versions: one anonymously published as the letterpress for a large folio volume (1810), another as an appendix to a poetical volume (1820), and two independent editions (1822, 1823). Furthermore, in 1842 Wordsworth allowed his text to be incorporated into an extended volume compiled by the local publishers Hudson and Nicholson in Kendal, which went through five editions until 1859. In addition to these ten editions, Wordsworth's *Guide* was widely extracted, adapted, and referenced throughout the nineteenth and early twentieth century. More than any other publication and for almost two hundred years, Wordsworth's *Guide* has shaped tourism in the English Lake District and modern attitudes towards the natural landscape.

Wordsworth's *Guide* is not a mere tourist guide in any routine sense; as is clearly stated in the opening, its principal object is to 'furnish a Guide or Companion for the *Minds* of Persons of taste, and feeling for Landscape, who might be inclined to explore the District of the Lakes with that degree of attention to which its beauty may fairly lay claim' (p. 4). The book accordingly has two aspects: practical information for tourists, and more philosophical reflections on how we should relate to landscape and the environment. The most influential observation in the *Guide* is arguably its claim that the Lake District is 'a sort of national property, in which every man has a right and interest who has an eye to perceive and a heart to enjoy' (p. 68). This notion provided a rationale for the foundation of the National Trust in 1895 and the establishment of the Lake District National Park in 1951. The 2017 nomination document for the Lake District as a World Heritage site quoted Wordsworth's statement about 'national property' and cited his contribution to 'the idea that landscape has a value, and that everyone has a right to appreciate and enjoy it'. In the twenty-first century we can see how Wordsworth's *Guide* has had far-reaching influence on the 'modern concept of legally-protected landscapes' and sustainable tourism.[1]

---

[1] UNESCO, Executive Summary. https://whc.unesco.org/en/list/422.

As Wordsworth opposed the construction of the Kendal and Windermere Railway (1844–5), it is often assumed that he was also hostile to tourism. However, he recognized that tourism was the Lake District's 'staple' industry, and that protecting the region's 'beauty and its character of retirement' would be vital for promoting and sustaining tourism in years to come (p. 137). To that end, his *Guide* aims to teach us how best we can 'worthily enjoy' the Lake District with due respect for its natural beauty and quietness and without upsetting the fragile relationship between human beings and nature. Wordsworth's writing reflects the development of tourism in the Lake District, and also does much to encourage modern ideas of sustainable tourism.

A Brief History of Lake District Tourism, 1750–1810

Lake District tourism began a few decades before Wordsworth's birth (7 April 1770) and developed rapidly during his lifetime thanks to the vogue for the picturesque, improvement of roads, and the arrival of railways. The Vale of Keswick's appeal to early visitors was encouraged by William Bellers's engravings of the area (1752), John Dalton's *Descriptive Poem* (1755), and John Brown's *Description of the Lake at Keswick* (1767). Extracted in many later guidebooks and travel books, Dalton and Brown brought Keswick's romantic scenery to public attention and set the fashion for describing landscapes in picturesque terms.

While Dalton and Brown were Cumbrian natives, the poet Thomas Gray was one of the first tourists to travel to the Lakes specifically for sightseeing. Primed by reading Dalton and Brown, Gray made a tour in October 1769, basing himself at Keswick for six out of his ten days in the Lakes, and making forays to Borrowdale, Grange, Lodore Falls, Crow Park, Derwentwater, Castlerigg, and Bassenthwaite. Gray's travel journal, originally taking the form of letters to Thomas Warton, was posthumously published in William Mason's 1775 edition of the *Poems of Thomas Gray*. Through this volume, and through excerpts in Thomas West's guide and numerous other travel books and articles, Gray's account was widely circulated, providing a model for prose writing about Lake District scenery. His terror at the wild craggy landscape of Borrowdale has often been ridiculed by later writers, whereas his description of the paradisal view of Grasmere from Dunmail Raise has been much admired: 'Not a single red tile, no flaring gentleman's house or garden-wall, break in upon the repose of this little unsuspected paradise'.[2] With these words, Gray initiated the idea of Grasmere as an idyllic sanctuary at the centre of the Lake District,[3] and anticipated Wordsworth's 'almost visionary mountain republic' of independent 'estatesmen' (pp. 51, 67); 'how much the charm of what *was*, depended upon what was *not*' (p. 52), remarks Wordsworth, making Gray's description a cornerstone of his argument for protecting the Lake District landscape from unnecessary development.

Also inspired by Dalton and Brown's descriptions, the lawyer William Hutchinson made a Lake District tour in 1773 and published *An Excursion to the Lakes* in the following year. As a landscape connoisseur, Hutchinson compared three lakes, Windermere, Derwentwater, and Ullswater, with reference to the paintings of Claude Lorrain, Salvator Rosa, and Poussin. More energetic and adventurous than Gray, Hutchinson went boating on Derwentwater in the moonlight and climbed Skiddaw in a storm. Hutchinson's lively and evocative descriptions and his spirited personal response to landscape would prove influential for Wordsworth's *Guide*.

When Thomas West published his *Guide to the Lakes* in 1778, the Lake District was beginning to attract lovers of picturesque scenery. Covering a much wider area than Hutchinson's and giving practical information about approaches, routes, and road conditions, West's volume was in many ways the first modern tourist guide to the region. He recommended approaching the Lake District from the south (by crossing the Lancaster Sands, then travelling from Furness, along Windermere, up to Keswick) for the aesthetic effect of moving gradually from beautiful to sublime landscapes (Wordsworth would follow West in this respect). West also established a way of travelling through and seeing the Lake District by visiting 'viewing stations', where tourists could view the landscape through a 'Claude glass'. Sometimes called 'Gray's glass' after the poet, this small convex mirror was an indispensable item for picturesque travellers, who

---

[2] William Mason, ed., *The Poems of Mr. Gray, to which are Prefixed Memoirs of his Life and Writings* (York, 1775), p. 365.

[3] John Murdoch (preface), *The Discovery of the Lake District: A Northern Arcadia and Its Uses* (Victoria and Albert Museum, 1984), p. 16.

would turn their backs on the scene to enjoy the framed view reflected in a tinted mirror. West advised travellers where to take views and how to appreciate them, citing earlier visitors including Brown, Hutchinson, and Gray.[4] In later editions of West's guide this material was included in the appendices, amounting to an anthology of early writings on the Lake District.[5] With extensive revisions by William Cockin, West's guide reached its eleventh edition by 1821; it proved widely influential, particularly when the protracted war with France (1793–1815) deflected tourists from European to domestic locations.

Alongside West was William Gilpin, another pioneer of the picturesque. A native of Cumbria, Gilpin was a perceptive writer, whose *Observations, Relative Chiefly to Picturesque Beauty, Made in the Year 1772: on Several Parts of England; Particularly the Mountains, and Lakes of Cumberland, and Westmoreland* (1786) attended to subtle shifts of light and shade, how the surface of water appears, changes of weather, and ephemeral phenomena such as fogs and mists—in all of these ways Gilpin foreshadowed Wordsworth. But Gilpin's obsession with the picturesque inevitably proved a limitation, and soon provoked satirical reactions, including James Plumptre's *The Lakers* (1798), William Combe and Thomas Rowlandson's *The Tour of Doctor Syntax* (1812), and Wordsworth's 'The Brothers' (1800):

> These Tourists, Heaven preserve us! needs must live
> A profitable life: some glance along,
> Rapid and gay, as if the earth were air,
> And they were butterflies to wheel about
> Long as their summer lasted; some, as wise,
> Upon the forehead of a jutting crag
> Sit perch'd with book and pencil on their knee,
> And look and scribble, scribble on and look,
> Until a man might travel twelve stout miles,
> Or reap an acre of his neighbour's corn . . . (1–10)

[4] Peter Crosthwaite's *Seven Maps of the Lakes* (1783) shows West's stations with several other pieces of information, helping tourists to travel with West's guide.
[5] Norman Nicholson, *The Lakers: The Adventures of the First Tourists* (Hale, 1955), p. 63.

Carelessly 'glancing along', none of these tourists actually settle for long enough to contemplate and experience the landscape they have come to enjoy.

It was time for a change. In *A Fortnight's Ramble to the Lakes* (1792) Joseph Budworth had implicitly criticized picturesque tourists by declaring that he would not use West's guide. Avoiding the well-worn routes to West's viewing stations, Budworth set off up the mountains, ascending Helm Crag, Coniston Old Man, Helvellyn, and Skiddaw, thereby becoming a pioneer fell-walker. At Buttermere he 'discovered' and brought to public attention the rustic beauty of 'the Maid of Buttermere'. Budworth's book was effectively a straw in the wind, and soon others would follow him in quest of new ways of enjoying the Lake District.[6]

Wordsworth's Guide and Lake District Tourism

The vogue for the picturesque attracted many artists to the Lake District, including Thomas Gainsborough, Joseph Farington, Francis Towne, J. M. W. Turner, William Green, and John Constable. In 1777 Farington travelled in the footsteps of Thomas Gray and published a set of twenty views of the sites Gray had visited. Originally issued separately in the 1780s, Farington's views were later compiled into a single volume, *Views of the Lakes &c. in Cumberland and Westmorland* (1789). In publishing this volume, Farington accompanied his plates with letterpress—that is, verbal descriptions of the scenes depicted—to enhance the book's appeal. This form of publication anticipated the format of Joseph Wilkinson's *Select Views in Cumberland, Westmoreland, and Lancashire* (1810), and it is an interesting coincidence that the anonymous letterpress for Farington's volume was written by William Cookson, Wordsworth's maternal uncle.[7]

---

[6] For a more detailed history of how the Lake District was 'discovered' by artists and writers and how tourism developed there in the eighteenth century, see Peter Bicknell, ed., *The Illustrated Wordsworth's Guide to the Lakes* (Webb & Bower, 1984) and *The Picturesque Scenery of the Lake District, 1752–1855: A Bibliographical Study* (St Paul's Bibliographies, 1990); Murdoch, *Discovery of the Lake District*; and Cecilia Powell and Stephen Hebron, *Savage Grandeur and Noblest Thought: Discovering the Lake District 1750–1820* (Wordsworth Trust, 2010).

[7] Powell and Hebron, *Savage Grandeur*, 65. Cookson's letterpress combines topographical and historical information with 'lyrical description'.

Farington's *Views* proved a popular souvenir for visitors to the Lakes for more than two decades; Crosthwaite, the map publisher at Keswick, remarked in 1806 that it sold 'better than ever'.[8] Several other similar volumes appeared, including Peter Holland's *Select Views* (1792) and John Smith's *Views of the Lakes* (1795). Wordsworth's artist friend William Green of Ambleside was also working on a similar project that would result in *Seventy Eight Studies from Nature* (1809) and *A Description of Sixty Studies from Nature* (1810).

Joseph Wilkinson's plan was to publish his own volume of select views consisting of forty-eight soft-ground etchings, based on drawings he had made during his stay in Ormathwaite under Skiddaw, just north of Keswick.[9] While his forty-eight plates cover a large part of the Lake District, many views were taken from the vicinity of Keswick. When Wilkinson invited Wordsworth to write the letterpress for his forthcoming publication the poet was initially reluctant to do so as the *Select Views* would compete with Green's volume (*PrW* ii. 124). Eventually, however, he agreed and by the end of June 1809 had started drafting the letterpress, now recognized as the earliest version of what would become the *Guide to the Lakes*. Wordsworth had accepted this commission partly for financial reasons, but he also had a longstanding interest in this kind of writing: back in August 1807 he was reported to be 'preparing a manual to guide travellers in their tour amongst the Lakes' (Moorman ii. 158). It is uncertain whether the manual Wordsworth had been preparing in 1807 was the prototype of the text he was now working on for Wilkinson, but evidently the idea of such a text had already occurred to him. Within five months, by November 1809, he had completed the introductory essay: this text would later become a core part of his *Guide* where it is titled 'Description of the Scenery of the Lakes'. In a letter to Lady Beaumont Wordsworth says that he wanted 'to give a model of the manner in which topographical descriptions ought to be executed, in order to their being either useful or intelligible, by evolving truly and distinctly one appearance from another' (*LMY* i. 404); Dorothy Wordsworth speaks of her brother's description as 'the only regular

    [8] John R. Murray, *A Tour of the English Lakes with Thomas Gray and Joseph Farington RA* (Frances Lincoln, 2011), p. 59.

    [9] For details of the production of *Select Views*, see Moorman ii. 155–64; Nicholas Mason, Paul Westover, and Shannon Stimpson, 'Introduction' and Nicholas Mason, 'The Serial Publication of *Select Views*', in *RCDE*.

and . . . *scientific* account of the present and past state and appearance of the country that has yet appeared' (*LMY* i. 372). Unsatisfied with existing accounts, Wordsworth had determined to show how the Lake District landscape was formed by long interactions between human beings and nature—and to advise on how we should protect it for future generations.

Following the introduction, Wordsworth worked on Section I and Section II, roughly corresponding respectively to the first paragraph of 'Miscellaneous Observations' and 'Directions and Information for Tourists' in the 1835 edition of the *Guide*.[10] He was still at work when publication of Wilkinson's *Select Views* started in January 1810. The forty-eight plates were to be issued by subscription in twelve monthly instalments; in principle, four plates were to be distributed on the first day of each month,[11] accompanied by a four-page leaflet of unsigned letterpress—and no more: Wordsworth's text was cut at every fourth page regardless of content and even in the middle of a sentence (Reed i. 33). In this serial publication, Wordsworth's text was evidently of secondary significance. At least one subscriber, however, was an enthusiastic reader; immediately after the fifth distribution of plates on 1 May 1810, Lady Beaumont sent a letter of thanks to Wordsworth, who promptly replied with gratitude:

I am very happy that you have read the Introduction with so much pleasure, and must thank you for your kindness in telling me of it. I thought the part about the Cottages well-done; and also liked a sentence where I transport the Reader to the top of one of the Mountains, or rather to the Cloud chosen for this station, and give a sketch of the impressions which the Country might be supposed to make on a feeling mind, contemplating its appearance before it was inhabited.[12]

The verbal 'sketch' about the uninhabited era of the Lake District was included in the pages distributed on 1 March, and the 'part about the Cottages', on 1 May. The alacrity of this correspondence between Lady Beaumont and Wordsworth suggests their shared excitement about the poet's new mode of writing.[13]

[10] Section II of *Select Views* is reproduced in Appendix I.

[11] Due to an accident to the plate of Furness Abbey, the August instalment included only three plates, while in September five plates were included. For more detail, see the Chronology of the Serialization of *Select Views* compiled by Mason at the *RCDE* website.

[12] WW and DW to Lady Beaumont, 10 May 1810 (*LMY* i. 404).

[13] Lady Beaumont might have read Wordsworth's 'Introduction' in manuscript, as surmised by Mason ('The Serial Publication of *Select Views*', paragraph 8).

Wordsworth's 'Introduction' (thirty-four pages in all) was pub-
lished in eight monthly instalments between January and August
1810, and was followed by Section I, 'Of the Best Time for Visiting
the Lakes' (two pages) in September. The untitled Section II,
a sequence of tours in the Lake District, was not yet finished, how-
ever, as Wordsworth was irked that '[he could] not do the thing in
[his] own way'.[14] Eventually he lost interest in this commissioned
work, and in November subscribers were advised that 'the letterpress
has been delayed and will be included in the next number' (Reed i.
33). It was only with the help of Dorothy Wordsworth, who 'com-
pose[d] a description or two' (*LMY* i. 449), that the text of Section II
(six pages) was eventually finished and issued with the last instalment
of the plates on 1 December 1810.

While Dorothy helped finish the final section for Wilkinson's vol-
ume, Wordsworth was thinking about publishing a more substantial
tourist guide of his own. He had actually brooded over the plan for
some time: in November 1809, Dorothy remarked that 'if he were to
write a Guide to the Lakes and prefix this preface [i.e. the Introduction
for Wilkinson's *Select Views*], it would sell better, and bring him more
money than any of his higher labours'. She adds that Wordsworth
himself '[had] some thoughts of doing this' (*LMY* i. 372). After the
publication of *Select Views*, Wordsworth worked on a new expanded
guide between September 1811 and November 1812 (*PrW* ii. 127–9).
This draft 'Guide to the Lakes', adopting the text from *Select Views*,
combined a general introduction with descriptions of all parts of the
Lake District.

In the letterpress for *Select Views*, Wordsworth had tended to focus
on 'unfrequented paths . . . out of the common road' (p. 120) such as
Langdale, Blea Tarn, Buttermere, Crummock, Wasdale, Scale Force,
Ennerdale, Scafell, Great Gable, Styhead, Grisedale, and Brothers
Water. In a similar vein, in his newly projected draft guide of 1811–12,
he added accounts of a walk from Coniston to Seathwaite via Walna
Scar, the Duddon Valley, Yewdale, Tilberthwaite, Hawkshead, Borrow-
dale, and Furness. By recommending excursions that were only

[14] W.W. to M.W. [22 July 1810], *LSN* 25. Wordsworth's verbal descriptions of specific
places are not always congruent with the visual renditions by Wilkinson; and the forty-
eight prints were originally issued in a different order from that given in the table of
contents. For the order of Wilkinson's plates, their publication dates, and for the relation
between the text and the plates, see the note to *Select Views*, reproduced in Appendix I.

accessible on foot or horseback (as opposed to horse-drawn coaches), he attempted to lure tourists onto less-frequented scenic routes. Of the Duddon Valley, for instance, he remarks that it 'lies wholly out of the beaten track, but nothing is risked in recommending it to the Traveller of taste & feeling' (*PrW* ii. 298). Indeed, the role of a guide, in his view, was to turn travellers' attention to something 'deeper' and less discernible, that might 'easily escape the notice of the cursory Spectator' (p. 107)—as in these remarks about Yewdale:

Upon [the traveller's] entrance into this little valley, I would willingly afford him the help of my own memory so that he might hear, as I have done, its brook murmuring in deeper stillness and see its circle of woods and dewy fields with the first dimness of Evening settled upon them. (*PrW* ii. 313)

In this sketch of 'murmuring' amid 'the first dimness of Evening', the new, Wordsworthian note is clearly heard. The 1811–12 draft guide thus included several evocative passages, intriguing episodes, and personal responses—but the project was abandoned unfinished. Towards the end of 1812 Lord Lonsdale's offer of an annual pension solved Wordsworth's financial problems, enabling him to turn his attention to the completion of one of his 'higher labours': *The Excursion* (*PrW* ii. 130). A few passages of the 1811–12 draft guide were later incorporated in the endnote to the Duddon Sonnets volume of 1820, but the full manuscript had to wait until 1974 when W. J. B. Owen and Jane Smyser reproduced it as 'An Unpublished Tour' in the *Prose Works of William Wordsworth*.[15]

Seven years would pass before Wordsworth returned to his *Guide* material, and those seven years saw momentous changes. In 1814 the Napoleonic Wars came to a temporary end, and Wordsworth published *The Excursion*. Despite some bad reviews, the poem soon began to attract attention and was quoted in guidebooks such as T. H. Horne's *The Lakes of Lancashire, Westmorland, and Cumberland* (1816), illustrated by Joseph Farington; John Robinson's *A Guide to the Lakes* (1819); and T. H. A. Fielding and John Walton's *A Picturesque Tour of the English Lakes* (1821). Also included were excerpts from Wordsworth's 'The Brothers', 'To Joanna', 'Nutting', 'Fidelity', 'The Idle Shepherd-Boys', and 'Composed at —— Castle' (that is, the

---

[15] Another unpublished essay, 'The Sublime and the Beautiful', is also considered a part of this draft guidebook and included in *PrW*, vol. 2.

sonnet beginning 'Degenerate Douglas!'). By connecting Wordsworth's poems and places, these volumes encouraged travellers to see Lakeland landscapes interwoven with his poetry, preparing for a new mode of tourism that was shaped more by literary texts than by eighteenth-century picturesque aesthetics. A new Wordsworthian 'taste and feeling for landscape' was gradually being cultivated.

When Wordsworth published a second version of his guide in April 1820, it was as an appendix to *The River Duddon, a Series of Sonnets*, containing his description of topographical and historical aspects of the Lake District from *Select Views* (1810). Titled 'A Topographical Description of the Country of the Lakes, in the North of England', this was not at all like the draft he had been working on in 1811–12. Stripped of tourist-friendly information, routes, and descriptions of specific places, the 1820 version was primarily intended to help readers understand the poems in the volume. On the other hand, the thirty-three sonnets on the River Duddon served as a kind of poetical guide to the valley; much as *The Excursion* had beckoned travellers to Langdale and Grasmere, this sonnet sequence invited them to the remote valley of Dunnerdale, encouraging them to trace the course of the river with Wordsworth's sonnets in hand. In 1867, James Payn asserted that 'there is no better guide-book for even the most prosaic to take with him' than *The River Duddon*.[16]

The poems and 'Topographical Description' in the Duddon volume enjoyed good reviews, and this probably encouraged Wordsworth to prepare his first separate edition of the guide—*A Description of the Scenery of the Lakes, in the North of England*, published in June 1822. Coming after the *Select Views* letterpress and the 1820 'Topographical Description', this book was effectively a third edition. Compact, reasonably priced, equipped with a folding map and 'Directions, and Information for the Tourist', this stand-alone volume was intended for practical use. Wordsworth was already regarded as the poet of the Lake District, and readers had also been primed by travel books and guides that quoted his writings. The 1822 edition sold rapidly and within a year all 500 copies had been purchased. By December 1822 Wordsworth was already thinking of a revised edition. This was

---

[16] James Payn, *Lakes in Sunshine* (1867), p. 67. For details of how the Duddon Sonnets promoted tourism in the Duddon Valley, see Saeko Yoshikawa, 'The Duddon Sonnets and Duddon Tourism', *The Wordsworth Circle* 51.1 (2020), pp. 104–19.

published in June 1823, although sales were disappointingly slow: interest had apparently been satisfied. Longman advertised the book each summer and it took twelve years to shift all 1,000 copies.[17]

Still, in 1835, when stock of the fourth edition of 1823 had almost sold out, Wordsworth again thought of preparing a new revised volume. While the previous four editions had been issued by London-based publishers, it struck him that this new one should be printed and published locally. He wrote to the Kendal booksellers Hudson and Nicholson: 'this little Book would have a considerable sale, if any Publisher Resident in the Country would undertake to circulate it through the Lake district, and in the leading Towns of the North' (*LLY* iii. 48). He concluded urgently: 'Let me have your answer as soon as you can, as I wish to go to press instantly in order to secure the advantage of the sale of the approaching season'. This was 7 May 1835 and, within two and a half months, a fifth edition, now titled *A Guide through the District of the Lakes in the North of England*, was published at Kendal by Hudson and Nicholson.[18] This new book was structurally different from the previous ones: the practical part, 'Directions and Information for the Tourist', was expanded and moved from the end of the book to the front, before the 'Description of the Scenery of the Lakes', which was subdivided into three sections: 'View of the Country as Formed by Nature', 'Aspect of the Country as Affected by Its Inhabitants', and 'Changes, and Rules of Taste for Preventing Their Bad Effects'. Following these two parts were 'Miscellaneous Observations', 'Excursions to the Top of Scawfell and on the Banks of Ullswater', and 'Ode: The Pass of Kirkstone' (the publishers also inserted, 'with permission of the Author', an 'Itinerary of the Lakes'). The book was advertised in six local papers at Kendal, Carlisle, and Whitehaven and by late September 1838, local sales amounted to nearly 1,000 copies of a print run of 1,500 (while about eighty were sold by Longman in

---

[17] Reed i. 73, W. J. B. Owen, 'Costs, Sales, and Profits of Longman's Editions of Wordsworth', *Library*, 5th series, 12 (1957), 93–107 (p. 103).

[18] Hudson and Nicholson also ran a paper-mill in Burneside, two miles north of Kendal; accordingly, the 1835 *Guide* was printed on locally made paper. Mark Cropper, *The Leaves We Write On: James Cropper: A History in Paper-Making* (Ellergreen Press, 2004), p. 25.

London by that time).[19] With focused marketing, the 1835 edition achieved a remarkable commercial success.

While the 1823 edition had taken twelve years to sell 1,000 copies, the 1835 edition sold the same number in three. What was the difference between them? Enhanced practicality would be one answer: with the publisher's 'Itinerary' giving information about distances and inns, the fifth edition was a book to be used, and was accordingly titled '*A Guide*'. One newspaper review commended the revised 'Directions to Tourists' as 'both copious and instructive', recommending the *Guide* as 'a valuable acquisition to every tourist' (*Westmorland Gazette*, 25 July 1835). Another remarked: 'This Guide, besides possessing the advantage of the most approved routes and an excellent itinerary, which has been altered and much improved in this edition, will supply the rambler with a highly poetical description of the various beauties of the Lake district' (*Carlisle Patriot*, 15 August 1835).

Given that the *Carlisle Patriot* commended the book's 'poetical description', strong sales of the 1835 edition might also be attributed to Wordsworth's growing reputation as the poet of the Lakes who had made his home at Rydal Mount. Edward Baines's *A Companion to the Lakes* (1829, 1830), *Leigh's Guide* (1830, 1832) and Thomas Rose's *Westmorland, Cumberland, Durham, and Northumberland* (1832) were important in the promotion of Wordsworth's presence in the Lake District—the first two featured Rydal Mount as a tourist attraction, and Rose's book was remarkable for including numerous poems by Wordsworth. After the 'Topographical Description' appeared in the Duddon Volume (1820), Wordsworth's accounts of the Lake District had been referenced or extracted in travel articles and guidebooks, including John Brigg's *Lonsdale Magazine*, vol. 3 (1822), Charles Cooke's *Tourist and Traveller's Companion to the Lakes* (1827), John Wilson's 'Christopher at the Lakes' (1832), John Robinson's *Views of the Lakes in the North of England* (1833), and a magazine *The Mirror of Literature* (1835). Before the fifth edition of 1835, then, Wordsworth's 'Description of the Scenery of the Lakes', the main part of the *Guide to the Lakes*, had already been widely cited in tourist literature.

---

[19] Reed i. 104, Owen, 'Costs, Sales, and Profits', p. 106.

A third reason for the success of the 1835 edition was yet another practical feature. In the 1830s Britain was on the threshold of the railway age and the 'railway mania' that pushed this new means of transport into all corners of the country. In summer 1835 the *Carlisle Journal* for 22 August noted that a West Coast trunk railway from London to Scotland had been proposed to rival the eastern route projected from London to Edinburgh via York. Surveys to connect the Lancaster and Carlisle Railway with London began in November 1835, and Kendal was among the candidates for a station on the line. Locals expected that the railway would bring still more tourists to the Lake District, boosting the economy of gateway towns, including Kendal. Pitching to this new market, in the 1830s and 1840s local publishers issued *Allison's Northern Tourist's Guide* (Penrith, 1837), William Ford's *Description of the Scenery* (Carlisle, 1839), Jonathan Otley's *Descriptive Guide* (Keswick, 1842), *Atkinson's Handbook* (Kendal, 1847), and, of course, Wordsworth's 1835 *Guide*.

The Afterlife of Wordsworth's Guide

When 1,500 copies of the fifth edition of Wordsworth's *Guide* were exhausted in mid-1842, Hudson and Nicholson immediately published a new edition. As early as September 1838, they had suggested to Wordsworth a new expanded edition with more material for the benefit of tourists (*LLY* iv. 309n.). Wordsworth agreed, provided that in the new edition 'all that related to *mind*' should be 'printed entire and separated from other matter' (*LLY* iv. 310). What he meant was that the core part of the *Guide*—his 'Description of the Scenery of the Lakes'—should be separated from the '*guide matter*' (*LLY* iv. 310). The new edition, now titled *A Complete Guide to the Lakes*, consisted of an introduction (a reprint of the first half of the 'Miscellaneous Observations', on the frame of mind that the tourist should bring to the Lakes), 'Directions and Information for the Tourist' (revised and amplified), 'Description of the Scenery of the Lakes' (incorporating the latter half of the 'Miscellaneous Observations'), and newly added Adam Sedgwick's essays on the geology of the district and a glossary of place-names.[20]

---

[20] For the development of Wordsworth's text for the different versions of the *Guide*, see the table in Appendix III.

Five hundred and fifty copies of the 1842 edition sold out rapidly, and a further run of 1,200 copies was published in 1843. Wordsworth was now particularly keen on effective marketing: in his letter to the publisher John Hudson, 20 June 1844, he suggested that the new edition of the *Complete Guide* should be placed at bookstores in Carlisle 'so that it might catch the eye of persons coming from Scotland or Newcastle'. He had in mind the tourists who now arrived by rail and by coastal steamers; he goes on to remark:

I think it would be well to do the same at Whitehaven. A large iron steamboat will by next November be launched there that, it is calculated, will perform the voyage between Liverpool and Whitehaven in six hours; at present there are steamboats between those places three times a week that bring many passengers for a Peep at the Lakes. Of course you have an Agent at Ulverstone, it would be well also to have the Book exposed to sale at Penrith; and no doubt you have *that* done at Bowness and at Keswick.

'[W]ere it sufficiently put in the way of Tourists', Wordsworth believed, the *Complete Guide* 'would be greatly preferred to any other by most persons' (*LLY* iv. 554). He was surprisingly astute and far-sighted about the commercial advantages that accompanied the railways, and this is all the more surprising given that his letter to Hudson was written just four months before the publication of his controversial sonnet 'Is then no nook of English ground secure' in the *Morning Post* on 16 October 1844. Wordsworth's sonnet and his two letters to the *Morning Post* (see Appendix II) opposed the projected Kendal and Windermere Railway, although, as we have just seen, his broader attitude towards railways was ambiguous. Tourists were welcome to come to the peripheral gateway towns of the Lake District by rail and steamer, where they should purchase his *Complete Guide* and then proceed on foot or by coach, not by railway, so as not to mar the natural beauty and tranquillity they had come so far to enjoy.

Hudson's *Complete Guide* proved popular. It was issued in a third edition in 1846 and had sold nearly 3,000 copies by the time of Wordsworth's death in April 1850. Continuously updated in response to the rapidly changing transport system, Hudson's editions (1842–59) became influential in disseminating Wordsworthian views of nature among ever-increasing numbers of railway tourists. Amid these changes, Wordsworth's descriptions of natural phenomena in the Lake District remained intact in all the editions of Hudson's *Complete*

Guide. Furthermore, in addition to the eleven passages of Wordsworth's poetry quoted in the 1835 edition, Hudson's extracted lines from 'To Joanna', 'Yew-trees', 'Song at the Feast of Brougham Castle', 'Fidelity', and 'Lowther! in thy majestic Pile are seen'. The fourth edition of 1853, published after the poet's death, added about twenty more verse quotations, including lines from 'The Idle Shepherd-Boys', *An Evening Walk*, 'Poor Robin', 'Wansfell', 'The Poet's Walk', 'The Nab-Well', 'To a Daisy', 'To a Butterfly', Book Five of *The Excursion*, and *Home at Grasmere*, as well as Books Two and Four of *The Prelude* (recently published in 1850).[21]

In 1859 the publisher Thomas B. Hudson, successor of John Hudson, issued a fifth edition of the *Complete Guide*, embellished with ten steel engravings of Lake District views, ten outline views of mountains, and two decorative maps. At the same time, he published an abridged, cheaper edition: *Hudson's New Handbook for Visitors to the English Lakes, with an Introduction by the Late William Wordsworth*. Although the *Complete Guide* was 'for many years a favourite with tourists', Thomas B. Hudson remarked in its preface, 'on account of its size and price, [it] has been without the reach of the *Million* who visit the delightful scenery'. Thanks to cheap excursion trains, in the mid-Victorian decades the Lake District was becoming a popular weekend resort for a much wider range of people, including mill workers, mechanics, clerks, and shopkeepers. It was for these railway excursionists that Thomas B. Hudson published the *New Handbook*, including only the introduction and the 'Directions and Information for the Tourist' from the *Complete Guide*, omitting all of Wordsworth's 'Description of the Scenery' and Sedgwick's geological essays. That is to say, of Wordsworth's 1835 text only the first part of the 'Miscellaneous Observations' was retained intact—so the *New Handbook* could hardly now be called a Wordsworth publication. Mark Reed's authoritative Wordsworth bibliography regards the fifth 1859 edition of the *Complete Guide* as the last independent nineteenth-century edition of Wordsworth's *Guide*.[22] Still, Thomas B. Hudson shrewdly continued to use Wordsworth's name in its title, as the poet

[21] Many of these poems were taken from the *Memoirs of William Wordsworth* (1851) written by the poet's nephew Christopher Wordsworth (Jr).

[22] The exception is the one reprinted by J. Garnett in 1878, after the copyright of the 1835 edition had expired in 1877 (Reed i. 555). For the publication history of the *Guide*, see Appendix III.

was now firmly established as the principal authority on the Lake District and his name was marketable.

Thomas B. Hudson's abridged *New Handbook* was taken over by the Kendal publisher Titus Wilson in 1860, went through ten editions until the early 1870s, and then, with some changes in the title and arrangement, it was transformed into *Shaw's Tourist's Picturesque Guide to the English Lakes* (1873). In the 1880s it was reissued as *Ward and Lock's Pictorial and Historical Guide to the English Lakes* (1884), and, slightly changing its title, went through more than twenty further editions until the mid-twentieth century. Wordsworth's name continued to be printed on the title page until the early 1890s. When Ernest De Selincourt's annotated edition of *Guide to the Lakes* was published in 1906, one review in a local paper wondered '[h]ow many local people . . . [had] ever seen Wordsworth's guide to the Lakes, let alone read it'.[23] A good number of them, in fact: since its first anonymous publication in 1810, the various versions of Wordsworth's *Guide* had continued to be widely and formatively influential. While Wordsworth's volume itself had 'dropped out of notice during recent years', another review observed, 'writers on the Lake District . . . [had] been wont to suppose that they [could not] rightly treat their subject except in terms of Wordsworth or in terms as Wordsworthian as possible'.[24]

The Reception of Wordsworth's Guide

During the Victorian era, Wordsworth's *Guide* was quoted and recommended by many other guides and travel articles. The *Penny Magazine*, which enjoyed a sale of 200,000 copies at its peak in the 1830s, recommended in one of its 1837 articles that the *Guide* 'should be read by all persons, for the author's general view of the moral and physical circumstances of the country'.[25] Ford's *Description of the Scenery* (1839) and George Mogridge's *Loiterings among the Lakes* (1849) extracted at length from the *Guide*, and Charles Mackay's *Scenery and Poetry* (1846) deemed Wordsworth's book 'the most approved of all'. Wordsworth also inspired a succession of practical,

---

[23] 'Wordsworth's Guide to the Lakes', *Lakes Herald*, 2 February 1906.
[24] 'Wordsworth's Guide to the Lakes', *Sheffield Independent*, 3 February 1906.
[25] 'English Lakes', *Penny Magazine*, 6 (1837), 296.

tourist-friendly guides, including various versions of *Black's* guides (1841–1929) and *Murray's Handbook* (1866). Drawing on Wordsworth's *Guide* in writing about the physical features, geology, history, and social aspects of the Lake District, *Murray's* remarked: 'There is scarcely a crag, mountain, ghyll, waterfall, lake, or tarn, that does not derive an additional charm from the interest which Wordsworth has thrown around it' (p. xi). Thirty-five years later, in 1901, A. G. Bradley grumbled that younger generations had not read Wordsworth, except for the passages 'quoted in the guide-books'.[26] If this was the case, it could be said that Wordsworth's reputation and readership survived into the twentieth century thanks to the proliferation of guidebooks to the Lake District.

In what ways, then, does Wordsworth's *Guide* encourage us to appreciate the Lakeland landscape? For one thing, Wordsworth wants us to visit the region with a reflective mind. 'After all', he writes, 'it is upon the *mind* which a traveller brings along with him that his acquisitions, whether of pleasure or profit, must principally depend' (p. 72). Ford used Wordsworth's statement as the epigraph to his own guidebook and Hudson's, *Shaw's*, and *Ward and Lock's* continued to extract it in their introductions. Appealing less to the eyes of readers than to their minds, Wordsworth's *Guide* offers lyrical evocations of scenery intended to suggest how visitors might best enjoy the Lakeland landscape. An impressive example is his description of a placid lake on a calm autumnal day, after the equinoxial gales: 'while looking on the unruffled waters', he tells us, 'the imagination, by their aid, is carried into recesses of feeling otherwise impenetrable. The reason of this is, that the heavens are not only brought down into the bosom of the earth, but that the earth is mainly looked at, and thought of, through the medium of a purer element' (p. 36). The lake is presented in perfect rest, its 'unruffled waters' inviting a reflective or introspective mood; the lake and the mind are merged together, both becoming objects of contemplation. The ensuing passage is a seamless continuation of observation and contemplation of 'the quiet of a time' that enables the natural scenery to satisfy 'the most intense cravings for the tranquil, the lovely, and the perfect, to which man, the noblest of her creatures, is subject' (p. 37). Virginia Woolf drew from this passage an impression that 'sights which rejoice the eye also

[26] A. G. Bradley, *Highways and Byways in the Lake District* (1901), p. 226.

minister to the soul'.[27] In a word, Wordsworth's *Guide* demonstrates
how the Lake scenery pleases the eye and inspires the imagination.

In conveying the 'placid and quiet feeling which belongs peculiarly
to the lake', the *Guide* also extracts a passage from 'There was a Boy'
(p. 26) to evoke a Wordsworthian correspondence between the mind
and the outer world. Similarly, to create a sense of the solitude of
a mountain tarn, Wordsworth quotes from 'Fidelity' to suggest how
the sound of 'a leaping fish' sends 'a lonely cheer' and 'the raven's
croak' rings austerely among the crags. Summoning 'mists that
spread the flying shroud', this verse quotation also reminds readers of
the tragic death of Charles Gough and his faithful dog (p. 32).
Extracts from 'Long Meg and her Daughters' and *The Excursion* also
help to populate the landscape with human stories.

Wordsworth was influential in deflecting tourists' interests from
picturesque beauties to the literary associations of the Lake District,
although he was not alone in this respect. Quoting poetic descriptions
or adverting to literary associations were not the invention of
Wordsworth's *Guide*; rather, it was his poems and personal presence
in the Lake District that encouraged other guidebook writers to seek
for literary associations, transforming what had been 'picturesque
scenes' into 'Wordsworthian landscapes'. For instance, the passage
from Book Two of *The Excursion* describing the deep 'urn-like' valley
surrounding Blea Tarn had been extracted in Edward Baines's second
edition (1830) and Thomas Rose's volume (1832) *before* it was quoted
by Wordsworth himself in the fifth 1835 edition of the *Guide*
(Wordsworth evidently took the hint). In preparing the new *Complete
Guide* published by Hudson in 1842, Wordsworth agreed to include
five more extracts from his poetry, all of which had already been
quoted in *Black's Picturesque Guide* (1841). Hudson's also borrowed
some passages from a travel essay 'English Lakes' in the *Penny
Magazine* (1837) that had drawn on the 1823 fourth edition of
Wordsworth's *Guide*. In this way, Wordsworth's and other guidebooks
conversed with and inspired each other, shaping literary geographies
in which locations such as Dungeon Ghyll Force, Long Meg and her
Daughters Stone Circle, Aira Force, Rydal Lower Waterfall, Helm
Crag, and Grasmere were associated respectively with 'The Idle

[27] Virginia Woolf, 'Wordsworth and the Lakes', *Times Literary Supplement*, 15 June
1906.

Shepherd-Boys', 'Long Meg and her Daughters', 'The Somnambulist', *An Evening Walk*, *The Waggoner*, and *Home at Grasmere*. Several places in Langdale and Grasmere were routinely associated with passages from *The Excursion*.

The *Guide* also testifies to Wordsworth's powers of observation. He offers readers perceptions of nature's subtler beauties: lichens, mosses, and wayside flowers; a rivulet that is 'scarcely noticeable in a season of dry weather'; a lonely mountain tarn, rarely visited from year to year; the 'natural harmony' of colours in grasses, rocks, shrubs, trees, leaves, and cottages; the effects produced by frost and snow; bird-songs intermingled with the sound of water; and how weather can transform scenery—these details were admired by many, and extracted in *Onwhyn's Pocket Guide* (1841), Mogridge's *Loiterings among the Lakes* (1849), B. L. Blanchard's *Adams's Pocket Descriptive Guide* (1852), and Edwin Waugh's *In the Lake Country* (1880). Wordsworth's attention to the process of interaction between humans and the non-human—weather-beaten cottages 'grown' out of the native rock and clothed in 'a vegetable garb', or circular chimneys in harmony with living columns of smoke—inspired several Lakeland books and articles, including the *Penny Magazine* (1837), Ford's *Description of the Scenery* (1839), and even G. D. Abraham's *Motor Ways in Lakeland* (1913).

Wordsworth's descriptions of weather—the magical effects of mists, rain, storms, a burst of light, shifting shadows, clouds and vapours—appealed to readers' imaginations. He describes 'the showers, darkening, or brightening, as they fly from hill to hill' as 'not less grateful to the eye than finely interwoven passages of gay and sad music are touching to the ear' (p. 35). The shifting shades of the silent rain are captured through musical imagery, to present 'a soft eye music' ('Airey-Force Valley', 14). Admitting that the climate of the Lake District is not always favourable, Wordsworth tries to persuade his readers that '[t]he rain here comes down heartily, and is frequently succeeded by clear, bright weather, when every brook is vocal, and every torrent sonorous' (p. 35). This passage, celebrating the virtues of wet Lakeland weather, stimulated several Victorian guidebooks. Ford (1839) recalled a passage from *The Excursion* describing mountain streams after rain: 'Descending from the region of the clouds | And starting from the hollows of the earth | More multitudinous every moment—rend | Their way

before them' (iv. 528–31); and Payn (1867) was induced to extract
the opening lines of 'Resolution and Independence', capturing the
freshness and brightness of a landscape after a shower. In another
passage, Wordsworth admires 'the sight or sound of a storm coming
on or clearing away', claiming that '[i]nsensible must he be who
would not congratulate himself upon the bold bursts of sunshine,
the descending vapours, wandering lights and shadows, and the
invigorated torrents and water-falls, with which broken weather, in
a mountainous region, is accompanied' (p. 71). Prompted by this
passage, the *Penny Magazine* article (1837) remarks that 'Even the
stormiest [days] are most likely to present those occasional revela-
tions of grandeur' (p. 295), and extracts at length lines from Book
Two of *The Excursion* describing a visionary city created by the
'blind vapour' after a storm (ii. 859–95). So it was that Wordsworth's
verse and prose, reverberating in numerous Victorian guidebooks,
shaped the land of mists, clouds, and storms into a celebratory
scene suffused with his poetry.

It was in vapours, lights, and shadows that Wordsworth saw the
essence of his native country:

Such clouds, cleaving to their stations, or lifting up suddenly their glitter-
ing heads from behind rocky barriers, or hurrying out of sight with speed
of the sharpest edge—will often tempt an inhabitant to congratulate him-
self on belonging to a country of mists and clouds and storms, and make
him think of the blank sky of Egypt, and of the cerulean vacancy of Italy, as
an unanimated and even a sad spectacle. (pp. 35–6)

This rhapsodic celebration of the Lakeland weather may now seem
overdone, but it expresses Wordsworth's personal attachment to his
native place and his powerful sense of belonging. Along with more
lasting, geographical features such as mountains, rocks, lakes, and
rivers, in Wordsworth's view more ephemeral phenomena like rain
and mists composed the unique character of the Lake District. He
was also aware of the cycle of waters over and across the terrain,
transforming from rain and streams, through tarns and lakes, to
vapours and clouds, circulating through the earth and sky, unifying
and vivifying the landscape and affecting human feelings. These
aspects of Wordsworth's *Guide* have informed nature writings by
authors such as Richard Jefferies and Edward Thomas, and aspects of
modern ecological thought.

Here we should note Dorothy Wordsworth's contributions, too. She had helped to finish the long passage describing Wasdale for *Select Views* (1810, omitted from the 1835 edition; see p. 115); and offered the accounts of excursions to the summit of Scafell Pike and on the Banks of Ullswater. Her observant eyes capture the 'steelly brightness' of a lake, 'the earth . . . steaming with exhalations', and 'the lake, clouds, and mists . . . all in motion to the sound of sweeping winds' (pp. 88, 93). Virginia Woolf cites the following passage as an example of highly imaginative description: 'the lemon-coloured leaves of the birches, as the breeze turned them to the sun, sparkle, or rather *flash*, like diamonds, and the leafless purple twigs were tipped with globes of shining crystal' (p. 93). This is actually from the pen of Dorothy.

The account of a dramatic change of weather on the top of Scafell Pike was another popular quotation, praised by Harriet Martineau as 'the best account we have of the greatest mountain-excursion in England'.[28] This passage, based on Dorothy's account and revised by Wordsworth, relates how the summit of Scafell Pike discloses a sub-lime, dynamic prospect of mountains and vales in rapidly changing weather:

side by side with Eskdale, . . . the sister Vale of Donnerdale terminated by the Duddon Sands. . . . the Den of Wastdale . . . a gulph immeasurable: Grasmire and the other mountains of Crummock—Ennerdale and its mountains; and the Sea beyond! . . . Great Gavel, Helvellyn, and Skiddaw, . . . wrapped in storm; . . . Langdale, and the mountains in that quarter, . . . all bright in sunshine. . . . the struggles of gloom and sunshine . . . the Pikes of Langdale . . . decorated by two splendid rainbows. (pp. 84–5)

In a similar aerial view, Wordsworth had asked his readers to stand in imagination upon a cloud, hanging midway between Great Gable and Scafell, and to contemplate 'a number of vallies, not fewer than eight, diverging from the point . . . like spokes from the nave of a wheel' (p. 19). The 'wheel' analogy, by which we can grasp the layout of the whole region, became popular in books on the Lake District. If this analogy served to fix the image of a coherent district in tourists' minds, Dorothy's prospect from the summit of Scafell Pike brought

[28] Harriet Martineau, *The English Lakes* (1858), p. 139.

that idea brightly and compellingly to life, animated by the dynamic movements of clouds, vapours, lights, and rainbows.

Wordsworth's *Guide* was formative in promoting the Lake District as a single area, with its own climate, geology, 'wheel'-like topographical features. Here, Wordsworth claimed, people's lives had been shaped through a long process of negotiation with the natural environment; the *Guide* gives many pages to the social history of the Lake District, as well as its natural history. In addition, Wordsworth's poetry, widely inserted in this and other guides, gave the district a cultural identity for the Victorians and subsequent generations: 'Wordsworthshire'.

Significance of Wordsworth's Guide in the Modern World

In 1906 De Selincourt published a new annotated edition of Wordsworth's *Guide*, with the 1844–5 *Morning Post* letters and sonnets on the Kendal and Windermere Railway as an appendix. Now, the *Guide* began to assume fresh significance—for this was the decade when motorcars and new roads arrived in the Lake District. In a 1907 newspaper article one visitor to the Lake District complained about reckless drivers, referring to Wordsworth's sonnet, 'Is then no nook of English ground secure'.[29] As controversies over road-making and motorcars became heated, De Selincourt's edition served as a timely reminder of Wordsworth's protests against railway speculations in an earlier age.

When in the mid-1840s Wordsworth intervened in the Kendal and Windermere Railway controversy, he was criticized for being anti-democratic and elitist (as he was seen to be trying to exclude urban working-class tourists from the Lake District). Four decades later, as railway controversies in the Lake District revived in the 1880s, Wordsworth's ideas began to gain popular support. In 1883, citing the sonnet, 'Is then no nook of English ground secure', Hardwick Drumond Rawnsley acknowledged Wordsworth's inspiration in the successful campaign against the projected Braithwaite and Buttermere Railway, claiming that the Lake District should now be preserved for all visitors to the region. By the 1880s the Lake District had been surrounded by railways, and many of the ever-increasing numbers of

---

[29] S. H. Leeder, 'To the Editor of the *Times*', *The Times*, 9 September 1907.

visitors had 'Wordsworth in hand', as Rawnsley observed.[30] These masses, Rawnsley believed, held the key to preventing further damage to the landscape by railways.[31] Successive proposals for extending railways into the centre of the district were repeatedly repelled, and although no one could stop the motorcar invasion, campaigners did succeed in blocking the construction of new roads, including one over Styhead Pass and another through Dora's Field under Rydal Mount. Since then, Wordsworth's preservationist ideas have been called on in every controversy over transport development in the Lake District.

Wordsworth's letters to the *Morning Post* certainly included class-biased views and self-contradictory passages that reflected his ambivalent attitude towards tourism and conservation—an ambivalence that has contributed to modern ideas of protecting scenic areas while also allowing increasing access to them. Like us, Wordsworth was concerned with how to promote and preserve the Lake District, and how to strike a balance between accessibility and conservation: in a word, how to manage 'sustainable tourism'.

The Kendal and Windermere Railway controversy was thus a formative cultural moment that raised far-reaching questions about whose property the Lake District was, and who could claim a right to decide what to do with it—whether the Lake District was primarily a resource for local residents, or a landscape that belonged to the nation as a whole. Wordsworth's belief was the latter; in his *Guide* and *Morning Post* letters, he repeated his idea that the Lake District belongs to everyone who has 'an eye to perceive and a heart to enjoy'. By reading his *Guide* and *Morning Post* letters together, we can better understand his intention to establish the Lake District as 'a sort of national property'.

Wordsworth was especially concerned to protect the Lake District's 'character of seclusion and retirement'. In his *Guide*, he often turns readers' attention to the 'tranquil sublimity' of mountain recesses, retired valleys, the 'placid and quiet feeling' of a lake, and the 'inaudible motion' of vapours. In the busy, bustling days of urbanized and

[30] H. D. Rawnsley, 'The Proposed Permanent Lake District Defence Society', *Transactions of the Cumberland Association for the Advancement of Literature and Science*, 8 (1882–3), p. 78.

[31] Saeko Yoshikawa, *William Wordsworth and Modern Travel: Railways, Motorcars and the Lake District 1830–1940* (Liverpool University Press, 2020), pp. 74–5.

motorized twentieth-century society, and especially after the havoc of the First World War, these Wordsworthian aspects of the Lake District began to appeal more than ever. During and immediately after that war, many started to think of landscapes as national heritage, and a vogue for open-air recreational activities during the inter-war period lent momentum to campaigns for 'National Parks'. Ironically, it was thanks to the expansion of the transport network (including motor charabancs and buses) that walking in rural areas became a favourite pastime for a much wider range of people. Numerous organizations were formed to encourage urban workers to spend weekends and holidays in the countryside. Many guidebooks and travel books from this period echo Wordsworth's *Guide*, recommending walkers to follow country lanes and pathways that lead to the 'hidden treasures' of the landscape.

One such guide was *Walking in the Lake District* (1933) by H. H. Symonds, who worked tirelessly for the establishment of the Lake District National Park. Symonds thought it important to encourage an 'emotional impetus' among the general public, 'without which skill and knowledge [would] win no victories' in national parks campaigns. He remarked in his preface to *Walking in the Lake District*:

[M]y hope is that the book may stir, or else maintain, your interest in the greatest of our future National Parks, and that you will do something to create these. Many now preach the gospel 'Preserve the countryside'. Let us then preserve it in the best possible way, by teaching as many as we can to use and value it; . . . we can only learn liberty by the use of liberty; and until we get this free access to the open country back again into our city life, we shall be still unsatisfied. (pp. vii–viii)

While calling for 'free access' Symonds warned his readers not to travel by motorcars, which would do 'the district a disservice'. They should use public transport to gateway points, from where they should take to their feet—exactly as Wordsworth had recommended. So Wordsworth's 'democratic' and 'egalitarian' desire to protect the 'repose and quiet' of the Lake District 'for the sake of everyone' became a practical and reasonable goal—a goal that was achieved when the Lake District National Park was finally established in August 1951, a century after Wordsworth's death.

Many modern readers will share Wordsworth's idea that natural beauty and tranquillity sustain Lakeland tourism; that these qualities are vulnerable; and that they should accordingly be protected. A responsible attitude to the natural environment is one of Wordsworth's principal legacies. In the *Guide*, Wordsworth repeatedly explains how interactions between human activities and the natural environment have created the Lake District landscape, and he claims that, as a consequence, we are responsible for its protection and preservation. His opinions on architecture, gardening, plantation, and land management have become standards that are followed in the Lake District to this day.

One of the most conspicuous features of Wordsworth's *Guide* is a sense that the landscape is endangered because of the rapid transformation of agricultural and land-owning systems caused by industrial, economic, and social changes.[32] While readers are advised how best to appreciate the Lake District, Wordsworth's biographer Stephen Gill has said, they are also cautioned that its essential qualities are already vanishing. Strikingly, Wordsworth's *Guide* voiced the first public warning that this extraordinary region of England was endangered.[33] In his historical account of the Lake District, Wordsworth starts by asking readers to imagine a time 'before the country had been penetrated by any inhabitants' (p. 39), by way of encouraging a sharper awareness of the impact humans have had on the environment.[34] Here he seems to anticipate a concept of intense current concern: the Anthropocene. The *Oxford English Dictionary* defines this word as 'the epoch of geological time during which human activity is considered to be the dominant influence on the environment, climate, and ecology of the earth'; *OED* dates the first use of the word to 2000, but the idea that human beings can cause environmental change emerged during the eighteenth century and was a powerful influence on Wordsworth.[35]

---

[32] John Wyatt, *Wordsworth's Poems of Travel, 1819–42: 'Such Sweet Wayfaring'* (Macmillan, 1999), pp. 53–4; James McKusick, *Green Writing* (St Martin's Press, 2000), p. 74.

[33] Stephen Gill, 'Wordsworth and *The River Duddon*', *Essays in Criticism*, 57.1 (2007), pp. 34, 36.

[34] For Wordsworth's interest in the history of the pre-inhabited earth and geology, see John Wyatt, *Wordsworth and the Geologists* (Cambridge University Press, 1995); Theresa Kelley, *Wordsworth's Revisionary Aesthetics* (Cambridge University Press, 1988); Noah Heringman, *Romantic Rocks, Aesthetic Geology* (Cornell University Press, 2004).

[35] Ian Whyte, 'William Wordsworth's *Guide to the Lakes* and the Geographical Tradition', *Area*, 32.1 (2000), p. 104.

So what is the significance of Wordsworth's *Guide* for us now in the twenty-first century? Beyond its role as a travel guide, Wordsworth's book is an essay on landscape aesthetics, social history, and natural history, as well as a lyrical portrayal of the Lake District. It addresses how humans should live in harmony with nature, with a hope that 'a better taste should prevail'. There have been various readings of the text from diverse viewpoints: aesthetics, landscape, vernacular archi- tecture, politics (republicanism, nationalism), social history (the decline of yeomanry and industrialization), feminism, ecocriticism, geology, geography and place-writing, tourism studies, heritage stud- ies, genre studies and so on. We can read the *Guide* to examine Wordsworth's politics, ideology, aesthetics, and poetics, or his social, scientific, and environmental interests. But here I would like to reaf- firm the significance of the *Guide* in the context of today's sustainable tourism in the Lake District. It is sometimes claimed that Wordsworth's addressee in the *Guide*—'every man'—was 'a gentleman tourist' of the mid-nineteenth century, an 'educated man of taste and feeling'. But in the twenty-first century, we should understand Wordsworth's phrase 'every man' more inclusively as 'everyone', regardless of their social or financial status, education, nationality, ethnicity, race, or age. It has often been pointed out that, ironically, Wordsworth, who wanted to protect the beauty and tranquillity of the Lake District, actually became a threat by promoting tourism through his guide- book and his poetry. It would be more accurate to say that over two centuries Wordsworth's *Guide* has taught us how to enjoy the natural environment without destroying it, how to be responsible for its pro- tection through sustainable tourism, and how to appreciate and value the Lake District as a site that, largely owing to Wordsworth's influ- ence, is now a focus of World Cultural Heritage.

NOTE ON THE TEXT

OF the five lifetime editions of Wordsworth's *Guide to the Lakes* published in 1810, 1820, 1822, 1823, and 1835 the present text is taken from the 1835 edition: *A Guide through the District of the Lakes in the North of England*. Part of the first version (1810) is reproduced in Appendix I. For the publication history of successive editions of the *Guide*, please refer to the Introduction and Appendix III. Readers who would like to explore textual changes through the five editions should consult EdS; *PrW*, vol. 2; and the parallel texts reproduced in *RCDE*. Wordsworth's spellings for place-names, often different from those now current, have been retained. In the Introduction and the Explanatory Notes I use modern spellings except when quoting from Wordsworth's text. Other archaic and unique spellings have been retained, too, except for typographical errors which have been corrected in the light of Owen and Smyser's edition of 1974.

SELECT BIBLIOGRAPHY

For guidebooks to the Lake District, see Appendix IV: Two Hundred Years of Lake District Tourism 1750–1950.

Annotated Editions of Wordsworth's Guide to the Lakes

Bicknell, Peter, ed., *The Illustrated Wordsworth's Guide to the Lakes* (Exeter: Webb & Bower, 1984) [reproduces the fifth edition of 1835, along with numerous visual representations of the Lake District].

De Selincourt, Ernest, ed., *Guide to the Lakes* (1906; Oxford University Press, 1977); reprinted with a new preface by Stephen Gill (London: Frances Lincoln, 2004) [reproduces the fifth edition, with some additional materials and scholarly notes].

Mason, Nicholas, Paul Westover, and Shannon Stimpson, eds, *William Wordsworth's Guide to the Lakes: A Romantic Circles Digital Edition*. https://romantic-circles.org/editions/guide_lakes (April 2015, revised, June 2020) [in addition to an annotated 1835 text and an informative introduction, this digital edition includes a complete text of Wordsworth's 1810 letterpress and Wilkinson's engravings, a parallel-text comparison of the five editions of 1810, 1820, 1822, 1823, and 1835, excerpts from related letters, annotated bibliography, maps and photographic images of various locations].

Owen, W. J. B., and Jane Smyser, eds, *The Prose Works of William Wordsworth*, 3 vols (Oxford: Clarendon Press, 1974) [vol. 2 includes a thoroughly annotated version of the 1835 fifth edition with related texts, including Section II of *Select Views*, the 'Unpublished Tour' of 1810–11, and Wordsworth's essay on 'The Sublime and the Beautiful'; vol. 3 includes *Kendal and Windermere Railway: Two Letters Re-printed from the Morning Post* (1845)].

Writings by William and Dorothy Wordsworth and S. T. Coleridge

Coleridge, Samuel Taylor, *The Collected Letters of Samuel Taylor Coleridge*, ed. Earl Leslie Griggs, 6 vols (Oxford: Clarendon Press, 1956–71).

Coleridge, Samuel Taylor, *The Notebooks of Samuel Taylor Coleridge*, ed. Kathleen Coburn, 5 vols (Princeton: Princeton University Press, 1957–2002).

Wordsworth, Dorothy, *Journals of Dorothy Wordsworth*, ed. Ernest De Selincourt, 2 vols (1941, London: Macmillan, 1952).

Wordsworth, Dorothy, *The Grasmere and Alfoxden Journals*, ed. Pamela Woof (Oxford: Oxford University Press, 2008).

Wordsworth, William, *Poetical Works of William Wordsworth*, ed. Ernest De Selincourt, rev. Helen Darbishire, 5 vols (Oxford: Clarendon Press, 1952–63).

Wordsworth, William, *The Prelude: 1799, 1805, 1850*, ed. Jonathan Wordsworth, M. H. Abrams, and Stephen Gill (New York: Norton, 1979).

Wordsworth, William, *The Major Works*, ed. Stephen Gill (Oxford: Oxford University Press, 2008).

Wordsworth, William, *The Poems of William Wordsworth: Collected Reading Texts from the Cornell Wordsworth*, ed. Jared Curtis, 3 vols (Penrith: Humanities E-Books, 2009).

Wordsworth, William and Dorothy, *The Letters of William and Dorothy Wordsworth* (Oxford: Clarendon Press, 1963–93): *The Early Years,* ed. Chester L. Shaver (1967); *The Middle Years, pt. 1*, ed. Mary Moorman (1969); *The Middle Years*, ed. Mary Moorman and Alan G. Hill (1970); *The Later Years*, ed. Alan G. Hill, 4 vols (1978–88); *A Supplement of New Letters*, ed. Alan G. Hill (1993).

Biographies and Reference Works

Barker, Juliet, *Wordsworth: A Life* (London: Viking, 2000).

Bicknell, Peter, *The Picturesque Scenery of the Lake District, 1752–1855: A Bibliographical Study* (Winchester, Mich.: St Paul's Bibliographies, 1990).

Curtis, Jared, ed., *The Fenwick Notes of William Wordsworth* (London: Bristol Classical Press, 1993); revised, electronic edition (Penrith: Humanities-Ebooks, 2007).

Gill, Stephen, *William Wordsworth: A Life* (1989), 2nd edn (Oxford: Oxford University Press, 2020).

Lindop, Grevel, *A Literary Guide to the Lake District* (1993), 3rd edn (Ammanford: Sigma, 2015).

McCracken, David, *Wordsworth and the Lake District: A Guide to the Poems and Their Places* (Oxford: Oxford University Press, 1984).

Moorman, Mary, *William Wordsworth: A Biography*, 2 vols (Oxford: Clarendon Press, 1957, 1965).

Rawnsley, H. D., 'Reminiscences of Wordsworth among the Peasantry of Westmoreland', in *Wordsworthiana*, ed. William Knight (London: Macmillan, 1889), 79–120.

Rawnsley, H. D., *Literary Associations of the English Lakes*, 2 vols (Glasgow: MacLehose, 1894).

Reed, Mark L., *Wordsworth: The Chronology of the Early Years, 1770–1799; Middle Years, 1800–1815* (Cambridge, Mass.: Harvard University Press, 1967, 1975).

Reed, Mark L., *A Bibliography of William Wordsworth, 1787–1930*, 2 vols (Cambridge: Cambridge University Press, 2013).

Wordsworth, Christopher, *Memoirs of William Wordsworth*, 2 vols (London: Moxon, 1851).

Selected Critical Studies

Bate, Jonathan, *Romantic Ecology: Wordsworth and the Environmental Tradition* (London: Routledge, 1991).

Bode, Christoph, 'Putting the Lake District on the (Mental) Map: William Wordsworth's *Guide to the Lakes*', *Journal for the Study of British Cultures*, 4.1 (1997), 95–111.

Carlson, Julia S., *Romantic Marks and Measures: Wordsworth's Poetry in Fields of Print* (Philadelphia: University of Pennsylvania Press, 2016).

Chandler, David, 'The Influence of Southey's *Letters from England* on Wordsworth's *Guide to the Lakes*', *Notes and Queries*, 50.3 (2003), 288–91.

Freeman, Michael, *Railways and the Victorian Imagination* (New Haven: Yale University Press, 1999).

Fulford, Tim, *The Late Poetry of the Lake Poets: Romanticism Revised* (Cambridge: Cambridge University Press, 2013).

Garrett, James, *Wordsworth and the Writing of the Nation* (Aldershot: Ashgate, 2008).

Gill, Stephen, *Wordsworth and the Victorians* (Oxford: Clarendon Press, 1998).

Gill, Stephen, 'Wordsworth and *The River Duddon*', *Essays in Criticism*, 57.1 (2007), 22–41.

Hazucha, Andrew, 'Neither Deep nor Shallow but National: Eco-Nationalism in Wordsworth's *Guide to the Lakes*', *Interdisciplinary Studies in Literature and Environment*, 9.2 (2002), 61–73.

Heringman, Noah, *Romantic Rocks, Aesthetic Geology* (Ithaca: Cornell University Press, 2004).

Hess, Scott, *William Wordsworth and the Ecology of Authorship: The Roots of Environmentalism in Nineteenth-Century Culture* (Charlottesville: University of Virginia Press, 2012).

Hill, Gerard M-F, *A Guide to the Lakes of Cumberland, Westmorland and Lancashire by Thomas West* ([Cumbria]: Unipress Cumbria, 2008).

Kelley, Theresa M., *Wordsworth's Revisionary Aesthetics* (Cambridge: Cambridge University Press, 1988).

Kim, Benjamin, 'Generating a National Sublime: Wordsworth's *The River Duddon* and *The Guide to the Lakes*', *Studies in Romanticism*, 45.1 (2006): 49–75.

Labbe, Jacqueline M., *Romantic Visualities: Landscape, Gender, and Romanticism* (Basingstoke: Palgrave Macmillan, 1998).

McKusick, James C., *Green Writing: Romanticism and Ecology* (New York: St Martin's Press, 2000).

Mason, Nicholas, 'Larches, Llandaff, and Forestry Politics in Wordsworth's *Guide to the Lakes*', *Studies in Romanticism*, 61.3 (2022), 429–60.

Murdoch, John, preface, *The Discovery of the Lake District: A Northern Arcadia and Its Uses* (London: Victoria and Albert Museum, 1984).

Murray, John R., ed., *A Tour of the English Lakes with Thomas Gray and Joseph Farington RA* (London: Frances Lincoln, 2011).

Nabholtz, John R., 'Wordsworth's *Guide to the Lakes* and the Picturesque Tradition', *Modern Philology*, 61 (1964), 288–97.

Nicholson, Norman, *The Lakers: The Adventures of the First Tourists* (London: Hale, 1955).

Oda, Tomoya, 'A Slip of Wordsworth's Pen in his *Guide through the District of the Lakes*', *Notes and Queries*, n.s. 55.4 (2008), 424–5.

Ottum, Lisa, 'Discriminating Vision: Rereading Place in Wordsworth's *Guide to the Lakes*', *Prose Studies*, 34.3 (2012), 167–84.

Ousby, Ian, *The Englishman's England: Taste, Travel and the Rise of Tourism* (1990; London: Pimlico, 2002).

Owen, W. J. B., 'Wordsworth's Aesthetics of Landscape', *The Wordsworth Circle*, 7.2 (1976), 70–82.

Porter, Dahlia, 'Maps, Lists, Views: How the Picturesque Wye Transformed Topography', *Romanticism*, 19.2 (2013), 163–78.

Powell, Cecilia, and Stephen Hebron, *Savage Grandeur and Noblest Thoughts: Discovering the Lake District 1750–1820* (Grasmere: Wordsworth Trust, 2010).

Readman, Paul, *Storied Ground: Landscape and the Shaping of English National Identity* (Cambridge: Cambridge University Press, 2018).

Simonsen, Peter, *Wordsworth and Word-Preserving Arts: Typographic Inscription, Ekphrasis and Posterity in the Later Work* (Basingstoke: Palgrave Macmillan, 2007).

Smethurst, Paul, *Travel Writing and the Natural World, 1768–1840* (Basingstoke: Palgrave Macmillan, 2012).

Squire, Shelach J., 'Wordsworth and Lake District Tourism: Romantic Reshaping of Landscape', *Canadian Geographer*, 32.3 (1988), 237–47.

Thompson, Ian, *The English Lakes: A History* (London: Bloomsbury, 2010).

Walton, John K., and Jason Wood, eds, *The Making of a Cultural Landscape: The English Lake District as Tourist Destination, 1750–2010* (Farnham, Surrey: Ashgate, 2013).

Whyte, Ian, 'William Wordsworth's *Guide to the Lakes* and the Geographical Tradition', *Area*, 32.1 (2000), 101–6.

Woolf, Virginia. 'Wordsworth and the Lakes', *Times Literary Supplement* (15 June 1906).

Wyatt, John, *Wordsworth and the Geologists* (Cambridge: Cambridge University Press, 1995).

Wyatt, John, *Wordsworth's Poems of Travel, 1819–42: 'Such Sweet Wayfaring'* (Basingstoke: Macmillan, 1999).

Yoshikawa, Saeko, *William Wordsworth and the Invention of Tourism, 1820–1900* (Farnham, Surrey: Ashgate, 2014).

Yoshikawa, Saeko, *William Wordsworth and Modern Travel: Railways, Motorcars and the Lake District, 1830–1940* (Liverpool: Liverpool University Press, 2020).

A CHRONOLOGY OF
WILLIAM WORDSWORTH

1770 (7 Apr.) William Wordsworth (W) born at Cockermouth, Cumbria.

1771 (25 Dec.) Dorothy Wordsworth (DW) born at Cockermouth, Cumbria.

1778 (c.8 Mar.) Mother, Ann Wordsworth, dies.

1779 W sent to Hawkshead Grammar School.

1783 (30 Dec.) Father, John Wordsworth, dies.

1787 W enters St John's College, Cambridge.

1788–9 Composition of *An Evening Walk*. In summer W walks in Yorkshire, Lancashire, and Dovedale, on his way back to Hawkshead. (14 July 1789) Fall of Bastille, beginning of French Revolution.

1790 (July–Oct.) W on a walking tour through France and Switzerland with Robert Jones.

1791 W in London until Nov., when he returns to France and sees Revolutionary fervour in Paris.

1792 W influenced by Michel Beaupuy. Love affair with Annette Vallon and (Dec.) birth of their daughter Caroline. Composition of *Descriptive Sketches*. W returns to England to seek a livelihood.

1793 (Jan.) Louis XVI executed. (Feb.) War is declared between England and France. (Feb.) *An Evening Walk* and *Descriptive Sketches* published in London.

1794 W reunited with DW; (Apr.–May) they walk from Kendal to stay at Windy Brow, Keswick. (28 July) Execution of Robespierre. (Aug.–Sept.) W stays at Rampside and sees Peele Castle; nurses Raisley Calvert, who leaves W £900 on his death in Jan. 1795.

1795 (Aug.) W meets Samuel Taylor Coleridge (STC) and Southey in Bristol; settles with DW at Racedown in Dorset.

1797 W and DW move to Alfoxden, Somerset, to be nearer STC. First version of 'The Ruined Cottage' and plans for joint composition with STC.

1798 The *annus mirabilis*. 'The Ruined Cottage' completed. *Lyrical Ballads* published. W, DW, and STC go to Germany and over winter W writes autobiographical verse, the foundation of *The Prelude*, in Goslar. French invasion of republican Switzerland.

1799   (Apr.) W and DW return to England and stay with the
        Hutchinsons in Yorkshire. (Nov.) W and STC make a tour in the
        Lakes. (Dec.) W and DW travel from Yorkshire, through
        Wensleydale, to move into Dove Cottage, Grasmere.

1800   W begins *Home at Grasmere*, works on poems for the second
        edition of *Lyrical Ballads*, including 'The Brothers', published
        Jan. 1801, and writes Preface. (Jan.–Sept.) Brother John stays at
        Dove Cottage.

1802   (Apr.) Publication of further edition of *Lyrical Ballads*. (Aug.)
        Peace of Amiens enables W to visit Annette and Caroline. (4 Oct.)
        W marries Mary Hutchinson, and returns to Grasmere with
        Mary and DW.

1803   War begins again and fear of invasion grows. (June) Birth of first
        son, John. (from mid-Aug.) W, DW, STC tour Scotland. (Sept.)
        W and DW meet Walter Scott.

1804   Much composition, especially on *The Prelude*. Napoleon crowned
        Emperor.

1805   W's brother John, Captain of the *Earl of Abergavenny*, drowned.
        W completes *The Prelude*.

1807   *Poems in Two Volumes* published and ridiculed in reviews. On
        return journey from Coleorton, W visits Bolton Abbey, Gordale,
        and Malham with DW; composes *The White Doe of Rylstone*.
        (Aug.) W tells Lady Holland that he is preparing a guidebook.

1808   Ws leave Dove Cottage for larger house in Grasmere, Allan Bank.

1810   Son, William, born. Joseph Wilkinson's *Select Views* published,
        including W's anonymous letterpress, first version of *Guide to the
        Lakes*.

1811   Ws move from Allan Bank to the Rectory, Grasmere.

1812   Deaths of children, Thomas and Catherine.

1813   (May) Move to Rydal Mount. W becomes Distributor of Stamps
        for Westmorland; completes *The Excursion*.

1814   (Feb.) Napoleon abdicates. *The Excursion* published, attacked by
        reviewers. (July–Sept.) Tour of Scotland.

1815   Napoleon defeated at Waterloo. *The White Doe of Rylstone*
        published. First collected edition of poems published with
        Preface.

1819   *The Waggoner* and *Peter Bell* published.

1820   *The River Duddon*, with the *Topographical Description*, published.
        (July–Oct.) W tours on the Continent with Mary, DW, and others.

1822   *A Description of the Scenery of the Lakes*, 3rd edn, *Memorials of a Tour on the Continent*, *Ecclesiastical Sketches*, published.

1823   *A Description of the Scenery of the Lakes*, 4th edn.

1828–9 'The Wishing Gate' published in *The Keepsake for 1829*.

1831   (Sept.–Oct.) W tours Scotland and sees Walter Scott for the last time.

1833   W takes a steamboat from Whitehaven to visit the Isle of Man and Scotland; visits Eden Valley and sees viaducts under construction; writes 'Steamboats, Viaducts, Railways', published in 1835.

1835   *Yarrow Revisited*, including several poems set in the Lake District, published. *A Guide through the District of the Lakes*, 5th edn, published.

1837   Death of William IV, succeeded by Victoria. W tours France and Italy with Crabb Robinson.

1842   W's *Guide* compiled into Hudson's *Complete Guide to the Lakes*.

1843   W becomes Poet Laureate on Southey's death; dictates Fenwick Notes. Hudson's *Complete Guide*, 2nd edn, published.

1844   (Oct–Dec.) W's sonnets and letters published in the *Morning Post*, in opposition to the projected Kendal and Windermere Railway; W publishes them as a pamphlet in Jan.–Feb. 1845.

1845   One-volume collected edition of W's poems published, with an image of Rydal Mount on its frontispiece.

1846   Hudson's *Complete Guide*, 3rd edn.

1847   (Apr.) Kendal and Windermere Railway, Cockermouth and Workington Railway opened in April. (July) Death of daughter Dora.

1850   (23 Apr.) Death of W. (July) *The Prelude* published.

1851   *Memoirs of William Wordsworth* by his nephew Christopher Wordsworth published.

1853   Hudson's *Complete Guide*, 4th edn, includes excerpts from the *Memoirs* and new extracts from W's poetry.

1855   (25 Jan.) Death of DW.

1859   (17 Jan.) Death of Mary Wordsworth. Hudson's *Complete Guide*, 5th edn.

A GUIDE THROUGH THE
DISTRICT OF THE LAKES (1835)

A Guide through the District of the Lakes in the North of England

with a Description of the Scenery, &c.
For the Use of Tourists and Residents.
Fifth Edition, with Considerable Additions.

CONTENTS.

DIRECTIONS AND INFORMATION FOR THE TOURIST

DESCRIPTION OF THE SCENERY OF THE LAKES

SECTION FIRST
VIEW OF THE COUNTRY AS FORMED BY NATURE

SECTION SECOND
ASPECT OF THE COUNTRY AS AFFECTED BY ITS INHABITANTS

SECTION THIRD
CHANGES, AND RULES OF TASTE FOR PREVENTING THEIR BAD EFFECTS

MISCELLANEOUS OBSERVATIONS

EXCURSIONS

ODE

ITINERARY

DIRECTIONS AND INFORMATION
FOR
THE TOURIST

IN preparing this Manual, it was the Author's principal wish to furnish a Guide or Companion for the *Minds* of Persons of taste, and feeling for Landscape, who might be inclined to explore the District of the Lakes with that degree of attention to which its beauty may fairly lay claim. For the more sure attainment, however, of this primary object, he will begin by undertaking the humble and tedious task of supplying the Tourist with directions how to approach the several scenes in their best, or most convenient, order. But first, supposing the approach to be made from the south, and through Yorkshire, there are certain interesting spots which may be confidently recommended to his notice, if time can be spared before entering upon the Lake District; and the route may be changed in returning.

There are three approaches to the Lakes through Yorkshire;* the least adviseable is the great north road* by Catterick and Greta Bridge, and onwards to Penrith. The Traveller, however, taking this route,* might halt at Greta Bridge, and be well recompenced if he can afford to give an hour or two to the banks of the Greta, and of the Tees, at Rokeby. Barnard Castle also, about two miles up the Tees, is a striking object, and the main North Road might be rejoined at Bowes. Every one has heard of the great fall of the Tees above Middleham,* interesting for its grandeur, as the avenue of rocks that leads to it, is to the geologist. But this place lies so far out of the way as scarcely to be within the compass of our notice. It might, however, be visited by a Traveller on foot, or on horseback, who could rejoin the main road upon Stanemoor.

The second road* leads through a more interesting tract of country, beginning at Ripon, from which place see Fountain's Abbey, and thence by Hackfall, and Masham, to Jervaux Abbey, and up the vale of Wensley; turning aside before Askrigg is reached, to see Aysgarthforce, upon the Ure; and again, near Hawes, to Hardraw Scar, of which, with its waterfall, Turner has a fine drawing. Thence over the fells to Sedbergh, and Kendal.

The third approach from Yorkshire is through Leeds. Four miles beyond that town are the ruins of Kirkstall Abbey, should that road to

Skipton be chosen; but the other by Otley may be made much more interesting by turning off at Addington to Bolton Bridge, for the sake of visiting the Abbey and grounds.* It would be well, however, for a party previously to secure beds, if wanted, at the inn, as there is but one, and it is much resorted to in summer.

The Traveller on foot, or horseback, would do well to follow the banks of the Wharf upwards, to Burnsall, and thence cross over the hills to Gordale—a noble scene, beautifully described in Gray's Tour, and with which no one can be disappointed. Thence to Malham, where there is a respectable village inn, and so on, by Malham Cove,* to Settle.

Travellers in carriages must go from Bolton Bridge to Skipton, where they rejoin the main road; and should they be inclined to visit Gordale, a tolerable road turns off beyond Skipton. Beyond Settle, under Giggleswick Scar, the road passes an ebbing and flowing well, worthy the notice of the Naturalist. Four miles to the right of Ingleton, is Weathercote Cave, a fine object, but whoever diverges for this, must return to Ingleton. Near Kirkby Lonsdale observe the view from the bridge over the Lune,* and descend to the channel of the river, and by no means omit looking at the Vale of Lune from the Church-yard.*

The journey towards the lake country through Lancashire,* is, with the exception of the Vale of the Ribble, at Preston, uninteresting; till you come near Lancaster, and obtain a view of the fells and mountains of Lancashire and Westmorland; with Lancaster Castle, and the Tower of the Church seeming to make part of the Castle, in the foreground.

They who wish to see the celebrated ruins of Furness Abbey, and are not afraid of crossing the Sands,* may go from Lancaster to Ulverston; from which place take the direct road to Dalton; but by all means return through Urswick, for the sake of the view from the top of the hill, before descending into the grounds of Conishead Priory. From this quarter the Lakes would be advantageously approached by Coniston; thence to Hawkshead, and by the Ferry over Windermere, to Bowness: a much better introduction than by going direct from Coniston to Ambleside, which ought not to be done, as that would greatly take off from the effect of Windermere.

Let us now go back to Lancaster. The direct road thence to Kendal is 22 miles, but by making a circuit of eight miles, the Vale of the Lune to Kirkby Lonsdale will be included. The whole tract is pleasing; there is one view mentioned by Gray and Mason* especially so. In West's Guide* it is thus pointed out:—'About a quarter of a mile beyond the third mile-stone, where the road makes a turn to the right, there is a gate on the left which leads into a field where the station meant, will be found.' Thus far for those who approach the Lakes from the South.

Travellers from the North would do well to go from Carlisle by Wigton, and proceed along the Lake of Bassenthwaite to Keswick; or, if convenience should take them first to Penrith, it would still be better to cross the country to Keswick, and begin with that vale, rather than with Ulswater. It is worth while to mention, in this place, that the banks of the river Eden, about Corby, are well worthy of notice, both on account of their natural beauty, and the viaducts* which have recently been carried over the bed of the river, and over a neighbouring ravine. In the Church of Wetheral, close by, is a fine piece of monumental sculpture by Nollekens.* The scenes of Nunnery, upon the Eden, or rather that part of them which is upon Croglin, a mountain stream there falling into the Eden, are, in their way, unrivalled. But the nearest road thither, from Corby, is so bad, that no one can be advised to take it in a carriage. Nunnery may be reached from Corby by making a circuit and crossing the Eden at Armathwaite bridge. A portion of this road, however, is bad enough.

As much the greatest number of Lake Tourists begin by passing from Kendal to Bowness, upon Windermere, our notices shall commence with that Lake. Bowness is situated upon its eastern side,* and at equal distance from each extremity of the Lake of

Windermere.

The lower part of this Lake is rarely visited, but has many interesting points of view, especially at Storr's Hall and at Fell-foot, where the Coniston Mountains peer nobly over the western barrier, which elsewhere, along the whole Lake, is comparatively tame. To one also who has ascended the hill from Grathwaite on the western side, the Promontory called Rawlinson's Nab, Storr's Hall, and the Troutbeck Mountains, about sun-set, make a splendid landscape. The view from the Pleasure-house of the Station near the Ferry* has suffered much from Larch plantations;* this mischief, however, is gradually disappearing, and the Larches, under the management of the proprietor, Mr. Curwen,* are giving way to the native wood. Windermere ought to be seen both from its shores and from its surface. None of the other

Lakes unfold so many fresh beauties to him who sails upon them. This is owing to its greater size, to the islands, and to its having *two* vales at the head, with their accompanying mountains of nearly equal dignity. Nor can the grandeur of these two terminations be seen at once from any point, except from the bosom of the Lake. The Islands may be explored at any time of the day; but one bright unruffled evening, must, if possible, be set apart for the splendour, the stillness, and solemnity of a three hour's voyage upon the higher division of the Lake, not omitting, towards the end of the excursion, to quit the expanse of water, and peep into the close and calm River at the head; which, in its quiet character, at such a time, appears rather like an overflow of the peaceful Lake* itself, than to have any more immediate connection with the rough mountains whence it has descended, or the turbulent torrents by which it is supplied. Many persons content themselves with what they see of Windermere during their progress in a boat from Bowness to the head of the Lake, walking thence to Ambleside. But the whole road from Bowness is rich in diversity of pleasing or grand scenery; there is scarcely a field on the road side, which, if entered, would not give to the landscape some additional charm. Low-wood Inn, a mile from the head of Windermere, is a most pleasant halting-place; no inn in the whole district is so agreeably situated for water views and excursions; and the fields above it, and the lane that leads to Troutbeck, present beautiful views towards each extremity of the Lake. From this place, and from

Ambleside,

Rides may be taken in numerous directions, and the interesting walks are inexhaustible;[1] a few out of the main road may be particularized:—the lane that leads from Ambleside to Skelgill;* the ride, or walk by Rothay Bridge, and up the stream under Loughrigg Fell, continued on the western side of Rydal Lake, and along the fell to the foot of Grasmere Lake,* and thence round by the church of Grasmere; or, turning round Loughrigg Fell by Loughrigg Tarn and the River Brathay, back to Ambleside. From Ambleside is

---

[1] Mr. Green's Guide to the Lakes,* in two vols., contains a complete Magazine of minute and accurate information of this kind, with the names of mountains, streams, &c.

another charming excursion by Clappersgate, where cross the Brathay, and proceed with the river on the right to the hamlet of Skelwith-fold; when the houses are passed, turn, before you descend the hill, through a gate on the right, and from a rocky point is a fine view of the Brathay River, Langdale Pikes, &c.; then proceed to Colwith-force, and up Little Langdale to Blea Tarn. The scene in which this small piece of water lies, suggested to the Author the following description, (given in his Poem of the Excursion) supposing the spectator to look down upon it, not from the road, but from one of its elevated sides.

'Behold!

Beneath our feet, a little lowly Vale,
A lowly Vale, and yet uplifted high
Among the mountains; even as if the spot
Had been, from eldest time by wish of theirs,
So placed, to be shut out from all the world!
Urn-like it was in shape, deep as an Urn;
With rocks encompassed, save that to the South
Was one small opening, where a heath-clad ridge
Supplied a boundary less abrupt and close;
A quiet treeless nook,[1] with two green fields,
A liquid pool that glittered in the sun,
And one bare Dwelling; one Abode, no more!
It seemed the home of poverty and toil,
Though not of want: the little fields, made green
By husbandry of many thrifty years,
Paid cheerful tribute to the moorland House.
—There crows the Cock, single in his domain:
The small birds find in spring no thicket there
To shroud them; only from the neighbouring Vales
The Cuckoo, straggling up to the hill tops,
Shouteth faint tidings of some gladder place.'*

From this little Vale return towards Ambleside by Great Langdale, stopping, if there be time, to see Dungeon-ghyll waterfall.

The Lake of

---

[1] No longer strictly applicable, on account of recent plantations.

Coniston

May be conveniently visited from Ambleside, but is seen to most advantage by entering the country over the Sands from Lancaster. The Stranger, from the moment he sets his foot on those Sands, seems to leave the turmoil and traffic of the world behind him; and, crossing the majestic plain whence the sea has retired, he beholds, rising apparently from its base, the cluster of mountains among which he is going to wander, and towards whose recesses, by the Vale of Coniston, he is gradually and peacefully led.* From the Inn at the head of Coniston Lake, a leisurely Traveller might have much pleasure in looking into Yewdale and Tilberthwaite, returning to his Inn from the head of Yewdale by a mountain track which has the farm of Tarn Hows, a little on the right: by this road is seen much the best view of Coniston Lake from the south. At the head of Coniston Water there is an agreeable Inn, from which an enterprising Tourist might go to the Vale of the Duddon, over Walna Scar,* down to Seathwaite, Newfield, and to the rocks where the river issues from a narrow pass into the broad Vale. The stream is very interesting for the space of a mile above this point, and below, by Ulpha Kirk, till it enters the Sands, where it is overlooked by the solitary Mountain Black Comb, the summit of which, as that experienced surveyor, Colonel Mudge, declared, commands a more extensive view than any point in Britain. Ireland he saw more than once, but not when the sun was above the horizon.

'Close by the Sea, lone sentinel,
　　Black-Comb his forward station keeps;
He breaks the sea's tumultuous swell,—
　　And ponders o'er the level deeps.

He listens to the bugle horn,
　　Where Eskdale's lovely valley bends;
Eyes Walney's early fields of corn;
　　Sea-birds to Holker's woods he sends.

Beneath his feet the sunk ship rests,
In Duddon Sands, its masts all bare:

*　　　*　　　*　　　*　　　*'

　　　　　The Minstrels of Windermere, by Chas. Farish, B.D.

The Tourist may either return to the Inn at Coniston by Broughton, or, by turning to the left before he comes to that town, or, which would be much better, he may cross from

Ulpha Kirk

Over Birker moor, to Birker-force, at the head of the finest ravine in the country; and thence up the Vale of the Esk, by Hardknot and Wrynose, back to Ambleside. Near the road, in ascending from Eskdale, are conspicuous remains of a Roman fortress.* Details of the Duddon and Donnerdale are given in the Author's series of Sonnets upon the Duddon and in the accompanying Notes.* In addition to its two Vales at its head, Windermere communicates with two lateral Vallies; that of Troutbeck, distinguished by the mountains at its head—by picturesque remains of cottage architecture; and, towards the lower part, by bold foregrounds formed by the steep and winding banks of the river. This Vale, as before mentioned, may be most conveniently seen from Low Wood. The other lateral Valley, that of Hawkshead, is visited to most advantage, and most conveniently, from Bowness; crossing the Lake by the Ferry*—then pass the two villages of Sawrey, and on quitting the latter, you have a fine view of the Lake of Esthwaite, and the cone of one of the Langdale Pikes in the distance.

Before you leave Ambleside give three minutes to looking at a passage of the brook* which runs through the town; it is to be seen from a garden on the right bank of the stream, a few steps above the bridge—the garden at present is rented by Mrs. Airey.—Stockgill-force, upon the same stream, will have been mentioned to you as one of the sights of the neighbourhood. And by a Tourist halting a few days in Ambleside, the *Nook* also might be visited; a spot where there is a bridge over Scandale-beck, which makes a pretty subject for the pencil.* Lastly, for residents of a week or so at Ambleside, there are delightful rambles over every part of Loughrigg Fell and among the enclosures on its sides; particularly about Loughrigg Tarn, and on its eastern side about Fox How and the properties adjoining to the northwards.

Road from Ambleside to Keswick.

The Waterfalls of Rydal are pointed out to every one. But it ought to be observed here, that Rydal-mere is no where seen to advantage from the *main road*. Fine views of it may be had from Rydal Park; but these grounds, as well as those of Rydal Mount and Ivy Cottage, from which also it is viewed to advantage, are private. A foot road passing behind Rydal Mount and under Nab Scar to Grasmere,* is very favourable to views of the Lake and the Vale, looking back towards Ambleside. The horse road also, along the western side of the Lake, under Loughrigg fell, as before mentioned, does justice to the beauties of this small mere, of which the Traveller who keeps the high road* is not at all aware.

Grasmere.

There are two small Inns* in the Vale of Grasmere, one near the Church,* from which it may be conveniently explored in every direction, and a mountain walk taken up Easedale to Easedale Tarn, one of the finest tarns in the country, thence to Stickle Tarn, and to the top of Langdale Pikes. See also the Vale of Grasmere from Butterlip How. A boat is kept by the innkeeper, and this circular Vale, in the solemnity of a fine evening, will make, from the bosom of the Lake, an impression that will be scarcely ever effaced.

The direct road from Grasmere to Keswick* does not (as has been observed of Rydal Mere) shew to advantage Thirlmere, or Wythburn Lake, with its surrounding mountains. By a Traveller proceeding at leisure, a deviation ought to be made from the main road, when he has advanced a little beyond the sixth mile-stone short of Keswick, from which point there is a noble view of the Vale of Legberthwaite, with Blencathra (commonly called Saddle-back) in front. Having previously enquired, at the Inn near Wythburn Chapel, the best way from this mile-stone to the bridge that divides the Lake, he must cross it, and proceed with the Lake on the right,* to the hamlet a little beyond its termination, and rejoin the main road upon Shoulthwaite Moss, about four miles from Keswick; or, if on foot, the Tourist may follow the stream that issues from Thirlmere down the romantic Vale of St. John's, and so (enquiring the way at some cottage) to Keswick, by a circuit of little more than a mile.* A more interesting tract of country is scarcely any where to be seen, than the road between Ambleside and Keswick, with the deviations that have been pointed out. Helvellyn may be conveniently ascended from the Inn at Wythburn.

The Vale of Keswick.

This Vale stretches, without winding, nearly North and South, from the head of Derwent Water to the foot of Bassenthwaite Lake. It communicates with Borrowdale on the South; with the river Greta, and Thirlmere, on the East, with which the Traveller has become acquainted on his way from Ambleside; and with the Vale of Newlands on the West—which last Vale he may pass through, in going to, or returning from, Buttermere. The best views of Keswick Lake* are from Crow Park; Frier's Crag; the Stable-field, close by; the Vicarage, and from various points in taking the circuit of the Lake. More distant views, and perhaps full as interesting, are from the side of Latrigg, from Ormathwaite, and Applethwaite; and thence along the road at the foot of Skiddaw towards Bassenthwaite, for about a quarter of a mile. There are fine bird's eye views from the Castle-hill; from Ashness, on the road to Watenlath, and by following the Watenlath stream downwards to the Cataract of Lodore.* This Lake also, if the weather be fine, ought to be circumnavigated. There are good views along the western side of Bassenthwaite Lake, and from Armathwaite at its foot; but the eastern side from the high road has little to recommend it. The Traveller from Carlisle, approaching by way of Ireby, has, from the old road on the top of Bassenthwaite-hawse, much the most striking view of the Plain and Lake of Bassenthwaite, flanked by Skiddaw, and terminated by Wallowcrag on the south-east of Derwent Lake; the same point commands an extensive view of Solway Frith and the Scotch Mountains.* They who take the circuit of Derwent Lake, may at the same time include BORROWDALE,* going as far as Bowder-stone,* or Rosthwaite. Borrowdale is also conveniently seen on the way to Wastdale over Styhead; or, to Buttermere, by Seatoller and Honister Crag; or, going over the Stake, through Langdale, to Ambleside. Buttermere may be visited by a shorter way through Newlands, but though the descent upon the Vale of Buttermere, by this approach, is very striking, as it also is to one entering by the head of the Vale, under Honister Crag, yet, after all, the best entrance from Keswick is from the lower part of the Vale, having gone over Whinlater to Scale Hill, where there is a roomy Inn, with very good accommodation. The Mountains of the Vale of

Buttermere and Crummock

Are no where so impressive as from the bosom of Crummock Water. Scale-force, near it, is a fine chasm, with a lofty, though but slender, fall of water.

From Scale Hill a pleasant walk may be taken to an eminence in Mr. Marshall's woods,* and another by crossing the bridge at the foot of the hill, upon which the Inn stands, and turning to the right, after the opposite hill has been ascended a little way, then follow the road for half a mile or so that leads towards Lorton, looking back upon Crummock Water, &c., between the openings of the fences. Turn back and make your way to

Loweswater.

But this small Lake is only approached to advantage from the other end; therefore any Traveller going by this road to Wastdale, must look back upon it. This road to Wastdale, after passing the village of Lamplugh Cross, presents suddenly a fine view of the Lake of Ennerdale,* with its Mountains; and, six or seven miles beyond, leads down upon Calder Abbey. Little of this ruin is left, but that little is well worthy of notice. At Calder Bridge are two comfortable Inns, and, a few miles beyond, accommodations may be had at the Strands, at the foot of Wastdale. Into

Wastdale

Are three horse-roads, viz. over the Stye from Borrowdale; a short cut from Eskdale by Burnmoor Tarn, which road descends upon the head of the Lake; and the principal entrance from the open country by the Strands at its foot. This last is much the best approach. Wastdale is well worth the notice of the Traveller who is not afraid of fatigue; no part of the country is more distinguished by sublimity. Wastwater* may also be visited from Ambleside; by going up Langdale, over Hardknot and Wrynose—down Eskdale and by Irton Hall to the Strands; but this road can only be taken on foot, or on horseback, or in a cart.

We will conclude with

Ullswater,

As being, perhaps, upon the whole, the happiest combination of beauty and grandeur, which any of the Lakes affords. It lies not more than ten miles from Ambleside, and the Pass of Kirkstone and the descent from it are very impressive; but, notwithstanding, this Vale, like the others, loses much of its effect by being entered from the head: so that it is better to go from Keswick through Matterdale, and descend upon Gowbarrow Park; you are thus brought at once upon a magnificent view of the two higher reaches of the Lake. Ara-force thunders down the Ghyll on the left, at a small distance from the road. If Ullswater be approached from Penrith, a mile and a half brings you to the winding vale of Eamont, and the prospects increase in interest till you reach Patterdale; but the first four miles along Ullswater by this road are comparatively tame; and in order to see the lower part of the Lake to advantage, it is necessary to go round by Pooley Bridge, and to ride at least three miles along the Westmorland side of the water, towards Martindale. The views, especially if you ascend from the road into the fields, are magnificent; yet this is only mentioned that the transient Visitant may know what exists; for it would be inconvenient to go in search of them. They who take this course of three or four miles *on foot*, should have a boat in readiness at the end of the walk, to carry them across to the Cumberland side of the Lake, near Old Church, thence to pursue the road upwards to Patterdale. The Church-yard Yew-tree still survives at Old Church,* but there are no remains of a Place of Worship, a New Chapel* having been erected in a more central situation, which Chapel was consecrated by the then Bishop of Carlisle, when on his way to crown Queen Elizabeth, he being the only Prelate who would undertake the office. It may be here mentioned that Bassenthwaite Chapel* yet stands in a bay as sequestered as the Site of Old Church; such situations having been chosen in disturbed times to elude marauders.

The Trunk, or Body of the Vale of Ullswater need not be further noticed, as its beauties show themselves: but the curious Traveller may wish to know something of its tributary Streams.

At Dalemain, about three miles from Penrith, a Stream is crossed called the Dacre, or Dacor, which name it bore as early as the time of the Venerable Bede.* This stream does not enter the Lake, but joins the Eamont a mile below. It rises in the moorish Country about

Penruddock, flows down a soft sequestered Valley, passing by the ancient mansions of Hutton John and Dacre Castle. The former is pleasantly situated, though of a character somewhat gloomy and monastic, and from some of the fields near Dalemain, Dacre Castle, backed by the jagged summit of Saddle-back, with the Valley and Stream in front, forms a grand picture. There is no other stream that conducts to any glen or valley worthy of being mentioned, till we reach that which leads up to Ara-force, and thence into Matterdale, before spoken of. Matterdale, though a wild and interesting spot, has no peculiar features that would make it worth the Stranger's while to go in search of them; but, in Gowbarrow Park, the lover of Nature might linger for hours. Here is a powerful Brook,* which dashes among rocks through a deep glen, hung on every side with a rich and happy intermixture of native wood; here are beds of luxuriant fern, aged hawthorns, and hollies decked with honeysuckles; and fallow-deer glancing and bounding over the lawns and through the thickets. These are the attractions of the retired views, or constitute a foreground for ever-varying pictures of the majestic Lake, forced to take a winding course by bold promontories, and environed by mountains of sublime form, towering above each other. At the outlet of Gowbarrow Park, we reach a third stream, which flows through a little recess called Glencoin, where lurks a single house, yet visible from the road. Let the Artist or leisurely Traveller turn aside to it, for the buildings and objects around them are romantic and picturesque. Having passed under the steeps of Styebarrow Crag, and the remains of its native woods, at Glenridding Bridge, a fourth Stream is crossed.

The opening on the side of Ullswater Vale, down which this Stream flows, is adorned with fertile fields, cottages, and natural groves, that agreeably unite with the transverse views of the Lake; and the Stream, if followed up after the enclosures are left behind, will lead along bold water-breaks and waterfalls to a silent Tarn* in the recesses of Helvellyn. This desolate spot was formerly haunted by eagles, that built in the precipice which forms its western barrier. These birds used to wheel and hover round the head of the solitary angler. It also derives a melancholy interest from the fate of a young man, a stranger, who perished some years ago, by falling down the rocks in his attempt to cross over to Grasmere. His remains were discovered by means of a faithful dog that had lingered here for the space of three months, self-supported, and probably retaining to the last an attachment to the skeleton of its

master.* But to return to the road in the main Vale of Ullswater.—At
the head of the Lake (being now in Patterdale) we cross a fifth Stream,
Grisdale Beck: this would conduct through a woody steep, where may
be seen some unusually large ancient hollies, up to the level area of the
Valley of Grisdale; hence there is a path for foot-travellers, and along
which a horse may be led, to Grasmere. A sublime combination of
mountain forms appears in front while ascending the bed of this valley,
and the impression increases till the path leads almost immediately
under the projecting masses of Helvellyn. Having retraced the banks of
the Stream to Patterdale, and pursued the road up the main Dale, the
next considerable stream* would, if ascended in the same manner, con-
duct to Deep-dale, the character of which Valley may be conjectured
from its name. It is terminated by a cove, a craggy and gloomy abyss,
with precipitous sides; a faithful receptacle of the snows that are driven
into it, by the west wind, from the summit of Fairfield. Lastly, having
gone along the western side of Brotherswater and passed Hartsop Hall,
a Stream soon after issues from a cove richly decorated with native
wood. This spot is, I believe, never explored by Travellers; but, from
these sylvan and rocky recesses, whoever looks back on the gleaming
surface of Brotherswater, or forward to the precipitous sides and lofty
ridges of Dove Crag,* &c., will be equally pleased with the beauty, the
grandeur, and the wildness of the scenery.*

Seven Glens or Vallies have been noticed, which branch off from
the Cumberland side of the Vale. The opposite side has only two
Streams of any importance, one of which* would lead up from the
point where it crosses the Kirkstone-road, near the foot of Brotherswater,
to the decaying hamlet of Hartsop, remarkable for its cottage archi-
tecture, and thence to Hayswater, much frequented by anglers. The
other,* coming down Martindale, enters Ullswater at Sandwyke,
opposite to Gowbarrow Park. No persons but such as come to
Patterdale, merely to pass through it, should fail to walk as far as
Blowick, the only enclosed land which on this side borders the higher
part of the Lake. The axe has here indiscriminately levelled a rich
wood of birches and oaks, that divided this favoured spot into a hun-
dred pictures. It has yet its land-locked bays, and rocky promontories;
but those beautiful woods are gone, which *perfected* its seclusion; and
scenes, that might formerly have been compared to an inexhaustible
volume, are now spread before the eye in a single sheet,—magnificent
indeed, but seemingly perused in a moment! From Blowick a narrow

track conducts along the craggy side of Place-fell, richly adorned with juniper, and sprinkled over with birches, to the village of Sandwyke, a few straggling houses, that with the small estates attached to them, occupy an opening opposite to Lyulph's Tower and Gowbarrow Park. In Martindale,[1] the road loses sight of the Lake, and leads over a steep hill, bringing you again into view of Ullswater. Its lowest reach, four miles in length, is before you; and the view terminated by the long ridge of Cross Fell in the distance. Immediately under the eye is a deep-indented bay, with a plot of fertile land, traversed by a small brook, and rendered cheerful by two or three substantial houses of a more ornamented and showy appearance than is usual in those wild spots.

From Pooley Bridge, at the foot of the Lake, Haweswater may be conveniently visited. Haweswater is a lesser Ullswater, with this advantage, that it remains undefiled by the intrusion of bad taste.

Lowther Castle is about four miles from Pooley Bridge, and, if during this Tour the Stranger has complained, as he will have had reason to do, of a want of majestic trees, he may be abundantly recompensed for his loss in the far-spreading woods which surround that mansion. Visitants, for the most part, see little of the beauty of these magnificent grounds, being content with the view from the Terrace; but the whole course of the Lowther, from Askham to the bridge under Brougham Hall, presents almost at every step some new feature of river, woodland, and rocky landscape. A portion of this tract has, from its beauty, acquired the name of the Elysian Fields;—but the course of the stream can only be followed by the pedestrian.

NOTE.—*Vide* pp. 10–11—About 200 yards beyond the last house on the Keswick side of Rydal village the road is cut through a low wooded rock, called Thrang Crag. The top of it, which is only a few steps on the south side, affords the best view of the Vale which is to be had by a Traveller who confines himself to the public road.*

---

[1] See p. 90.

DESCRIPTION
OF THE
SCENERY OF THE LAKES

SECTION FIRST

View of The Country as Formed by Nature

AT Lucerne, in Switzerland, is shewn a Model of the Alpine country which encompasses the Lake of the four Cantons. The Spectator ascends a little platform, and sees mountains, lakes, glaciers, rivers, woods, waterfalls, and vallies, with their cottages, and every other object contained in them, lying at his feet; all things being represented in their appropriate colours. It may be easily conceived that this exhibition affords an exquisite delight to the imagination, tempting it to wander at will from valley to valley, from mountain to mountain, through the deepest recesses of the Alps. But it supplies also a more substantial pleasure: for the sublime and beautiful region, with all its hidden treasures, and their bearings and relations to each other, is thereby comprehended and understood at once.

Something of this kind, without touching upon minute details and individualities which would only confuse and embarrass, will here be attempted, in respect to the Lakes in the north of England, and the vales and mountains enclosing and surrounding them. The delineation, if tolerably executed, will, in some instances, communicate to the traveller, who has already seen the objects, new information; and will assist in giving to his recollections a more orderly arrangement than his own opportunities of observing may have permitted him to make; while it will be still more useful to the future traveller, by directing his attention at once to distinctions in things which, without such previous aid, a length of time only could enable him to discover. It is hoped, also, that this Essay may become generally serviceable, by leading to habits of more exact and considerate observation than, as far as the writer knows, have hitherto been applied to local scenery.

To begin, then, with the main outlines of the country;—I know not how to give the reader a distinct image of these more readily, than by requesting him to place himself with me, in imagination, upon some given point; let it be the top of either of the mountains, Great Gavel, or Scawfell; or, rather, let us suppose our station to be a cloud hanging midway between those two mountains, at not more than half a mile's distance from the summit of each, and not many yards above their highest elevation; we shall then see stretched at our feet a number of vallies, not fewer than eight, diverging from the point, on which we are supposed to stand, like spokes from the nave of a wheel.* First, we note, lying to the south-east, the vale of Langdale,[1] which will conduct the eye to the long lake of Winandermere, stretched nearly to the sea; or rather to the sands of the vast bay of Morcamb, serving here for the rim of this imaginary wheel;—let us trace it in a direction from the south-east towards the south, and we shall next fix our eyes upon the vale of Coniston, running up likewise from the sea, but not (as all the other vallies do) to the nave of the wheel, and therefore it may be not inaptly represented as a broken spoke sticking in the rim. Looking forth again, with an inclination towards the west, we see immediately at our feet the vale of Duddon, in which is no lake, but a copious stream winding among fields, rocks, and mountains, and terminating its course in the sands of Duddon. The fourth vale, next to be observed, viz. that of the Esk, is of the same general character as the last, yet beautifully discriminated from it by peculiar features. Its stream passes under the woody steep upon which stands Muncaster Castle, the ancient seat of the Penningtons, and after forming a short and narrow æstuary enters the sea below the small town of Ravenglass.* Next, almost due west, look down into, and along the deep valley of Wastdale, with its little chapel and half a dozen neat dwellings scattered upon a plain of meadow and corn-ground intersected with stone walls apparently innumerable, like a large piece of lawless patch-work, or an array of mathematical figures, such as in the ancient schools of geometry might have been sportively and fantastically traced out upon sand. Beyond this little fertile plain lies, within a bed of steep mountains, the long, narrow, stern, and desolate lake of Wastdale; and, beyond this, a dusky tract of level ground conducts the eye to the Irish Sea. The stream that issues from Wast-water is

---

[1] Anciently spelt Langden, and so called by the old inhabitants to this day—*dean*, from which the latter part of the word is derived, being in many parts of England a name for a valley.

named the Irt, and falls into the æstuary of the river Esk. Next comes in view Ennerdale, with its lake of bold and somewhat savage shores. Its stream, the Ehen or Enna, flowing through a soft and fertile country, passes the town of Egremont, and the ruins of the castle,*—then, seeming, like the other rivers, to break through the barrier of sand thrown up by the winds on this tempestuous coast, enters the Irish Sea. The vale of Buttermere, with the lake and village of that name, and Crummock-water, beyond, next present themselves. We will follow the main stream, the Coker, through the fertile and beautiful vale of Lorton, till it is lost in the Derwent, below the noble ruins of Cockermouth Castle. Lastly, Borrowdale, of which the vale of Keswick is only a continuation, stretching due north, brings us to a point nearly opposite to the vale of Winandermere with which we began. From this it will appear, that the image of a wheel, thus far exact, is little more than one half complete; but the deficiency on the eastern side may be supplied by the vales of Wytheburn, Ullswater, Hawswater, and the vale of Grasmere and Rydal; none of these, however, run up to the central point between Great Gavel and Scawfell. From this, hitherto our central point, take a flight of not more than four or five miles* eastward to the ridge of Helvellyn, and you will look down upon Wytheburn and St. John's Vale, which are a branch of the vale of Keswick; upon Ulswater, stretching due east:—and not far beyond to the south-east (though from this point not visible) lie the vale and lake of Hawswater; and lastly, the vale of Grasmere, Rydal, and Ambleside, brings you back to Winandermere, thus completing, though on the eastern side in a somewhat irregular manner, the representative figure of the wheel.

Such, concisely given, is the general topographical view of the country of the Lakes in the north of England; and it may be observed, that, from the circumference to the centre, that is, from the sea or plain country to the mountain stations specified, there is—in the several ridges that enclose these vales, and divide them from each other, I mean in the forms and surfaces, first of the swelling grounds, next of the hills and rocks, and lastly of the mountains—an ascent of almost regular gradation, from elegance and richness, to their highest point of grandeur and sublimity.* It follows therefore from this, first, that these rocks, hills, and mountains, must present themselves to view in stages rising above each other, the mountains clustering together towards the central point; and next, that an observer familiar with the several vales, must, from their various position in relation to the sun, have had before his eyes every possible embellishment of beauty, dignity, and splendour, which light and shadow can bestow upon objects so diversified. For example, in the vale of Winandermere, if the spectator looks for gentle and lovely scenes, his eye is turned towards the south; if for the grand, towards the north: in the vale of Keswick, which (as hath been said) lies almost due north of this, it is directly the reverse. Hence, when the sun is setting in summer far to the north-west, it is seen, by the spectator from the shores or breast of Winandermere, resting among the summits of the loftiest mountains, some of which will perhaps be half or wholly hidden by clouds, or by the blaze of light which the orb diffuses around it; and the surface of the lake will reflect before the eye correspondent colours through every variety of beauty, and through all degrees of splendour.* In the vale of Keswick, at the same period, the sun sets over the humbler regions of the landscape, and showers down upon *them* the radiance which at once veils and glorifies,—sending forth, meanwhile, broad streams of rosy, crimson, purple, or golden light, towards the grand mountains in the south and south-east, which, thus illuminated, with all their projections and cavities, and with an intermixture of solemn shadows, are seen distinctly through a cool and clear atmosphere. Of course, there is as marked a difference between the *noontide* appearance of these two opposite vales. The bedimming haze that overspreads the south, and the clear atmosphere and determined shadows of the clouds in the north, at the same time of the day, are each seen in these several vales, with a contrast as striking. The reader will easily conceive in what degree the intermediate vales partake of a kindred variety.

I do not indeed know any tract of country in which, within so narrow a compass, may be found an equal variety in the influences of light and shadow upon the sublime or beautiful features of landscape; and it is owing to the combined circumstances to which the reader's attention has been directed. From a point between Great Gavel and Scawfell, a shepherd would not require more than an hour to descend into any one of eight of the principal vales by which he would be surrounded; and all the others lie (with the exception of Hawswater) at but a small distance. Yet, though clustered together, every valley has its distinct and separate character; in some instances, as if they had been formed in studied contrast to each other, and in others with the united pleasing differences and resemblances of a sisterly rivalship. This concentration of interest gives to the country a decided super-iority over the most attractive districts of Scotland and Wales, espe-cially for the pedestrian traveller. In Scotland and Wales are found, undoubtedly, individual scenes, which, in their several kinds, cannot be excelled. But, in Scotland, particularly, what long tracts of desolate country intervene! so that the traveller, when he reaches a spot de-servedly of great celebrity, would find it difficult to determine how much of his pleasure is owing to excellence inherent in the landscape itself; and how much to an instantaneous recovery from an oppres-sion left upon his spirits by the barrenness and desolation through which he has passed.

But to proceed with our survey;—and, first, of the MOUNTAINS.* Their *forms* are endlessly diversified, sweeping easily or boldly in simple majesty, abrupt and precipitous, or soft and elegant. In mag-nitude and grandeur they are individually inferior to the most cele-brated of those in some other parts of this island; but, in the combinations which they make, towering above each other, or lifting themselves in ridges like the waves of a tumultuous sea, and in the beauty and variety of their surfaces and colours, they are surpassed by none.

The general *surface* of the mountains is turf, rendered rich and green by the moisture of the climate. Sometimes the turf, as in the neighbourhood of Newlands, is little broken, the whole covering being soft and downy pasturage. In other places rocks predominate; the soil is laid bare by torrents and burstings of water from the sides of the mountains in heavy rains; and not unfrequently their perpendicular sides are seamed by ravines (formed also by rains and torrents) which, meeting in angular points, entrench and scar the surface with numer-ous figures like the letters W. and Y.

In the ridge that divides Eskdale from Wasdale, granite is found; but the MOUNTAINS are for the most part composed of the stone by mineralogists termed schist, which, as you approach the plain coun-try, gives place to lime-stone and free-stone; but schist being the sub-stance of the mountains, the predominant *colour* of their *rocky* parts is bluish, or hoary grey—the general tint of the lichens with which the bare stone is encrusted. With this blue or grey colour is frequently intermixed a red tinge, proceeding from the iron that interveins the stone, and impregnates the soil. The iron is the principle of

decomposition in these rocks; and hence, when they become pulver-
ized, the elementary particles crumbling down, overspread in many
places the steep and almost precipitous sides of the mountains with
an intermixture of colours, like the compound hues of a dove's neck.*
When in the heat of advancing summer, the fresh green tint of the
herbage has somewhat faded, it is again revived by the appearance of
the fern profusely spread over the same ground: and, upon this plant,
more than upon any thing else, do the changes which the seasons
make in the colouring of the mountains depend. About the first week
in October, the rich green, which prevailed through the whole sum-
mer, is usually passed away. The brilliant and various colours of the
fern are then in harmony with the autumnal woods; bright yellow or
lemon colour, at the base of the mountains, melting gradually, through
orange, to a dark russet brown towards the summits, where the plant,
being more exposed to the weather, is in a more advanced state of
decay.* Neither heath nor furze are *generally* found upon the *sides* of
these mountains, though in many places they are adorned by those
plants, so beautiful when in flower. We may add, that the mountains
are of height sufficient to have the surface towards the summit soft-
ened by distance, and to imbibe the finest aërial hues.* In common
also with other mountains, their apparent forms and colours are per-
petually changed by the clouds and vapours which float round them:
the effect indeed of mist or haze, in a country of this character, is like
that of magic.* I have seen six or seven ridges rising above each other,
all created in a moment by the vapours upon the side of a mountain,
which, in its ordinary appearance, shewed not a projecting point to
furnish even a hint for such an operation.

I will take this opportunity of observing, that they who have stud-
ied the appearances of nature feel that the superiority, in point of
visual interest, of mountainous over other countries—is more strik-
ingly displayed in winter than in summer. This, as must be obvious, is
partly owing to the *forms* of the mountains, which, of course, are not
affected by the seasons; but also, in no small degree, to the greater
variety that exists in their winter than their summer *colouring*. This
variety is such, and so harmoniously preserved, that it leaves little
cause of regret when the splendour of autumn is passed away. The
oak-coppices, upon the sides of the mountains, retain russet leaves;
the birch stands conspicuous with its silver stem and puce-coloured
twigs; the hollies, with green leaves and scarlet berries, have come

forth to view from among the deciduous trees, whose summer foliage
had concealed them: the ivy is now plentifully apparent upon the
stems and boughs of the trees, and upon the steep rocks. In place of
the deep summer-green of the herbage and fern, many rich colours
play into each other over the surface of the mountains; turf (the tints
of which are interchangeably tawny-green, olive, and brown,) beds of
withered fern, and grey rocks, being harmoniously blended together.
The mosses and lichens are never so fresh and flourishing as in win-
ter, if it be not a season of frost; and their minute beauties prodigally
adorn the foreground. Wherever we turn, we find these productions
of nature, to which winter is rather favourable than unkindly, scat-
tered over the walls, banks of earth, rocks, and stones, and upon the
trunks of trees, with the intermixture of several species of small fern,
now green and fresh; and, to the observing passenger, their forms and
colours are a source of inexhaustible admiration. Add to this the hoar-
frost and snow, with all the varieties they create, and which volumes
would not be sufficient to describe. I will content myself with one
instance of the colouring produced by snow, which may not be
uninteresting to painters. It is extracted from the memorandum-book
of a friend;* and for its accuracy I can speak, having been an eye-witness
of the appearance. 'I observed,' says he, 'the beautiful effect of the
drifted snow upon the mountains, and the perfect *tone* of colour.
From the top of the mountains downwards a rich olive was produced
by the powdery snow and the grass, which olive was warmed with
a little brown, and in this way harmoniously combined, by insensible
gradations, with the white. The drifting took away the monotony of
snow; and the whole vale of Grasmere, seen from the terrace walk in
Easedale, was as varied, perhaps more so, than even in the pomp of
autumn. In the distance was Loughrigg-Fell, the basin-wall of the lake:
this, from the summit downward, was a rich orange-olive; then the lake
of a bright olive-green, nearly the same tint as the snow-powdered
mountain tops and high slopes in Easedale; and lastly, the church,
with its firs, forming the centre of the view. Next to the church came
nine distinguishable hills, six of them with woody sides turned
towards us, all of them oak-copses with their bright red leaves and
snow-powdered twigs; these hills—so variously situated in relation to
each other, and to the view in general, so variously powdered, some
only enough to give the herbage a rich brown tint, one intensely white
and lighting up all the others—were yet so placed, as in the most

inobtrusive manner to harmonise by contrast with a perfect naked, snowless bleak summit in the far distance.'

Having spoken of the forms, surface, and colour of the mountains, let us descend into the VALES. Though these have been represented under the general image of the spokes of a wheel, they are, for the most part, winding; the windings of many being abrupt and intricate. And, it may be observed, that, in one circumstance, the general shape of them all has been determined by that primitive conformation through which so many became receptacles of lakes. For they are not formed, as are most of the celebrated Welsh vallies, by an approxima- tion of the sloping bases of the opposite mountains towards each other, leaving little more between than a channel for the passage of a hasty river; but the bottom of these vallies is mostly a spacious and gently declining area, apparently level as the floor of a temple, or the surface of a lake, and broken in many cases, by rocks and hills, which rise up like islands from the plain. In such of the vallies as make many windings, these level areas open upon the traveller in succession, divided from each other sometimes by a mutual approximation of the hills, leaving only passage for a river, sometimes by correspondent windings, without such approximation; and sometimes by a bold advance of one mountain towards that which is opposite it. It may here be observed with propriety that the several rocks and hills, which have been described as rising up like islands from the level area of the vale, have regulated the choice of the inhabitants in the situation of their dwellings. Where none of these are found, and the inclination of the ground is not sufficiently rapid easily to carry off the waters, (as in the higher part of Langdale, for instance,) the houses are not sprin- kled over the middle of the vales, but confined to their sides, being placed merely so far up the mountain as to be protected from the floods. But where these rocks and hills have been scattered over the plain of the vale, (as in Grasmere, Donnerdale, Eskdale, &c.) the beauty which they give to the scene is much heightened by a single cottage, or cluster of cottages, that will be almost always found under them, or upon their sides;* dryness and shelter having tempted the Dalesmen to fix their habitations there.

I shall now speak of the LAKES of this country. The form of the lake is most perfect when, like Derwent-water, and some of the smaller lakes, it least resembles that of a river;—I mean, when being looked at from any given point where the whole may be seen at once, the width of it bears such proportion to the length, that, however the outline may be diversified by far-receding bays, it never assumes the shape of a river, and is contemplated with that placid and quiet feeling which belongs peculiarly to the lake—as a body of still water under the influence of no current;* reflecting therefore the clouds, the light, and all the imagery of the sky and surrounding hills; expressing also and making visible the changes of the atmosphere,* and motions of the lightest breeze, and subject to agitation only from the winds—

> ————The visible scene
> Would enter unawares into his mind
> With all its solemn imagery, its rocks,
> Its woods, and that uncertain heaven received
> Into the bosom of the *steady* lake!*

It must be noticed, as a favourable characteristic of the lakes of this country, that, though several of the largest, such as Winandermere, Ulswater, Hawswater, do, when the whole length of them is commanded from an elevated point, lose somewhat of the peculiar form of the lake, and assume the resemblance of a magnificent river;* yet, as their shape is winding, (particularly that of Ulswater and Hawswater) when the view of the whole is obstructed by those barriers which determine the windings, and the spectator is confined to one reach, the appropriate feeling is revived; and one lake may thus in succession present to the eye the essential characteristic of many. But, though the forms of the large lakes have this advantage, it is nevertheless favourable to the beauty of the country that the largest of them are comparatively small; and that the same vale generally furnishes a succession of lakes, instead of being filled with one. The vales in North Wales, as hath been observed, are not formed for the reception of lakes; those of Switzerland, Scotland, and this part of the North of England, *are* so formed; but, in Switzerland and Scotland, the proportion of diffused water is often too great, as at the lake of Geneva for instance, and in most of the Scotch lakes. No doubt it sounds magnificent and flatters the imagination, to hear at a distance of expanses of water so many leagues in length and miles in width; and such ample room may be delightful to the fresh-water sailor, scudding with a lively breeze amid the rapidly-shifting scenery. But, who ever travelled along the banks of Loch-Lomond, variegated as the lower part is by islands, without feeling that a speedier termination of the long vista of blank water would be acceptable; and without wishing for an interposition of green meadows, trees, and cottages, and a sparkling stream to run by his side? In fact, a notion of grandeur, as connected with magnitude, has seduced persons of taste into a general mistake upon this subject. It is much more desirable, for the purposes of pleasure, that lakes should be numerous, and small or middle-sized, than large, not only for communication by walks and rides, but for variety, and for recurrence of similar appearances. To illustrate this by one instance:—how pleasing is it to have a ready and frequent opportunity of watching, at the outlet of a lake, the stream pushing its way among the rocks in lively contrast with the stillness from which it has escaped; and how amusing to compare its noisy and turbulent motions with the gentle playfulness of the breezes, that may be starting up or wandering here and there over the faintly-rippled surface of the broad water! I may add, as a general remark, that, in lakes of great width, the shores cannot be distinctly seen at the same time, and therefore contribute little to mutual illustration and ornament; and, if the opposite shores are out of sight of each other, like those of the American and Asiatic lakes, then unfortunately the traveller is reminded of a nobler object; he has the blankness of a sea-prospect without the grandeur and accompanying sense of power.

As the comparatively small size of the lakes in the North of England is favourable to the production of variegated landscape, their *boundary-line* also is for the most part gracefully or boldly indented. That uniformity which prevails in the primitive frame of the lower grounds among all chains or clusters of mountains where large bodies of still water are bedded, is broken by the *secondary* agents of nature, ever at work to supply the deficiences of the mould in which things were originally cast. Using the word *deficiences*, I do not speak with reference to those stronger emotions which a region of mountains is peculiarly fitted to excite. The bases of those huge barriers may run for a long space in straight lines, and these parallel to each other; the opposite sides of a profound vale may ascend as exact counterparts, or in mutual reflection, like the billows of a troubled sea; and the impression be, from its very simplicity, more awful and sublime. Sublimity is the result of Nature's first great dealings with the superficies of the earth; but the general tendency of her subsequent operations is towards the production of beauty; by a multiplicity of symmetrical parts uniting in a consistent whole. This is every where exemplified along the margins of these lakes. Masses of rock, that have been precipitated from the heights into the area of waters, lie in some places like stranded ships;* or have acquired the compact structure of jutting piers; or project in little peninsulas crested with native wood. The smallest rivulet—one whose silent influx is scarcely noticeable in a season of dry weather—so faint is the dimple made by it on the surface of the smooth lake—will be found to have been not useless in shaping, by its deposits of gravel and soil in time of flood, a curve that would not otherwise have existed. But the more powerful brooks, encroaching upon the level of the lake, have, in course of time, given birth to ample promontories of sweeping outline that contrasts boldly with the longitudinal base of the steeps on the opposite shore; while their flat or gently-sloping surfaces never fail to introduce, into the midst of desolation and barrenness, the elements of fertility, even where the habitations of men may not have been raised. These alluvial promontories, however, threaten, in some places, to bisect the waters which they have long adorned; and, in course of ages, they will cause some of the lakes to dwindle into numerous and insignificant pools; which, in their turn, will finally be filled up. But, checking these intrusive calculations, let us rather be content with appearances as they are, and pursue in imagination the meandering shores, whether rugged steeps, admitting of no cultivation, descend into the water; or gently-sloping lawns and woods, or flat and fertile meadows stretch between the margin of the lake and the mountains. Among minuter recommendations will be noticed, especially along bays exposed to the setting-in of strong winds, the curved rim of fine blue gravel, thrown up in course of time by the waves, half of it perhaps gleaming from under the water, and the corresponding half of a lighter hue; and in other parts bordering the lake, groves, if I may so call them, of reeds and bulrushes; or plots of water-lilies lifting up their large target-shaped leaves to the breeze, while the white flower is heaving upon the wave.*

To these may naturally be added the birds that enliven the waters.* Wild-ducks in spring-time hatch their young in the islands, and upon reedy shores;—the sand-piper, flitting along the stony margins, by its restless note attracts the eye to motions as restless:—upon some jutting rock, or at the edge of a smooth meadow, the stately heron may be described with folded wings, that might seem to have caught their delicate hue from the blue waters, by the side of which she watches for her sustenance. In winter, the lakes are sometimes resorted to by wild swans;* and in that season habitually by widgeons, goldings,* and other aquatic fowl of the smaller species. Let me be allowed the aid of verse to describe the evolutions which these visitants sometimes perform, on a fine day towards the close of winter.

> Mark how the feather'd tenants of the flood,
> With grace of motion that might scarcely seem
> Inferior to angelical, prolong
> Their curious pastime! shaping in mid air
> (And sometimes with ambitious wing that soars
> High as the level of the mountain tops,)
> A circuit ampler than the lake beneath,
> Their own domain;—but ever, while intent
> On tracing and retracing that large round,
> Their jubilant activity evolves
> Hundreds of curves and circlets, to and fro,
> Upward and downward, progress intricate
> Yet unperplex'd, as if one spirit swayed
> Their indefatigable flight.—'Tis done—
> Ten times, or more, I fancied it had ceased;
> But lo! the vanish'd company again
> Ascending;—they approach—I hear their wings
> Faint, faint, at first, and then an eager sound
> Past in a moment—and as faint again!
> They tempt the sun to sport amid their plumes;
> They tempt the water or the gleaming ice,
> To shew them a fair image;—'tis themselves,
> Their own fair forms, upon the glimmering plain,
> Painted more soft and fair as they descend
> Almost to touch;—then up again aloft,
> Up with a sally and a flash of speed,
> As if they scorn'd both resting-place and rest!*

The ISLANDS, dispersed among these lakes, are neither so numerous nor so beautiful as might be expected from the account that has been given of the manner in which the level areas of the vales are so frequently diversified by rocks, hills, and hillocks, scattered over them; nor are they ornamented (as are several of the lakes in Scotland

and Ireland) by the remains of castles or other places of defence; nor
with the still more interesting ruins of religious edifices. Every one
must regret that scarcely a vestige is left of the Oratory, consecrated
to the Virgin, which stood upon Chapel-Holm in Windermere, and
that the Chauntry has disappeared, where mass used to be sung, upon
St. Herbert's Island, Derwent-water. The islands of the last-men-
tioned lake are neither fortunately placed nor of pleasing shape; but if
the wood upon them were managed with more taste, they might
become interesting features in the landscape. There is a beautiful
cluster on Winandermere;* a pair pleasingly contrasted upon Rydal;
nor must the solitary green island of Grasmere* be forgotten. In the
bosom of each of the lakes of Ennerdale and Devockwater is a single
rock, which, owing to its neighbourhood to the sea, is—

> 'The haunt of cormorants and sea-mews' clang,'*

a music well suited to the stern and wild character of the several
scenes! It may be worth while here to mention (not as an object of
beauty, but of curiosity) that there occasionally appears above the sur-
face of Derwent-water, and always in the same place, a considerable
tract of spongy ground covered with aquatic plants, which is called
the Floating, but with more propriety might be named the Buoyant,
Island;* and, on one of the pools near the lake of Esthwaite, may
sometimes be seen a mossy Islet, with trees upon it, shifting about
before the wind, a lusus naturæ frequent on the great rivers of
America, and not unknown in other parts of the world.

> ——'fas habeas invisere Tiburis arva,
> Albuneæque lacum, atque umbras terrasque natantes.'[1]*

This part of the subject may be concluded with observing—that,
from the multitude of brooks and torrents that fall into these lakes,
and of internal springs by which they are fed, and which circulate
through them like veins, they are truly living lakes, '*vivi lacus*;'* and
are thus discriminated from the stagnant and sullen pools frequent
among mountains that have been formed by volcanoes, and from the
shallow meres found in flat and fenny countries. The water is also of
crystalline purity; so that, if it were not for the reflections of the
incumbent mountains by which it is darkened, a delusion might
be felt, by a person resting quietly in a boat on the bosom of

---

[1] See that admirable Idyllium, the Catillus and Salia, of Landor.

Winandermere or Derwent-water, similar to that which Carver so beautifully describes when he was floating alone in the middle of lake Erie or Ontario,* and could almost have imagined that his boat was suspended in an element as pure as air, or rather that the air and water were one.

Having spoken of Lakes I must not omit to mention, as a kindred feature of this country, those bodies of still water called TARNS.* In the economy of nature these are useful, as auxiliaries to Lakes; for if the whole quantity of water which falls upon the mountains in time of storm were poured down upon the plains without intervention, in some quarters, of such receptacles, the habitable grounds would be much more subject than they are to inundation. But, as some of the collateral brooks spend their fury, finding a free course toward and also down the channel of the main stream of the vale before those that have to pass through the higher tarns and lakes have filled their several basins, a gradual distribution is effected; and the waters thus reserved, instead of uniting, to spread ravage and deformity, with those which meet with no such detention, contribute to support, for a length of time, the vigour of many streams without a fresh fall of rain. Tarns are found in some of the vales, and are numerous upon the mountains. A Tarn, in a *Vale*, implies, for the most part, that the bed of the vale is not happily formed; that the water of the brooks can neither wholly escape, nor diffuse itself over a large area. Accordingly, in such situations, Tarns are often surrounded by an unsightly tract of boggy ground; but this is not always the case, and in the cultivated parts of the country, when the shores of the Tarn are determined, it differs only from the Lake in being smaller, and in belonging mostly to a smaller valley, or circular recess. Of this class of miniature lakes, Loughrigg Tarn, near Grasmere, is the most beautiful example. It has a margin of green firm meadows, of rocks, and rocky woods, a few reeds here, a little company of water-lilies there, with beds of gravel or stone beyond; a tiny stream issuing neither briskly nor sluggishly out of it; but its feeding rills, from the shortness of their course, so small as to be scarcely visible. Five or six cottages are reflected in its peaceful bosom; rocky and barren steeps rise up above the hanging enclosures; and the solemn pikes of Langdale overlook, from a distance, the low cultivated ridge of land that forms the northern boundary of this small, quiet, and fertile domain. The *mountain* Tarns can only be recommended to the notice of the inquisitive traveller who

has time to spare. They are difficult of access and naked; yet some of
them are, in their permanent forms, very grand; and there are acci-
dents of things which would make the meanest of them interesting. At
all events, one of these pools is an acceptable sight to the mountain
wanderer; not merely as an incident that diversifies the prospect, but
as forming in his mind a centre or conspicuous point to which objects,
otherwise disconnected or insubordinated, may be referred. Some
few have a varied outline, with bold heath-clad promontories; and, as
they mostly lie at the foot of a steep precipice, the water where the sun
is not shining upon it,* appears black and sullen; and, round the mar-
gin, huge stones and masses of rock are scattered; some defying con-
jecture as to the means by which they came thither;* and others
obviously fallen from on high—the contribution of ages! A not
unpleasing sadness is induced by this perplexity, and these images of
decay; while the prospect of a body of pure water unattended with
groves and other cheerful rural images by which fresh water is usually
accompanied, and unable to give furtherance to the meagre vegeta-
tion around it—excites a sense of some repulsive power strongly put
forth, and thus deepens the melancholy natural to such scenes. Nor is
the feeling of solitude often more forcibly or more solemnly impressed
than by the side of one of these mountain pools: though desolate and
forbidding, it seems a distinct place to repair to; yet where the visit-
ants must be rare, and there can be no disturbance. Water-fowl flock
hither; and the lonely Angler may here be seen; but the imagination,
not content with this scanty allowance of society, is tempted to attri-
bute a voluntary power to every change which takes place in such
a spot, whether it be the breeze that wanders over the surface of the
water, or the splendid lights of evening resting upon it in the midst of
awful precipices.

> 'There, sometimes does a leaping fish
> Send through the tarn a lonely cheer;
> The crags repeat the raven's croak
> In symphony austere:
> Thither the rainbow comes, the cloud,
> And mists that spread the flying shroud
> And sunbeams, and the sounding blast.'*

It will be observed that this country is bounded on the south and
west by the sea, which combines beautifully, from many elevated

points, with the inland scenery; and, from the bay of Morcamb, the sloping shores and back-ground of distant mountains are seen, composing pictures equally distinguished for amenity and grandeur. But the æstuaries on this coast are in a great measure bare at low water;[1] and there is no instance of the sea running far up among the mountains, and mingling with the Lakes, which are such in the strict and usual sense of the word, being of fresh water. Nor have the streams, from the shortness of their course, time to acquire that body of water necessary to confer upon them much majesty. In fact, the most considerable, while they continue in the mountain and lake-country, are rather large brooks than rivers. The water is perfectly pellucid, through which in many places are seen, to a great depth, their beds of rock, or of blue gravel, which give to the water itself an exquisitely cerulean colour: this is particularly striking in the rivers Derwent and Duddon,* which may be compared, such and so various are their beauties, to any two rivers of equal length of course in any country. The number of the torrents and smaller brooks is infinite, with their water-falls and water-breaks; and they need not here be described. I will only observe that, as many, even of the smallest rills, have either found, or made for themselves, recesses in the sides of the mountains or in the vales, they have tempted the primitive inhabitants to settle near them for shelter; and hence, cottages so placed, by seeming to withdraw from the eye, are the more endeared to the feelings.

The Woods consist chiefly of oak, ash, and birch, and here and there Wych-elm, with underwood of hazel, the white and black thorn, and hollies; in moist places alders and willows abound; and yews among the rocks. Formerly the whole country must have been covered with wood to a great height up the mountains; where native Scotch firs[2] must have grown in great profusion, as they do in the northern part of Scotland to this day. But not one of these old inhabitants has existed, perhaps, for some hundreds of years; the beautiful traces,

[1] In fact there is not an instance of a harbour on the Cumberland side of the Solway frith that is not dry at low water; that of Ravenglass, at the mouth of the Esk, as a natural harbour is much the best. The Sea appears to have been retiring slowly for ages from this coast. From Whitehaven to St. Bees extends a track of level ground, about five miles in length, which formerly must have been under salt water, so as to have made an island of the high ground that stretches between it and the Sea.

[2] This species of fir is in character much superior to the American which has usurped its place: Where the fir is planted for ornament, let it be by all means of the aboriginal species, which can only be procured from the Scotch nurseries.

however, of the universal sylvan[1] appearance the country formerly had, yet survive in the native coppice-woods that have been protected by inclosures, and also in the forest-trees and hollies, which, though disappearing fast, are yet scattered both over the inclosed and uninclosed parts of the mountains. The same is expressed by the beauty and intricacy with which the fields and coppice-woods are often intermingled: the plough of the first settlers having followed naturally the veins of richer, dryer, or less stony soil; and thus it has shaped out an intermixture of wood and lawn, with a grace and wildness which it would have been impossible for the hand of studied art to produce. Other trees have been introduced within these last fifty years, such as beeches, larches, limes, &c. and plantations of firs, seldom with advantage, and often with great injury to the appearance of the country; but the sycamore (which I believe was brought into this island from Germany, not more than two hundred years ago) has long been the favourite of the cottagers; and, with the fir, has been chosen to screen their dwellings;* and is sometimes found in the fields whither the winds or the waters may have carried its seeds.

The want most felt, however, is that of timber trees. There are few *magnificent* ones to be found near any of the lakes; and unless greater care be taken, there will, in a short time, scarcely be left an ancient oak that would repay the cost of felling. The neighbourhood of Rydal, notwithstanding the havoc which has been made, is yet nobly distinguished.* In the woods of Lowther, also, is found an almost matchless store of ancient trees, and the majesty and wildness of the native forest.

Among the smaller vegetable ornaments must be reckoned the bilberry, a ground plant, never so beautiful as in early spring, when it is seen under bare or budding trees, that imperfectly intercept the sunshine, covering the rocky knolls with a pure mantle of fresh verdure, more lively than the herbage of the open fields;—the broom that spreads luxuriantly along rough pastures, and in the month of June interveins the steep copses with its golden blossoms;*—and the juniper, a rich evergreen, that thrives in spite of cattle, upon the unenclosed parts of the mountains:—the Dutch myrtle diffuses fragrance in moist places; and there is an endless variety of brilliant flowers in

---

[1] A squirrel (so I have heard the old people of Wytheburn say) might have gone from their chapel to Keswick without alighting on the ground.

the fields and meadows, which, if the agriculture of the country were more carefully attended to, would disappear. Nor can I omit again to notice the lichens and mosses: their profusion, beauty, and variety exceed those of any other country I have seen.

It may now be proper to say a few words respecting climate, and 'skiey influences,'* in which this region, as far as the character of its landscapes is affected by them, may, upon the whole, be considered fortunate. The country is, indeed, subject to much bad weather, and it has been ascertained that twice as much rain falls here as in many parts of the island; but the number of black drizzling days, that blot out the face of things, is by no means *proportionally* great. Nor is a continuance of thick, flagging, damp air, so common as in the West of England and Ireland. The rain here comes down heartily, and is frequently succeeded by clear, bright weather,* when every brook is vocal, and every torrent sonorous; brooks and torrents, which are never muddy, even in the heaviest floods, except, after a drought, they happen to be defiled for a short time by waters that have swept along dusty roads, or have broken out into ploughed fields. Days of unsettled weather, with partial showers, are very frequent; but the showers, darkening, or brightening, as they fly from hill to hill, are not less grateful to the eye than finely interwoven passages of gay and sad music are touching to the ear.* Vapours exhaling from the lakes and meadows after sun-rise, in a hot season, or, in moist weather, brooding upon the heights, or descending towards the valleys with inaudible motion, give a visionary character to everything around them; and are in themselves so beautiful, as to dispose us to enter into the feelings of those simple nations (such as the Laplanders of this day) by whom they are taken for guardian deities of the mountains; or to sympathise with others who have fancied these delicate apparitions to be the spirits of their departed ancestors.* Akin to these are fleecy clouds resting upon the hill-tops; they are not easily managed in picture, with their accompaniments of blue sky; but how glorious are they in nature! how pregnant with imagination for the poet! and the height of the Cumbrian mountains is sufficient to exhibit daily and hourly instances of those mysterious attachments. Such clouds, cleaving to their stations, or lifting up suddenly their glittering heads from behind rocky barriers, or hurrying out of sight with speed of the sharpest edge—will often tempt an inhabitant to congratulate himself on belonging to a country of mists and clouds and storms, and make him think of the blank sky of Egypt, and of the cerulean vacancy of Italy, as an unanimated and even a sad spectacle.* The atmosphere, however, as in every country subject to much rain, is frequently unfavourable to landscape, especially when keen winds succeed the rain which are apt to produce coldness, spottiness, and an unmeaning or repulsive detail in the distance;—a sunless frost, under a canopy of leaden and shapeless clouds, is, as far as it allows things to be seen, equally disagreeable.

It has been said that in human life there are moments worth ages. In a more subdued tone of sympathy may we affirm, that in the climate of England there are, for the lover of nature, days which are worth whole months,—I might say—even years. One of these favoured days sometimes occurs in spring-time, when that soft air is breathing over the blossoms and new-born verdure, which inspired Buchanan with his beautiful Ode to the first of May; the air, which, in the luxuriance of his fancy, he likens to that of the golden age,—to that which gives motion to the funereal cypresses on the banks of Lethe;—to the air which is to salute beatified spirits when expiatory fires shall have consumed the earth with all her habitations. But it is in autumn that days of such affecting influence most frequently intervene;—the atmosphere seems refined, and the sky rendered more crystalline, as the vivifying heat of the year abates; the lights and shadows are more delicate; the colouring is richer and more finely harmonized; and, in this season of stillness, the ear being unoccupied, or only gently excited, the sense of vision becomes more susceptible of its appropriate enjoyments. A resident in a country like this which we are treating of, will agree with me, that the presence of a lake is indispensable to exhibit in perfection the beauty of one of these days; and he must have experienced, while looking on the unruffled waters, that the imagination, by their aid, is carried into recesses of feeling otherwise impenetrable. The reason of this is, that the heavens are not only brought down into the bosom of the earth, but that the earth is mainly looked at, and thought of, through the medium of a purer element.* The happiest time is when the equinoxial gales are departed; but their fury may probably be called to mind by the sight of a few shattered boughs, whose leaves do not differ in colour from the faded foliage of the stately oaks from which these relics of the storm depend: all else speaks of tranquillity;—not a breath of air, no restlessness of insects, and not a moving object perceptible—except the clouds gliding in the depths of the lake, or the traveller passing along, an inverted image, whose motion seems governed by the quiet of a time,* to which its archetype, the living person, is, perhaps, insensible:—or it may happen, that the figure of one of the larger birds, a raven or a heron, is crossing silently among the reflected clouds, while the voice of the real bird, from the element aloft, gently awakens* in the spectator the recollection of appetites and instincts, pursuits and occupations, that deform and agitate the world,—yet have no power to prevent nature from putting on an aspect capable of satisfying the most intense cravings for the tranquil, the lovely, and the perfect, to which man, the noblest of her creatures, is subject.

Thus far, of climate, as influencing the feelings through its effect on the objects of sense. We may add, that whatever has been said upon the advantages derived to these scenes from a changeable atmosphere, would apply, perhaps still more forcibly, to their appearance under the varied solemnities of night. Milton, it will be remembered, has given a *clouded* moon to Paradise* itself. In the night-season also, the narrowness of the vales, and comparative smallness of the lakes, are especially adapted to bring surrounding objects home to the eye and to the heart. The stars, taking their stations above the hill-tops,* are contemplated from a spot like the Abyssinian recess of Rasselas,* with much more touching interest than they are likely to excite when looked at from an open country with ordinary undulations: and it must be obvious, that it is the *bays* only of large lakes that can present such contrasts of light and shadow as those of smaller dimensions display from every quarter. A deep contracted valley, with diffused waters, such a valley and plains level and wide as those of Chaldea, are the two extremes in which the beauty of the heavens and their connexion with the earth are most sensibly felt. Nor do the advantages I have been speaking of imply here an exclusion of the aerial effects of distance. These are insured by the height of the mountains, and are found, even in the narrowest vales, where they lengthen in perspective, or act (if the expression may be used) as telescopes for the open country.

The subject would bear to be enlarged upon: but I will conclude this section with a night-scene suggested by the Vale of Keswick. The Fragment is well known; but it gratifies me to insert it, as the Writer was one of the first who led the way to a worthy admiration of this country.

'Now sunk the sun, now twilight sunk, and night
Rode in her zenith; not a passing breeze
Sigh'd to the grove, which in the midnight air
Stood motionless, and in the peaceful floods
Inverted hung: for now the billows slept
Along the shore, nor heav'd the deep; but spread
A shining mirror to the moon's pale orb,
Which, dim and waning, o'er the shadowy cliffs,
The solemn woods, and spiry mountain tops,
Her glimmering faintness threw: now every eye,
Oppress'd with toil, was drown'd in deep repose,
Save that the unseen Shepherd in his watch,
Propp'd on his crook, stood listening by the fold,
And gaz'd the starry vault, and pendant moon;
Nor voice, nor sound, broke on the deep serene;
But the soft murmur of swift-gushing rills,
Forth issuing from the mountain's distant steep,
(Unheard till now, and now scarce heard) proclaim'd
All things at rest, and imag'd the still voice
Of quiet, whispering in the ear of night.'[1]

[1] Dr. Brown, the author of this fragment, was from his infancy brought up in Cumberland, and should have remembered that the practice of folding sheep by night is unknown among these mountains, and that the image of the Shepherd upon the watch is out of its place, and belongs only to countries, with a warmer climate, that are subject to ravages from beasts or prey. It is pleasing to notice a dawn of imaginative feeling in these verses. Tickel, a man of no common genius, chose, for the subject of a Poem, Kensington Gardens, in preference to the Banks of the Derwent, within a mile or two of which he was born. But this was in the reign of Queen Anne, or George the first. Progress must have been made in the interval; though the traces of it, except in the works of Thomson and Dyer, are not very obvious.

SECTION SECOND

Aspect of The Country, as Affected by its Inhabitants

HITHERTO I have chiefly spoken of the features by which nature has discriminated this country from others. I will now describe, in general terms, in what manner it is indebted to the hand of man. What I have to notice on this subject will emanate most easily and perspicuously from a description of the ancient and present inhabitants, their occupations, their condition of life, the distribution of landed property among them, and the tenure by which it is holden.

The reader will suffer me here to recall to his mind the shapes of the vallies, and their position with respect to each other, and the forms and substance of the intervening mountains. He will people the vallies with lakes and rivers: the coves and sides of the mountains with pools and torrents; and will bound half of the circle which we have contemplated by the sands of the sea, or by the sea itself. He will conceive that, from the point upon which he stood, he looks down upon this scene before the country had been penetrated by any inhabitants:—to vary his sensations, and to break in upon their stillness, he will form to himself an image of the tides visiting and re-visiting the friths, the main sea dashing against the bolder shore, the rivers pursuing their course to be lost in the mighty mass of waters. He may see or hear in fancy the winds sweeping over the lakes, or piping with a loud voice among the mountain peaks; and, lastly, may think of the primeval woods shedding and renewing their leaves with no human eye to notice, or human heart to regret or welcome the change.* 'When the first settlers entered this region (says an animated writer) they found it overspread with wood; forest trees, the fir, the oak, the ash, and the birch had skirted the fells, tufted the hills, and shaded the vallies, through centuries of silent solitude; the birds and beasts of prey reigned over the meeker species; and the *bellum inter omnia* maintained the balance of nature in the empire of beasts.'*

Such was the state and appearance of this region when the aboriginal colonists of the Celtic tribes were first driven or drawn towards it, and became joint tenants with the wolf, the boar, the wild bull, the red deer, and the leigh, a gigantic species of deer which has been long extinct;* while the inaccessible crags were occupied by the falcon, the raven, and the eagle. The inner parts were too secluded, and of too little value, to participate much of the benefit of Roman manners; and though these conquerors encouraged the Britons to the improvement of their lands in the plain country of Furness and Cumberland, they seem to have had little connexion with the mountains, except for military purposes, or in subservience to the profit they drew from the mines.

When the Romans retired from Great Britain, it is well known that these mountain-fastnesses furnished a protection to some unsubdued Britons, long after the more accessible and more fertile districts had been seized by the Saxon or Danish invader. A few, though distinct, traces of Roman forts or camps, as at Ambleside, and upon Dunmallet,* and a few circles of rude stones attributed to the Druids,[1]* are the only vestiges that remain upon the surface of the

[1] It is not improbable that these circles were once numerous, and that many of them may yet endure in a perfect state, under no very deep covering of soil. A friend of the Author, while making a trench in a level piece of ground, not far from the banks of the Eamont, but in no connexion with that river, met with some stones which seemed to him formally arranged; this excited his curiosity, and proceeding, he uncovered a perfect circle of stones, from two to three or four feet high, with a *sanctum sanctorum*,—the whole a complete place of Druidical worship of small dimensions, having the same sort of relation to Stonehenge, Long Meg and her Daughters near the river Eden, and Karl Lofts near Shap (if this last be not Danish), that a rural chapel bears to a stately church, or to one of our noble cathedrals. This interesting little monument having passed, with the field in which it was found, into other hands, has been destroyed. It is much to be regretted, that the striking relic of antiquity at Shap has been in a great measure destroyed also.

The DAUGHTERS of LONG MEG are placed not in an oblong, as the STONES of SHAP, but in a perfect circle, eighty yards in diameter, and seventy-two in number, and from above three yards high, to less than so many feet: a little way out of the circle stands LONG MEG herself—a single stone eighteen feet high.

When the Author first saw this monument, he came upon it by surprize, therefore might over-rate its importance as an object; but he must say, that though it is not to be compared with Stonehenge, he has not seen any other remains of those dark ages, which can pretend to rival it in singularity and dignity of appearance.

> A weight of awe not easy to be borne
> Fell suddenly upon my spirit, cast
> From the dread bosom of the unknown past,
> When first I saw that sisterhood forlorn;—
> And Her, whose strength and stature seem to scorn
> The power of years—pre-eminent, and placed
> Apart, to overlook the circle vast.
> Speak, Giant-mother! tell it to the Morn,

country, of these ancient occupants; and, as the Saxons and Danes, who succeeded to the possession of the villages and hamlets which had been established by the Britons, seem at first to have confined themselves to the open country,—we may descend at once to times long posterior to the conquest by the Normans, when their feudal polity was regularly established. We may easily conceive that these narrow dales and mountain sides, choked up as they must have been with wood, lying out of the way of communication with other parts of the Island, and upon the edge of a hostile kingdom,* could have little attraction for the high-born and powerful; especially as the more open parts of the country furnished positions for castles and houses of defence, sufficient to repel any of those sudden attacks, which, in the then rude state of military knowledge, could be made upon them. Accordingly, the more retired regions (and to such I am now confining myself) must have been neglected or shunned even by the persons whose baronial or signioral rights extended over them, and left, doubtless, partly as a place of refuge for outlaws and robbers, and partly granted out for the more settled habitation of a few vassals following the employment of shepherds or woodlanders. Hence these lakes and inner vallies are unadorned by any remains of ancient grandeur, castles, or monastic edifices, which are only found upon the skirts of the country, as Furness Abbey, Calder Abbey, the Priory of Lannercost, Gleaston Castle,—long ago a residence of the Flemings,—and the numerous ancient castles of the Cliffords, the Lucys, and the Dacres.* On the southern side of these mountains, (especially in that part known by the name of Furness Fells, which is more remote from the borders,) the state of society would necessarily be more settled; though it also was fashioned, not a little, by its neighbourhood to a hostile kingdom. We will, therefore, give a sketch of the economy of the Abbots in the distribution of lands among their tenants, as similar plans were doubtless adopted by other Lords, and as the consequences have affected the face of the country materially to the present day, being, in fact, one of the principal causes which give

> While she dispels the cumbrous shades of night;
> Let the Moon hear, emerging from a cloud,
> When, how, and wherefore, rose on British ground
> That wondrous Monument, whose mystic round
> Forth shadows, some have deemed, to mortal sight
> The inviolable God that tames the proud.*

it such a striking superiority, in beauty and interest, over all other parts of the island.

'When the Abbots of Furness,' says an author before cited, 'enfranchised their villains, and raised them to the dignity of customary tenants, the lands, which they had cultivated for their lord, were divided into whole tenements; each of which, besides the customary annual rent, was charged with the obligation of having in readiness a man completely armed for the king's service on the borders, or elsewhere; each of these whole tenements was again subdivided into four equal parts; each villain had one; and the party tenant contributed his share to the support of the man of arms, and of other burdens. These divisions were not properly distinguished; the land remained mixed; each tenant had a share through all the arable and meadow-land, and common of pasture over all the wastes. These sub-tenements were judged sufficient for the support of so many families; and no further division was permitted. These divisions and sub-divisions were convenient at the time for which they were calculated: the land, so parcelled out, was, of necessity more attended to, and the industry greater, when more persons were to be supported by the produce of it. The frontier of the kingdom, within which Furness was considered, was in a constant state of attack and defence; more hands, therefore, were necessary to guard the coast, to repel an invasion from Scotland, or make reprisals on the hostile neighbour. The dividing the lands in such manner as has been shown, increased the number of inhabitants, and kept them at home till called for: and, the land being mixed, and the several tenants united in equipping the plough, the absence of the fourth man was no prejudice to the cultivation of his land, which was committed to the care of three.

'While the villains of Low Furness were thus distributed over the land, and employed in agriculture; those of High Furness were charged with the care of flocks and herds, to protect them from the wolves which lurked in the thickets, and in winter to browze them with the tender sprouts of hollies and ash. This custom was not till lately discontinued in High Furness; and holly-trees were carefully preserved for that purpose when all other wood was cleared off; large tracts of common being so covered with these trees, as to have the appearance of a forest of hollies. At the Shepherd's call, the flocks surrounded the holly-bush, and received the croppings at his hand, which they greedily nibbled up, bleating for more. The Abbots of Furness enfranchised these pastoral vassals, and permitted them to enclose *quillets* to their houses, for which they paid encroachment rent.'—West's *Antiquities of Furness*.*

However desirable, for the purposes of defence, a numerous population might be, it was not possible to make at once the same numerous allotments among the untilled vallies, and upon the sides of the mountains, as had been made in the cultivated plains. The enfranchised shepherd, or woodlander, having chosen there his place of residence, builds it of sods, or of the mountain-stone, and, with the permission of his lord, encloses, like Robinson Crusoe, a small croft or two immediately at his door for such animals as he wishes to protect. Others are happy to imitate his example, and avail themselves of the same privileges: and thus a population, mainly of Danish or Norse origin, as the dialect indicates,* crept on towards the more secluded parts of the vallies. Chapels, daughters of some distant mother church, are first erected in the more open and fertile vales, as those of Bowness and Grasmere, offsets of Kendal: which again, after a period, as the settled population increases, become mother-churches to smaller edifices, planted, at length, in almost every dale throughout the country. The inclosures, formed by the tenantry, are for a long time confined to the home-steads; and the arable and meadow land of the vales is possessed in common field; the several portions being marked out by stones, bushes, or trees: which portions, where the custom has survived, to this day are called *dales*, from the word *deylen*, to distribute; but, while the valley was thus lying open, enclosures seem to have taken place upon the sides of the mountains; because the land there was not intermixed, and was of little comparative value; and, therefore, small opposition would be made to its being appropriated by those to whose habitations it was contiguous. Hence the singular appearance which the sides of many of these mountains exhibit, intersected, as they are, almost to the summit, with stone walls. When first erected, these stone fences must have little disfigured the face of the country; as part of the lines would every where be hidden by the quantity of native wood then remaining; and the lines would also be broken (as they still are) by the rocks which interrupt and vary their course. In the meadows, and in those parts of the lower grounds where the soil has not been sufficiently drained, and could not afford a stable foundation, there, when the increasing value of land, and the inconvenience suffered from intermixed plots of ground in common field, had induced each inhabitant to enclose his own, they were compelled to make the fences of alders, willows, and other trees. These, where the native wood had disappeared, have frequently enriched the vallies with a sylvan appearance; while the intricate intermixture of property has given to the fences a graceful irregularity, which, where large properties are prevalent, and large capitals employed in agriculture, is unknown. This sylvan appearance is heightened by the number of ash-trees planted in rows along the quick fences, and along the walls, for the purpose of browzing the cattle at the approach of winter. The branches are lopped off and strewn upon the pastures; and when the cattle have stripped them of the leaves, they are used for repairing the hedges or for fuel.

We have thus seen a numerous body of Dalesmen creeping into possession of their home-steads, their little crofts, their mountain-enclosures; and, finally, the whole vale is visibly divided; except, perhaps, here and there some marshy ground, which, till fully drained, would not repay the trouble of enclosing. But these last partitions do not seem to have been general, till long after the pacification of the Borders, by the union of the two crowns: when the cause, which had first determined the distribution of land into such small parcels, had not only ceased,—but likewise a general improvement had taken place in the country, with a correspondent rise in the value of its produce. From the time of the union, it is certain that this species of feudal population must rapidly have diminished. That it was formerly much more numerous than it is at present, is evident from the multitude of tenements (I do not mean houses, but small divisions of land) which belonged formerly each to a several proprietor, and for which separate fines are paid to the manorial lord at this day. These are often in the proportion of four to one of the present occupants. 'Sir Launcelot Threlkeld, who lived in the reign of Henry VII., was wont to say, he had three noble houses, one for pleasure, Crosby, in Westmoreland, where he had a park full of deer; one for profit and warmth, wherein to reside in winter, namely, Yanwith, nigh Penrith; and the third, Threlkeld (on the edge of the vale of Keswick), well stocked with tenants to go with him to the wars.'* But, as I have said, from the union of the two crowns, this numerous vassalage (their services not being wanted) would rapidly diminish; various tenements would be united in one possessor; and the aboriginal houses, probably little better than hovels, like the kraels* of savages, or the huts of the Highlanders of Scotland, would fall into decay, and the places of many be supplied by substantial and comfortable buildings, a majority of which remain to this day scattered over the vallies, and are often the only dwellings found in them.

From the time of the erection of these houses, till within the last sixty years, the state of society, though no doubt slowly and gradually improving, underwent no material change. Corn was grown in these vales (through which no carriage-road had yet been made) sufficient upon each estate to furnish bread for each family, and no more: notwithstanding the union of several tenements, the possessions of each inhabitant still being small, in the same field was seen an intermixture of different crops; and the plough was interrupted by little rocks, mostly overgrown with wood, or by spongy places, which the tillers of the soil had neither leisure nor capital to convert into firm land. The storms and moisture of the climate induced them to sprinkle their upland property with outhouses of native stone, as places of shelter for their sheep, where, in tempestuous weather, food was distributed to them. Every family spun from its own flock the wool with which it was clothed; a weaver was here and there found among them; and the rest of their wants was supplied by the produce of the yarn, which they carded and spun in their own houses, and carried to market, either under their arms, or more frequently on pack-horses, a small train taking their way weekly down the valley or over the mountains to the most commodious town. They had, as I have said, their rural chapel, and of course their minister, in clothing or in manner of life, in no respect differing from themselves, except on the Sabbath-day; this was the sole distinguished individual among them; every thing else, person and possession, exhibited a perfect equality, a community of shepherds and agriculturists,* proprietors, for the most part, of the lands which they occupied and cultivated.

While the process above detailed was going on, the native forest must have been every where receding; but trees were planted for the sustenance of the flocks in winter,—such was then the rude state of agriculture; and, for the same cause, it was necessary that care should be taken of some part of the growth of the native woods. Accordingly, in Queen Elizabeth's time, this was so strongly felt, that a petition was made to the Crown, praying, 'that the Blomaries in High Furness might be abolished, on account of the quantity of wood which was consumed in them for the use of the mines, to the great detriment of the cattle.'* But this same cause, about a hundred years after, produced effects directly contrary to those which had been deprecated. The re-establishment, at that period, of furnaces upon a large scale, made it the interest of the people to convert the steeper and more stony of the enclosures, sprinkled over with remains of the native forest, into close woods, which, when cattle and sheep were excluded, rapidly sowed and thickened themselves. The reader's attention has been directed to the cause by which tufts of wood, pasturage, meadow, and arable land, with its various produce, are intricately intermingled in the same field; and he will now see, in like manner, how enclosures entirely of wood, and those of cultivated ground, are blended all over the country under a law of similar wildness.

An historic detail has thus been given of the manner in which the hand of man has acted upon the surface of the inner regions of this mountainous country, as incorporated with and subservient to the powers and processes of nature. We will now take a view of the same agency—acting, within narrower bounds, for the production of the few works of art and accommodations of life which, in so simple a state of society, could be necessary. These are merely habitations of man and coverts for beasts,* roads and bridges, and places of worship.

And to begin with the COTTAGES.* They are scattered over the vallies, and under the hill sides, and on the rocks; and, even to this day, in the more retired dales, without any intrusion of more assuming buildings:

> Cluster'd like stars some few, but single most,
> And lurking dimly in their shy retreats,
> Or glancing on each other cheerful looks,
> Like separated stars with clouds between.*   MS.

The dwelling-houses, and contiguous outhouses, are, in many instances, of the colour of the native rock, out of which they have been built; but, frequently the Dwelling or Fire-house, as it is ordinarily called, has been distinguished from the barn or byre by rough-cast and white wash, which, as the inhabitants are not hasty in renewing it, in a few years acquires, by the influence of weather, a tint at once sober and variegated.* As these houses have been, from father to son, inhabited by persons engaged in the same occupations, yet necessarily with changes in their circumstances, they have received without incongruity additions and accommodations adapted to the needs of each successive occupant, who, being for the most part proprietor, was at liberty to follow his own fancy: so that these humble dwellings remind the contemplative spectator of a production of nature, and may (using a strong expression) rather be said to have grown than to have been erected;—to have risen, by an instinct of their own, out of the native rock*—so little is there in them of formality, such is their wildness and beauty. Among the numerous recesses and projections in the walls and in the different stages of their roofs, are seen bold and harmonious effects of contrasted sunshine and shadow. It is a favourable circumstance, that the strong winds, which sweep down the vallies, induced the inhabitants, at a time when the materials for building were easily procured, to furnish many of these dwellings with substantial porches; and such as have not this defence, are seldom unprovided with a projection of two large slates over their thresholds. Nor will the singular beauty of the chimneys escape the eye of the attentive traveller. Sometimes a low chimney, almost upon a level with the roof, is overlaid with a slate, supported upon four slender pillars, to prevent the wind from driving the smoke down the chimney. Others are of a quadrangular shape, rising one or two feet above the roof; which low square is often surmounted by a tall cylinder, giving to the cottage chimney the most beautiful shape in which it is ever seen. Nor will it be too fanciful or refined to remark, that there is a pleasing harmony between a tall chimney of this circular form, and the living column of smoke, ascending from it through the still air.* These dwellings, mostly built, as has been said, of rough unhewn stone, are roofed with slates, which were rudely taken from the quarry before the present art of splitting them was understood, and are, therefore, rough and uneven in their surface, so that both the coverings and sides of the houses have furnished places of rest for the seeds of lichens, mosses, ferns, and flowers. Hence buildings, which in their very form call to mind the processes of nature, do thus, clothed in part with a vegetable garb, appear to be received into the bosom of the living principle of things,* as it acts and exists among the woods and fields; and, by their colour and their shape, affectingly direct the thoughts to that tranquil course of nature and simplicity, along which the humble-minded inhabitants have, through so many generations, been led. Add the little garden with its shed for bee-hives, its small bed of pot-herbs, and its borders and patches of flowers for Sunday posies, with sometimes a choice few too much prized to be plucked; an orchard of proportioned size; a cheese-press, often supported by some tree near the door; a cluster of embowering sycamores for summer shade; with a tall fir, through which the winds sing when other trees are leafless; the little rill or household spout murmuring in all seasons;—combine these incidents and images together, and you have the representative idea of a mountain-cottage in this country so beautifully formed in itself, and so richly adorned by the hand of nature.

Till within the last sixty years there was no communication between any of these vales by carriage-roads; all bulky articles were transported on pack-horses. Owing, however, to the population not being concentrated in villages, but scattered, the vallies themselves were intersected as now by innumerable lanes and path-ways leading from house to house and from field to field. These lanes, where they are fenced by stone walls, are mostly bordered with ashes, hazels, wild roses, and beds of tall fern at their base; while the walls themselves, if old, are overspread with mosses, small ferns, wild strawberries, the geranium, and lichens:* and, if the wall happen to rest against a bank of earth, it is sometimes almost wholly concealed by a rich facing of stone-fern. It is a great advantage to a traveller or resident, that these numerous lanes and paths, if he be a zealous admirer of nature, will lead him on into all the recesses of the country, so that the hidden treasures of its landscapes may, by an ever-ready guide, be laid open to his eyes.

Likewise to the smallness of the several properties is owing the great number of bridges over the brooks and torrents, and the daring and graceful neglect of danger or accommodation with which so many of them are constructed, the rudeness of the forms of some, and their endless variety. But, when I speak of this rudeness, I must at the same time add, that many of these structures are in themselves models of elegance, as if they had been formed upon principles of the most thoughtful architecture. It is to be regretted that these monuments of the skill of our ancestors, and of that happy instinct by which consummate beauty was produced, are disappearing fast; but sufficient specimens remain[1] to give a high gratification to the man of genuine taste. Travellers who may not have been accustomed to pay attention to things so inobtrusive, will excuse me if I point out the proportion between the span and elevation of the arch, the lightness of the parapet, and the graceful manner in which its curve follows faithfully that of the arch.

Upon this subject I have nothing further to notice, except the PLACES OF WORSHIP, which have mostly a little school-house adjoining.[2] The architecture of these churches and chapels, where they have not been recently rebuilt or modernised, is of a style not less appropriate and admirable than that of the dwelling-houses and other structures. How sacred the spirit by which our forefathers were directed! The *religio loci* is nowhere violated by these unstinted, yet unpretending, works of human hands. They exhibit generally a well-proportioned oblong, with a suitable porch, in some instances a steeple tower, and in others nothing more than a small belfry, in which one or two bells hang visibly. But these objects, though pleasing in their forms, must necessarily, more than others in rural scenery, derive their interest from the sentiments of piety and reverence for the modest virtues and simple manners of humble life with which they may be contemplated. A man must be very insensible who would not be touched with pleasure at the sight of the chapel of Buttermere,

[1] Written some time ago. The injury done since, is more than could have been calculated upon.

Singula de nobis anni praedantur euntes. This is in the course of things; but why should the genius that directed the ancient architecture of these vales have deserted them? For the bridges, churches, mansions, cottages, and their richly fringed and flat-roofed outhouses, venerable as the grange of some old abbey, have been substituted structures, in which baldness only seems to have been studied, or plans of the most vulgar utility. But some improvement may be looked for in future; the gentry *recently* have copied the old models, and successful instances might be pointed out, if I could take the liberty.*

[2] In some places scholars were formerly taught in the church, and at others the school-house was a sort of ante-chapel to the place of worship, being under the same roof; an arrangement which was abandoned as irreverent. It continues, however, to this day in Borrowdale. In the parish register of that chapelry is a notice, that a youth who had quitted the valley, and died in one of the towns on the coast of Cumberland, had requested that his body should be brought and interred at the foot of the pillar by which he had been accustomed to sit while a school-boy. One cannot but regret that parish registers so seldom contain any thing but bare names; in a few of this country, especially in that of Loweswater, I have found interesting notices of unusual natural occurrences—characters of the deceased, and particulars of their lives. There is no good reason why such memorials should not be frequent; these short and simple annals would in future ages become precious.*

so strikingly expressing, by its diminutive size, how small must be the congregation there assembled, as it were, like one family; and proclaiming at the same time to the passenger, in connection with the surrounding mountains, the depth of that seclusion in which the people live, that has rendered necessary the building of a separate place of worship for so few. A patriot, calling to mind the images of the stately fabrics of Canterbury, York, or Westminster, will find a heart-felt satisfaction in presence of this lowly pile, as a monument of the wise institutions of our country, and as evidence of the all-pervading and paternal care of that venerable Establishment, of which it is, perhaps, the humblest daughter. The edifice is scarcely larger than many of the single stones or fragments of rock which are scattered near it.*

We have thus far confined our observations on this division of the subject, to that part of these Dales which runs up far into the mountains.

As we descend towards the open country, we meet with halls and mansions, many of which have been places of defence against the incursions of the Scottish borderers; and they not unfrequently retain their towers and battlements. To these houses, parks are sometimes attached, and to their successive proprietors we chiefly owe whatever ornament is still left to the country of majestic timber.* Through the open parts of the vales are scattered, also, houses of a middle rank between the pastoral cottage and the old hall residence of the knight or esquire. Such houses differ much from the rugged cottages before described, and are generally graced with a little court or garden in front, where may yet be seen specimens of those fantastic and quaint figures which our ancestors were fond of shaping out in yew-tree, holly, or box-wood. The passenger will sometimes smile at such elaborate display of petty art,* while the house does not deign to look upon the natural beauty or the sublimity which its situation almost unavoidably commands.

Thus has been given a faithful description, the minuteness of which the reader will pardon, of the face of this country as it was, and had been through centuries, till within the last sixty years. Towards the head of these Dales was found a perfect Republic of Shepherds and Agriculturists,* among whom the plough of each man was confined to the maintenance of his own family, or to the occasional accommodation of his neighbour.[1] Two or three cows furnished each family with milk and cheese. The chapel was the only edifice that presided over these dwellings, the supreme head of this pure Commonwealth; the members of which existed in the midst of a powerful empire, like an ideal society or an organized community, whose constitution had been imposed and regulated by the mountains which protected it. Neither high-born nobleman, knight, nor esquire, was here; but many of these humble sons of the hills had a consciousness that the land, which they walked over and tilled, had for more than five hundred years been possessed by men of their name and blood;* and venerable was the transition, when a curious traveller, descending from the heart of the mountains, had come to some ancient manorial residence in the more open parts of the Vales, which, through the rights attached to its proprietor, connected the almost visionary mountain republic he had been contemplating with the substantial frame of society as existing in the laws and constitution of a mighty empire.

[1] One of the most pleasing characteristics of manners in secluded and thinly-peopled districts, is a sense of the degree in which human happiness and comfort are dependent on the contingency of neighbourhood. This is implied by a rhyming adage common here, '*Friends are far, when neighbours are nar*' (near). This mutual helpfulness is not confined to out-of-doors work; but is ready upon all occasions. Formerly, if a person became sick, especially the mistress of a family, it was usual for those of the neighbours who were more particularly connected with the party by amicable offices, to visit the house, carrying a present; this practice, which is by no means obsolete, is called *owning* the family, and is regarded as a pledge of a disposition to be otherwise serviceable in a time of disability and distress.

SECTION THIRD

Changes, and Rules of Taste For Preventing
Their Bad Effects

SUCH, as hath been said, was the appearance of things till within the last sixty years.* A practice, denominated Ornamental Gardening, was at that time becoming prevalent over England. In union with an admiration of this art, and in some instances in opposition to it, had been generated a relish for select parts of natural scenery:* and Travellers, instead of confining their observations to Towns, Manufactories, or Mines, began (a thing till then unheard of) to wander over the island in search of sequestered spots, distinguished as they might accidently have learned, for the sublimity or beauty of the forms of Nature there to be seen.—Dr. Brown, the celebrated Author of the Estimate of the Manners and Principles of the Times, published a letter to a friend, in which the attractions of the Vale of Keswick were delineated with a powerful pencil, and the feeling of a genuine Enthusiast. Gray, the Poet, followed: he died soon after his forlorn and melancholy pilgrimage to the Vale of Keswick, and the record left behind him of what he had seen and felt in this journey, excited that pensive interest with which the human mind is ever disposed to listen to the farewell words of a man of genius. The journal of Gray feelingly showed how the gloom of ill health and low spirits had been irradiated by objects, which the Author's powers of mind enabled him to describe with distinctness and unaffected simplicity. Every reader of this journal must have been impressed with the words which conclude his notice of the Vale of Grasmere:—'Not a single red tile, no flaring gentleman's house or garden-wall, breaks in upon the repose of this little unsuspected paradise; but all is peace, rusticity, and happy poverty, in its neatest and most becoming attire.'*

What is here so justly said of Grasmere applied almost equally to all its sister Vales. It was well for the undisturbed pleasure of the Poet that he had no forebodings of the change which was soon to take place; and it might have been hoped that these words, indicating how much the charm of what *was*, depended upon what was *not*, would of themselves have preserved the ancient franchises of this and other kindred mountain retirements from trespass; or (shall I dare to say?) would have secured scenes so consecrated from profanation. The lakes had now become celebrated; visitors flocked hither from all parts of England; the fancies of some were smitten so deeply, that they became settlers; and the Islands of Derwentwater and Winandermere, as they offered the strongest temptation, were the first places seized upon, and were instantly defaced by the intrusion.

The venerable wood that had grown for centuries round the small house called St. Herbert's Hermitage, had indeed some years before been felled by its native proprietor,* and the whole island planted anew with Scotch firs, left to spindle up by each other's side—a melancholy phalanx, defying the power of the winds,* and disregarding the regret of the spectator, who might otherwise have cheated himself into a belief, that some of the decayed remains of those oaks, the place of which was in this manner usurped, had been planted by the Hermit's own hand. This sainted spot, however, suffered comparatively little injury. At the bidding of an alien improver, the Hind's Cottage, upon Vicar's island, in the same lake, with its embowering sycamores and cattle-shed, disappeared from the corner where they stood; and right in the middle, and upon the precise point of the island's highest elevation, rose a tall square habitation, with four sides exposed, like an astronomer's observatory, or a warren-house reared upon an eminence for the detection of depredators, or, like the temple of Œolus,* where all the winds pay him obeisance. Round this novel structure, but at a respectful distance, platoons of firs were stationed, as if to protect their commander when weather and time should somewhat have shattered his strength. Within the narrow limits of this island were typified also the state and strength of a kingdom, and its religion as it had been, and was,—for neither was the druidical circle uncreated, nor the church of the present establishment; nor the stately pier, emblem of commerce and navigation; nor the fort to deal out thunder upon the approaching invader.* The taste of a succeeding proprietor rectified the mistakes as far as was practicable, and has ridded the spot of its puerilities.* The church, after having been docked of its steeple, is applied, both ostensibly and really, to the purpose for which the body of the pile was actually erected, namely, a boat-house; the fort is demolished; and, without indignation on the part of the spirits of the ancient Druids who officiated at the circle upon the opposite hill,* the mimic arrangement of stones, with its *sanctum sanctorum*, has been swept away.

The present instance has been singled out, extravagant as it is, because, unquestionably, this beautiful country has, in numerous other places, suffered from the same spirit, though not clothed exactly in the same form, nor active in an equal degree. It will be sufficient here to utter a regret for the changes that have been made upon the principal Island at Winandermere, and in its neighbourhood.* What could be more unfortunate than the taste that suggested the paring of the shores, and surrounding with an embankment this spot of ground, the natural shape of which was so beautiful! An artificial appearance has thus been given to the whole, while infinite varieties of minute beauty have been destroyed.* Could not the margin of this noble island be given back to nature? Winds and waves work with a careless and graceful hand: and, should they in some places carry away a portion of the soil, the trifling loss would be amply compensated by the additional spirit, dignity, and loveliness, which these agents and the other powers of nature would soon communicate to what was left behind.* As to the larch-plantations upon the main shore,—they who remember the original appearance of the rocky steeps, scattered over with native hollies and ash-trees, will be prepared to agree with what I shall have to say hereafter upon plantations[1] in general.*

But, in truth, no one can now travel through the more frequented tracts, without being offended, at almost every turn, by an introduction of discordant objects, disturbing that peaceful harmony of form and colour, which had been through a long lapse of ages most happily preserved.

All gross transgressions of this kind originate, doubtless, in a feeling natural and honourable to the human mind, viz. the pleasure which it receives from distinct ideas, and from the perception of order, regularity, and contrivance. Now, unpractised minds receive these impressions only from objects that are divided from each other by strong lines of demarcation; hence the delight with which such minds are smitten by formality and harsh contrast. But I would beg of those who are eager to create the means of such gratification, first carefully to study what already exists; and they will find, in a country so lavishly gifted by nature, an abundant variety of forms marked out with a precision that will satisfy their desires. Moreover, a new habit

---

[1] These are disappearing fast, under the management of the present Proprietor, and native wood is resuming its place.*

of pleasure will be formed opposite to this, arising out of the perception of the fine gradations by which in nature one thing passes away into another,* and the boundaries that constitute individuality disappear in one instance only to be revived elsewhere under a more alluring form. The hill of Dunmallet, at the foot of Ulswater, was once divided into different portions, by avenues of fir-trees, with a green and almost perpendicular lane descending down the steep hill through each avenue;*—contrast this quaint appearance with the image of the same hill overgrown with self-planted wood,—each tree springing up in the situation best suited to its kind, and with that shape which the situation constrained or suffered it to take. What endless melting and playing into each other of forms and colours does the one offer to a mind at once attentive and active; and how insipid and lifeless, compared with it, appear those parts of the former exhibition with which a child, a peasant perhaps, or a citizen unfamiliar with natural imagery, would have been most delighted!

The disfigurement which this country has undergone has not, however, proceeded wholly from the common feelings of human nature which have been referred to as the primary sources of bad taste in rural imagery; another cause must be added, that has chiefly shown itself in its effect upon buildings. I mean a warping of the natural mind occasioned by a consciousness that, this country being an object of general admiration, every new house would be looked at and commented upon either for approbation or censure. Hence all the deformity and ungracefulness that ever pursue the steps of constraint or affectation. Persons, who in Leicestershire or Northamptonshire would probably have built a modest dwelling like those of their sensible neighbours, have been turned out of their course; and, acting a part, no wonder if, having had little experience, they act it ill. The craving for prospect, also, which is immoderate, particularly in new settlers, has rendered it impossible that buildings, whatever might have been their architecture, should in most instances be ornamental to the landscape; rising as they do from the summits of naked hills in staring contrast to the snugness and privacy of the ancient houses.

No man is to be condemned for a desire to decorate his residence and possessions; feeling a disposition to applaud such an endeavour, I would show how the end may be best attained. The rule is simple; with respect to grounds—work, where you can, in the spirit of nature, with an invisible hand of art. Planting, and a removal of wood, may thus, and thus only, be carried on with good effect; and the like may be said of building, if Antiquity, who may be styled the co-partner and sister of Nature, be not denied the respect to which she is entitled. I have already spoken of the beautiful forms of the ancient mansions of this country, and of the happy manner in which they harmonise with the forms of nature. Why cannot such be taken as a model, and modern internal convenience be confined within their external grace and dignity. Expense to be avoided, or difficulties to be overcome, may prevent a close adherence to this model; still, however, it might be followed to a certain degree in the style of architecture and in the choice of situation, if the thirst for prospect were mitigated by those considerations of comfort, shelter, and convenience, which used to be chiefly sought after. But should an aversion to old fashions unfortunately exist, accompanied with a desire to transplant into the cold and stormy North, the elegancies of a villa formed upon a model taken from countries with a milder climate, I will adduce a passage from an English poet, the divine Spenser, which will show in what manner such a plan may be realised without injury to the native beauty of these scenes.

> 'Into that forest farre they thence him led,
> Where was their dwelling in a pleasant glade
> With MOUNTAINS round about environed,
> And MIGHTY WOODS which did the valley shade,
> And like a stately theatre it made,
> Spreading itself into a spacious plaine;
> And in the midst a little river plaide
> Emongst the pumy stones which seem'd to 'plaine
> With gentle murmure that his course they did restraine.
>
> Beside the same a dainty place there lay,
> Planted with mirtle trees and laurels green,
> In which the birds sang many a lovely lay
> Of God's high praise, and of their sweet loves teene,
> As it an earthly paradise had beene;
> In whose *enclosed shadow* there was pight
> A fair pavilion, *scarcely to be seen*,
> The which was all within most richly dight,
> That greatest princes living it mote well delight.'*

Houses or mansions suited to a mountainous region, should be 'not obvious, not obtrusive, but retired;'* and the reasons for this rule, though they have been little adverted to, are evident. Mountainous countries, more frequently and forcibly than others, remind us of the power of the elements, as manifested in winds, snows, and torrents, and accordingly make the notion of exposure very unpleasing; while shelter and comfort are in proportion necessary and acceptable. Far-winding vallies difficult of access, and the feelings of simplicity habitually connected with mountain retirements, prompt us to turn from ostentation as a thing there eminently unnatural and out of place. A mansion, amid such scenes, can never have sufficient dignity or interest to become principal in the landscape, and to render the mountains, lakes, or torrents, by which it may be surrounded, a subordinate part of the view. It is, I grant, easy to conceive, that an ancient castellated building, hanging over a precipice or raised upon an island, or the peninsula of a lake, like that of Kilchurn Castle, upon Loch Awe, may not want, whether deserted or inhabited, sufficient majesty to preside for a moment in the spectator's thoughts over the high mountains among which it is embosomed; but its titles are from antiquity—a power readily submitted to upon occasion as the vice-gerent of Nature:* it is respected, as having owed its existence to the necessities of things, as a monument of security in times of disturbance and danger long passed away,—as a record of the pomp and violence of passion, and a symbol of the wisdom of law;—it bears a countenance of authority, which is not impaired by decay.

> 'Child of loud-throated war, the mountain-stream
> Roars in thy hearing; but thy hour of rest
> Is come, and thou art silent in thy age!'*

To such honours a modern edifice can lay no claim; and the puny efforts of elegance appear contemptible, when, in such situations, they are obtruded in rivalship with the sublimities of Nature. But, towards the verge of a district like this of which we are treating, where the mountains subside into hills of moderate elevation, or in an undulating or flat country, a gentleman's mansion may, with propriety, become a principal feature in the landscape; and, itself being a work of art, works and traces of artificial ornament may, without censure, be extended around it, as they will be referred to the common centre, the house; the right of which to impress within certain limits a character of obvious ornament will not be denied, where no commanding forms of nature dispute it, or set it aside. Now, to a want of the perception of this difference, and to the causes before assigned, may chiefly be attributed the disfigurement which the Country of the Lakes has undergone, from persons who may have built, demolished, and planted, with full confidence, that every change and addition was or would become an improvement.

The principle that ought to determine the position, apparent size, and architecture of a house, viz. that it should be so constructed, and (if large) so much of it hidden, as to admit of its being gently incorporated into the scenery of nature—should also determine its colour. Sir Joshua Reynolds used to say, 'If you would fix upon the best colour for your house, turn up a stone, or pluck up a handful of grass by the roots, and see what is the colour of the soil where the house is to stand, and let that be your choice.' Of course, this precept given in conversation, could not have been meant to be taken literally. For example, in Low Furness, where the soil, from its strong impregnation with iron, is universally of a deep red, if this rule were strictly followed, the house also must be of a glaring red; in other places it must be of a sullen black; which would only be adding annoyance to annoyance. The rule, however, as a general guide, is good; and, in agricultural districts, where large tracts of soil are laid bare by the plough, particularly if (the face of the country being undulating) they are held up to view, this rule, though not to be implicitly adhered to, should never be lost sight of;—the colour of the house ought, if possible, to have a cast or shade of the colour of the soil. The principle is, that the house must harmonise with the surrounding landscape: accordingly, in mountainous countries, with still more confidence may it be said, 'look at the rocks and those parts of the mountains where the soil is visible, and they will furnish a safe direction.' Nevertheless, it will often happen that the rocks may bear so large a proportion to the rest of the landscape, and may be of such a tone of colour, that the rule may not admit, even here, of being implicitly followed. For instance, the chief defect in the colouring of the Country of the Lakes (which is most strongly felt in the summer season) is an over-prevalence of a bluish tint,* which the green of the herbage, the fern, and the woods, does not sufficiently counteract. If a house, therefore, should stand where this defect prevails, I have no hesitation in saying, that the colour of the neighbouring rocks would not be the best that could be chosen. A tint ought to be introduced approaching nearer to those which, in the technical language of painters, are called *warm*: this, if happily selected, would not disturb, but would animate the landscape. How often do we see this exemplified upon a small scale by the native cottages, in cases where the glare of white-wash has been subdued by time and enriched by weather-stains!* No harshness is then seen; but one of these cottages, thus coloured, will often form a central point to a landscape by which the whole shall be connected, and an influence of pleasure diffused over all the objects that compose the picture. But where the cold blue tint of the rocks is enriched by the iron tinge, the colour cannot be too closely imitated; and it will be produced of itself by the stones hewn from the adjoining quarry, and by the mortar, which may be tempered with the most gravelly part of the soil. The pure blue gravel, from the bed of the river, is, however, more suitable to the mason's purpose, who will probably insist also that the house must be covered with rough-cast, otherwise it cannot be kept dry; if this advice be taken, the builder of taste will set about contriving such means as may enable him to come the nearest to the effect aimed at.

The supposed necessity of rough-cast to keep out rain in houses not built of hewn stone or brick, has tended greatly to injure English landscape, and the neighbourhood of these Lakes especially, by furnishing such apt occasion for whitening buildings.* That white should be a favourite colour for rural residences is natural for many reasons. The mere aspect of cleanliness and neatness thus given, not only to an individual house, but, where the practice is general, to the whole face of the country, produces moral associations so powerful, that, in many minds, they take place of all others. But what has already been said upon the subject of cottages, must have convinced men of feeling and imagination, that a human dwelling of the humblest class may be rendered more deeply interesting to the affections, and far more pleasing to the eye, by other influences, than a sprightly tone of colour spread over its outside. I do not, however, mean to deny, that a small white building, embowered in trees, may, in some situations, be a delightful and animating object—in no way injurious to the landscape; but this only where it sparkles from the midst of a thick shade, and in rare and solitary instances; especially if the country be itself rich and pleasing, and abound with grand forms. On the sides of bleak and desolate moors, we are indeed thankful for the sight of white cottages and white houses plentifully scattered, where, without these, perhaps every thing would be cheerless: this is said, however, with hesitation, and with a wilful sacrifice of some higher enjoyments. But I have certainly seen such buildings glittering at sunrise, and in wandering lights, with no common pleasure. The continental traveller also will remember, that the convents hanging from the rocks of the Rhine, the Rhone, the Danube, or among the Appenines, or the mountains of Spain, are not looked at with less complacency when, as is often the case, they happen to be of a brilliant white. But this is perhaps owing, in no small degree, to the contrast of that lively colour with the gloom of monastic life, and to the general want of rural residences of smiling and attractive appearance, in those countries.

The objections to white, as a colour, in large spots or masses in landscape, especially in a mountainous country, are insurmountable. In nature, pure white is scarcely ever found but in small objects, such as flowers; or in those which are transitory, as the clouds, foam of rivers, and snow. Mr. Gilpin, who notices this, has also recorded the just remark of Mr. Locke, of N——, that white destroys the *gradations* of distance;* and, therefore, an object of pure white can scarcely ever be managed with good effect in landscape-painting. Five or six white houses, scattered over a valley, by their obtrusiveness, dot the surface, and divide it into triangles, or other mathematical figures, haunting the eye, and disturbing that repose which might otherwise be perfect. I have seen a single white house materially impair the majesty of a mountain; cutting away, by a harsh separation, the whole of its base, below the point on which the house stood. Thus was the apparent size of the mountain reduced, not by the interposition of another object in a manner to call forth the imagination, which will give more than the eye loses; but what had been abstracted in this case was left visible; and the mountain appeared to take its beginning, or to rise, from the line of the house, instead of its own natural base. But, if I may express my own individual feeling, it is after sunset, at the coming on of twilight, that white objects are most to be complained of.* The solemnity and quietness of nature at that time are always marred, and often destroyed by them. When the ground is covered with snow, they are of course inoffensive; and in moonshine they are always pleasing—it is a tone of light with which they accord: and the dimness of the scene is enlivened by an object at once conspicuous and cheerful. I will conclude this subject with noticing, that the cold, slaty colour, which many persons, who have heard the white condemned, have adopted in its stead, must be disapproved of for the reason already given. The flaring yellow runs into the opposite extreme, and is still more censurable. Upon the whole, the safest colour, for general use, is something between a cream and a dust-colour, commonly called stone colour;—there are, among the Lakes, examples of this that need not be pointed out.[1]

The principle taken as our guide, viz. that the house should be so formed, and of such apparent size and colour, as to admit of its being gently incorporated with the works of nature, should also be applied to the management of the grounds and plantations, and is here more urgently needed; for it is from abuses in this department, far more even than from the introduction of exotics in architecture (if the phrase may be used), that this country has suffered. Larch and fir plantations* have been spread, not merely with a view to profit, but in many instances for the sake of ornament. To those who plant for profit, and are thrusting every other tree out of the way, to make room for their favourite, the larch, I would utter first a regret, that they should have selected these lovely vales for their vegetable manufactory, when there is so much barren and irreclaimable land in the neighbouring moors,* and in other parts of the island, which might have been had for this purpose at a far cheaper rate. And I will also beg leave to represent to them, that they ought not to be carried away by flattering promises from the speedy growth of this tree; because in rich soils and sheltered situations, the wood, though it thrives fast, is full of sap and of little value; and is, likewise, very subject to ravage from the attacks of insects, and from blight. Accordingly, in Scotland, where planting is much better understood, and carried on upon an incomparably larger scale than among us, good soil and sheltered situations are appropriated to the oak, the ash, and other deciduous trees; and the larch is now generally confined to barren and exposed ground. There the plant, which is a hardy one, is of slower growth; much less liable to injury; and the timber is of better quality. But the circumstances of many permit, and their taste leads them, to plant with little regard to profit; and there are others, less wealthy, who have such a lively feeling of the native beauty of these scenes, that they are laudably not unwilling to make some sacrifices to heighten it. Both these classes of persons, I would entreat to enquire of themselves

---

[1] A proper colouring of houses is now becoming general. It is best that the colouring material should be mixed with the rough-cast, and not laid on as a *wash* afterwards.

wherein that beauty which they admire consists. They would then see that, after the feeling has been gratified that prompts us to gather round our dwelling a few flowers and shrubs, which from the circumstance of their not being native, may, by their very looks, remind us that they owe their existence to our hands, and their prosperity to our care; they will see that, after this natural desire has been provided for, the course of all beyond has been predetermined by the spirit of the place. Before I proceed, I will remind those who are not satisfied with the restraint thus laid upon them, that they are liable to a charge of inconsistency, when they are so eager to change the face of that country, whose native attractions, by the act of erecting their habitations in it, they have so emphatically acknowledged.* And surely there is not a single spot that would not have, if well managed, sufficient dignity to support itself, unaided by the productions of other climates, or by elaborate decorations which might be becoming elsewhere.

Having adverted to the feelings that justify the introduction of a few exotic plants, provided they be confined almost to the doors of the house, we may add, that a transition should be contrived, without abruptness, from these foreigners to the rest of the shrubs, which ought to be of the kinds scattered by Nature, through the woods—holly, broom, wild-rose, elder, dogberry, white and black thorn, &c.—either these only, or such as are carefully selected in consequence of their being united in form, and harmonising in colour with them, especially with respect to colour, when the tints are most diversified, as in autumn and spring. The various sorts of fruit-and-blossom-bearing trees usually found in orchards, to which may be added those of the woods,—namely, the wilding, black cherry tree, and wild cluster-cherry (here called heck-berry)—may be happily admitted as an intermediate link between the shrubs and the forest trees; which last ought almost entirely to be such as are natives of the country. Of the birch, one of the most beautiful of the native trees, it may be noticed, that, in dry and rocky situations, it outstrips even the larch, which many persons are tempted to plant merely on account of the speed of its growth. The Scotch fir is less attractive during its youth than any other plant; but, when full-grown, if it has had room to spread out its arms, it becomes a noble tree; and, by those who are disinterested enough to plant for posterity, it may be placed along with the sycamore near the house;* for, from their massiveness, both these trees unite well with buildings, and in some situations with rocks also; having, in their forms and apparent substances, the effect of something intermediate betwixt the immoveableness and solidity of stone, and the spray and foliage of the lighter trees. If these general rules be just, what shall we say to whole acres of artificial shrubbery and exotic trees among rocks and dashing torrents, with their own wild wood in sight—where we have the whole contents of the nurseryman's catalogue jumbled together—colour at war with colour, and form with form?—among the most peaceful subjects of Nature's kingdom, everywhere discord, distraction, and bewilderment! But this deformity, bad as it is, is not so obtrusive as the small patches and large tracts of larch-plantations that are overrunning the hill sides. To justify our condemnation of these, let us again recur to Nature. The process, by which she forms woods and forests, is as follows. Seeds are scattered indiscriminately by winds, brought by waters, and dropped by birds. They perish, or produce, according as the soil and situation upon which they fall are suited to them: and under the same dependence, the seedling or the sucker, if not cropped by animals, (which Nature is often careful to prevent by fencing it about with brambles or other prickly shrubs) thrives, and the tree grows, sometimes single, taking its own shape without constraint, but for the most part compelled to conform itself to some law imposed upon it by its neighbours. From low and sheltered places, vegetation travels upwards to the more exposed; and the young plants are protected, and to a certain degree fashioned, by those that have preceded them. The continuous mass of foliage which would be thus produced, is broken by rocks, or by glades or open places, where the browzing of animals has prevented the growth of wood. As vegetation ascends, the winds begin also to bear their part in moulding the forms of the trees; but, thus mutually protected, trees, though not of the hardiest kind, are enabled to climb high up the mountains. Gradually, however, by the quality of the ground, and by increasing exposure, a stop is put to their ascent; the hardy trees only are left: those also, by little and little, give way—and a wild and irregular boundary is established, graceful in its outline, and never contemplated without some feeling, more or less distinct, of the powers of Nature by which it is imposed.

Contrast the liberty that encourages, and the law that limits, this joint work of nature and time, with the disheartening necessities, restrictions, and disadvantages, under which the artificial planter must proceed, even he whom long observation and fine feeling have

best qualified for his task. In the first place his trees, however well
chosen and adapted to their several situations, must generally start all
at the same time; and this necessity would of itself prevent that fine
connection of parts, that sympathy and organization, if I may so
express myself, which pervades the whole of a natural wood, and
appears to the eye in its single trees, its masses of foliage, and their
various colours, when they are held up to view on the side of a moun-
tain; or when, spread over a valley, they are looked down upon from
an eminence. It is therefore impossible, under any circumstances, for
the artificial planter to rival the beauty of nature. But a moment's
thought will show that, if ten thousand of this spiky tree, the larch, are
stuck in at once upon the side of a hill, they can grow up into nothing
but deformity; that, while they are suffered to stand, we shall look in
vain for any of those appearances which are the chief sources of
beauty in a natural wood.

It must be acknowledged that the larch, till it has outgrown the size
of a shrub, shows, when looked at singly, some elegance in form and
appearance, especially in spring, decorated, as it then is, by the pink
tassels of its blossoms; but, as a tree, it is less than any other pleasing:
its branches (for *boughs* it has none) have no variety in the youth of the
tree, and little dignity, even when it attains its full growth; *leaves* it
cannot be said to have, consequently neither affords shade nor shelter.
In spring the larch becomes green long before the native trees; and its
green is so peculiar and vivid, that, finding nothing to harmonize
with it, wherever it comes forth, a disagreeable speck is produced. In
summer, when all other trees are in their pride, it is of a dingy life-
less hue; in autumn of a spiritless unvaried yellow, and in winter it
is still more lamentably distinguished from every other deciduous
tree of the forest, for they seem only to sleep, but the larch appears
absolutely dead. If an attempt be made to mingle thickets, or a cer-
tain proportion of other forest-trees, with the larch, its horizontal
branches intolerantly cut them down as with a scythe, or force them to
spindle up to keep pace with it. The terminating spike renders it impos-
sible that the several trees, where planted in numbers, should ever
blend together so as to form a mass or masses of wood. Add thousands
to tens of thousands, and the appearance is still the same—a collec-
tion of separate individual trees, obstinately presenting themselves
as such; and which, from whatever point they are looked at, if but
seen, may be counted upon the fingers. Sunshine, or shadow, has

MISCELLANEOUS
OBSERVATIONS

MR. WEST, in his well-known Guide to the Lakes, recommends, as the best season for visiting this country,* the interval from the beginning of June to the end of August; and, the two latter months being a time of vacation and leisure, it is almost exclusively in these that strangers resort hither. But that season is by no means the best; the colouring of the mountains and woods,* unless where they are diversified by rocks, is of too unvaried a green; and, as a large portion of the vallies is allotted to hay-grass, some want of variety is found there also. The meadows, however, are sufficiently enlivened after hay-making begins, which is much later than in the southern part of the island. A stronger objection is rainy weather,* setting in sometimes at this period with a vigour, and continuing with a perseverance, that may remind the disappointed and dejected traveller of those deluges of rain which fall among the Abyssinian mountains, for the annual supply of the Nile.* The months of September and October (particularly October) are generally attended with much finer weather; and the scenery is then, beyond comparison, more diversified, more splendid, and beautiful; but, on the other hand, short days prevent long excursions, and sharp and chill gales are unfavourable to parties of pleasure out of doors. Nevertheless, to the sincere admirer of nature, who is in good health and spirits, and at liberty to make a choice, the six weeks following the 1st of September may be recommended in preference to July and August. For there is no inconvenience arising from the season which, to such a person, would not be amply compensated by the *autumnal* appearance of any of the more retired vallies, into which discordant plantations and unsuitable buildings have not yet found entrance.—In such spots, at this season, there is an admirable compass and proportion of natural harmony in colour, through the whole scale of objects; in the tender green of the after-grass upon the meadows, interspersed with islands of grey or mossy rock, crowned by shrubs and trees; in the irregular inclosures of standing corn, or stubble-fields, in like manner broken; in the mountain-sides glowing with fern of divers colours; in the calm

blue lakes and river-pools; and in the foliage of the trees, through all
the tints of autumn,—from the pale and brilliant yellow of the birch
and ash, to the deep greens of the unfaded oak and alder, and of, the
ivy upon the rocks, upon the trees, and the cottages.* Yet, as most
travellers are either stinted, or stint themselves, for time, the space
between the middle or last week in May, and the middle or last
week of June, may be pointed out as affording the best combination
of long days, fine weather, and variety of impressions. Few of the
native trees are then in full leaf; but, for whatever may be wanting
in depth of shade, more than an equivalent will be found in the
diversity of foliage, in the blossoms of the fruit-and-berry-bearing
trees which abound in the woods, and in the golden flowers of the
broom and other shrubs, with which many of the copses are
intervened.* In those woods, also, and on these mountain-sides
which have a northern aspect, and in the deep dells, many of the
spring-flowers still linger; while the open and sunny places are
stocked with the flowers of the approaching summer. And, besides,
is not an exquisite pleasure still untasted by him who has not heard
the choir of linnets and thrushes chaunting their love-songs in the
copses, woods, and hedge-rows of a mountainous country; safe
from the birds of prey, which build in the inaccessible crags, and
are at all hours seen or heard wheeling about in the air? The num-
ber of these formidable creatures is probably the cause, why, in the
narrow vallies, there are no skylarks; as the destroyer would be en-
abled to dart upon them from the near and surrounding crags,
before they could descend to their ground-nests for protection. It
is not often that the nightingale resorts to these vales; but almost all
the other tribes of our English warblers are numerous; and their
notes, when listened to by the side of broad still waters,* or when
heard in unison with the murmuring of mountain-brooks, have the
compass of their power enlarged accordingly. There is also an
imaginative influence in the voice of the cuckoo, when that voice
has taken possession of a deep mountain valley, very different from
any thing which can be excited by the same sound in a flat country.*
Nor must a circumstance be omitted, which here renders the close
of spring especially interesting; I mean the practice of bringing
down the ewes from the mountains to yean in the vallies and
enclosed grounds. The herbage being thus cropped as it springs,
that first tender emerald green of the season, which would otherwise

have lasted little more than a fortnight, is prolonged in the pastures and meadows for many weeks: while they are farther enlivened by the multitude of lambs bleating and skipping about. These sportive creatures, as they gather strength, are turned out upon the open mountains, and with their slender limbs, their snow-white colour, and their wild and light motions, beautifully accord or contrast with the rocks and lawns, upon which they must now begin to seek their food. And last, but not least, at this time the traveller will be sure of room and comfortable accommodation, even in the smaller inns. I am aware that few of those who may be inclined to profit by this recommendation will be able to do so, as the time and manner of an excursion of this kind are mostly regulated by circumstances which prevent an entire freedom of choice. It will therefore be more pleasant to observe, that, though the months of July and August are liable to many objections, yet it often happens that the weather, at this time, is not more wet and stormy than they, who are really capable of enjoying the sublime forms of nature in their utmost sublimity, would desire. For no traveller, provided he be in good health, and with any command of time, would have a just privilege to visit such scenes, if he could grudge the price of a little confinement among them, or interruption in his journey, for the sight or sound of a storm coming on or clearing away. Insensible must he be who would not congratulate himself upon the bold bursts of sunshine, the descending vapours, wandering lights and shadows, and the invigorated torrents and water-falls, with which broken weather, in a mountainous region, is accompanied.* At such a time there is no cause to complain, either of the monotony of midsummer colouring, or the glaring atmosphere of long, cloudless, and hot days.

Thus far concerning the respective advantages and disadvantages of the different seasons for visiting this country. As to the order in which objects are best seen—a lake being composed of water flowing from higher grounds, and expanding itself till its receptacle is filled to the brim,—it follows, that it will appear to most advantage when approached from its outlet, especially if the lake be in a mountainous country; for, by this way of approach, the traveller faces the grander features of the scene, and is gradually conducted into its most sublime recesses. Now, every one knows that from amenity and beauty the transition to sublimity is easy and favourable; but the reverse is not so; for, after the faculties have been elevated, they are indisposed to humbler excitement.[1]*

It is not likely that a mountain will be ascended without disappointment, if a wide range of prospect be the object, unless either the summit be reached before sun-rise, or the visitant remain there until the time of sun-set, and afterwards. The precipitous sides of the mountain, and the neighbouring summits, may be seen with effect under any atmosphere which allows them to be seen at all; but *he* is the most fortunate adventurer, who chances to be involved in vapours which open and let in an extent of country partially, or, dispersing suddenly, reveal the whole region from centre to circumference.*

A stranger to a mountainous country may not be aware that his walk in the early morning ought to be taken on the eastern side of the vale, otherwise he will lose the morning light, first touching the tops and thence creeping down the sides of the opposite hills, as the sun ascends, or he may go to some central eminence, commanding both the shadows from the eastern, and the lights upon the western mountains. But, if the horizon line in the east be low, the western side may be taken for the sake of the reflections, upon the water, of light from the rising sun. In the evening, for like reasons, the contrary course should be taken.*

After all, it is upon the *mind* which a traveller brings along with him that his acquisitions, whether of pleasure or profit, must principally depend.*—May I be allowed a few words on this subject?

Nothing is more injurious to genuine feeling than the practice of hastily and ungraciously depreciating the face of one country by comparing it with that of another.* True it is Qui *bene* distinguit bene *docet*;* yet fastidiousness is a wretched travelling companion; and the best guide to which, in matters of taste we can entrust ourselves, is a disposition to be pleased. For example, if a traveller be among the Alps, let him surrender up his mind to the fury of the gigantic torrents,

---

[1] The only instances to which the foregoing observations do not apply, are Derwent-water and Lowes-water. Derwent is distinguished from all the other Lakes by being *surrounded* with sublimity: the fantastic mountains of Borrowdale to the south, the solitary majesty of Skiddaw to the north, the bold steeps of Wallow-crag and Lodore to the east, and to the west the clustering mountains of New-lands. Lowes-water is tame at the head, but towards its outlet has a magnificent assemblage of mountains. Yet as far as respects the formation of such receptacles, the general observation holds good: neither Derwent nor Lowes-water derive any supplies from the streams of those mountains that dignify the landscape towards the outlets.

and take delight in the contemplation of their almost irresistible violence, without complaining of the monotony of their foaming course, or being disgusted with the muddiness of the water—apparent even where it is violently agitated. In Cumberland and Westmorland, let not the comparative weakness of the streams prevent him from sympathizing with such impetuosity as they possess; and, making the most of the present objects, let him, as he justly may do, observe with admiration the unrivalled brilliancy of the water, and that variety of motion, mood, and character,* that arises out of the want of those resources by which the power of the streams in the Alps is supported.—Again, with respect to the mountains; though these are comparatively of diminutive size, though there is little of perpetual snow, and no voice of summer-avalanches is heard among them; and though traces left by the ravage of the elements are here comparatively rare and unimpressive, yet out of this very deficiency proceeds a sense of stability and permanence that is, to many minds, more grateful—

> 'While the coarse rushes to the sweeping breeze
> Sigh forth their ancient melodies.'*

Among the Alps are few places that do not preclude this feeling of tranquil sublimity.* Havoc, and ruin, and desolation, and encroachment, are everywhere more or less obtruded; and it is difficult, notwithstanding the naked loftiness of the *pikes*, and the snow-capped summits of the *mounts*, to escape from the depressing sensation, that the whole are in a rapid process of dissolution; and, were it not that the destructive agency must abate as the heights diminish, would, in time to come, be levelled with the plains. Nevertheless, I would relish to the utmost the demonstrations of every species of power at work to effect such changes.*

From these general views let us descend a moment to detail. A stranger to mountain imagery naturally on his first arrival looks out for sublimity in every object that admits of it; and is almost always disappointed. For this disappointment there exists, I believe, no general preventive; nor is it desirable that there should. But with regard to one class of objects, there is a point in which injurious expectations may be easily corrected. It is generally supposed that waterfalls are scarcely worth being looked at except after much rain, and that, the more swoln the stream, the more fortunate the spectator; but this however is true only of large cataracts with sublime accompaniments; and not even of these without some drawbacks.* In other instances, what becomes, at such a time, of that sense of refreshing coolness which can only be felt in dry and sunny weather, when the rocks, herbs, and flowers glisten with moisture diffused by the breath of the precipitous water?* But, considering these things as objects of sight only, it may be observed that the principal charm of the smaller waterfalls or cascades consists in certain proportions of form and affinities of colour, among the component parts of the scene; and in the contrast maintained between the falling water and that which is apparently at rest, or rather settling gradually into quiet in the pool below. The beauty of such a scene, where there is naturally so much agitation, is also heightened, in a peculiar manner, by the *glimmering*, and, towards the verge of the pool, by the *steady*, reflection of the surrounding images.* Now, all those delicate distinctions are destroyed by heavy floods, and the whole stream rushes along in foam and tumultuous confusion. A happy proportion of component parts is indeed noticeable among the landscapes of the North of England; and, in this characteristic essential to a perfect picture, they surpass the scenes of Scotland, and, in a still greater degree, those of Switzerland.

As a resident among the Lakes,* I frequently hear the scenery of this country compared with that of the Alps; and therefore a few words shall be added to what has been incidentally said upon that subject.

If we could recall, to this region of lakes, the native pine-forests, with which many hundred years ago a large portion of the heights was covered, then, during spring and autumn, it might frequently, with much propriety, be compared to Switzerland,—the elements of the landscape would be the same—one country representing the other in miniature. Towns, villages, churches, rural seats, bridges and roads: green meadows and arable grounds, with their various produce, and deciduous woods of diversified foliage which occupy the vales and lower regions of the mountains, would, as in Switzerland, be divided by dark forests from ridges and round-topped heights covered with snow, and from pikes and sharp declivities imperfectly arrayed in the same glittering mantle: and the resemblance would be still more perfect on those days when vapours, resting upon, and floating around the summits, leave the elevation of the mountains less dependent upon the eye than on the imagination. But the pine-forests have wholly disappeared; and only during late spring and early autumn is realized here that assemblage of the imagery of different seasons, which is exhibited through the whole summer among the Alps,—winter in the distance,—and warmth, leafy woods, verdure and fertility at hand, and widely diffused.

Striking, then, from among the permanent materials of the landscape, that stage of vegetation which is occupied by pine-forests, and, above that, the perennial snows, we have mountains, the highest of which little exceed 3,000 feet, while some of the Alps do not fall short of 14,000 or 15,000, and 8,000 or 10,000 is not an uncommon elevation. Our tracts of wood and water are almost as diminutive in comparison; therefore, as far as sublimity is dependent upon absolute bulk and height, and atmospherical influences in connection with these, it is obvious, that there can be no rivalship. But a short residence among the British Mountains will furnish abundant proof, that, after a certain point of elevation, viz. that which allows of compact and fleecy clouds settling upon, or sweeping over, the summits, the sense of sublimity depends more upon form and relation of objects to each other than upon their actual magnitude; and, that an elevation of 3,000 feet is sufficient to call forth in a most impressive degree the creative, and magnifying, and softening powers of the atmosphere. Hence, on the score even of sublimity, the superiority of the Alps is by no means so great as might hastily be inferred;—and, as to the *beauty* of the lower regions of the Swiss Mountains, it is noticeable—that, as they are all regularly mown, their surface has nothing of that mellow tone and variety of hues by which mountain turf, that is never touched by the scythe, is distinguished. On the smooth and steep slopes of the Swiss hills, these plots of verdure do indeed agreeably unite their colour with that of the deciduous trees, or make a lively contrast with the dark green pine-groves that define them, and among which they run in endless variety of shapes—but this is most pleasing *at first sight*; the permanent gratification of the eye requires finer gradations of tone, and a more delicate blending of hues into each other. Besides, it is only in spring and late autumn that cattle animate by their presence the Swiss lawns; and, though the pastures of the higher regions where they feed during the summer are left in their natural state of flowery herbage, those pastures are so remote, that their texture and colour are of no consequence in the composition of any picture in which a lake of the Vales is a feature. Yet in those lofty regions, how vegetation is invigorated by the genial climate of that country! Among the luxuriant flowers there met with,

groves, or forests, if I may so call them, of Monks-hood* are fre-
quently seen; the plant of deep, rich blue, and as tall as in our gardens;
and this at an elevation where, in Cumberland, Icelandic moss would
only be found, or the stony summits be utterly bare.

We have, then, for the colouring of Switzerland, *principally* a vivid
green herbage, black woods, and dazzling snows, presented in masses
with a grandeur to which no one can be insensible; but not often
graduated by Nature into soothing harmony, and so ill-suited to the
pencil, that though abundance of good subjects may be there found,
they are not such as can be deemed *characteristic* of the country; nor
is this unfitness confined to colour: the forms of the mountains,
though many of them in some points of view the noblest that can be
conceived, are apt to run into spikes and needles, and present a jagged
outline which has a mean effect, transferred to canvass. This must
have been felt by the ancient masters; for, if I am not mistaken, they
have not left a single landscape, the materials of which are taken from
the *peculiar* features of the Alps; yet Titian passed his life almost in
their neighbourhood; the Poussins and Claude must have been well
acquainted with their aspects; and several admirable painters, as
Tibaldi and Luino, were born among the Italian Alps.* A few experi-
ments have lately been made by Englishmen, but they only prove that
courage, skill, and judgement, may surmount any obstacles; and it
may be safely affirmed, that they who have done best in this bold
adventure, will be the least likely to repeat the attempt.* But, though
our scenes are better suited to painting than those of the Alps, I should
be sorry to contemplate either country in reference to that art, fur-
ther than as its fitness or unfitness for the pencil renders it more or
less pleasing to the eye of the spectator, who has learned to observe
and feel, chiefly from Nature herself.

Deeming the points in which Alpine imagery is superior to British
too obvious to be insisted upon, I will observe that the deciduous
woods, though in many places unapproachable by the axe, and tri-
umphing in the pomp and prodigality of Nature, have, in general,[1]
neither the variety nor beauty which would exist in those of the
mountains of Britain, if left to themselves. Magnificent walnut-trees
grow upon the plains of Switzerland; and fine trees, of that species,
are found scattered over the hill-sides: birches also grow here and

[1] The greatest variety of trees is found in the Valais.

there in luxuriant beauty; but neither these, nor oaks, are ever a prevailing tree, nor can even be said to be common; and the oaks, as far as I had an opportunity of observing, are greatly inferior to those of Britain. Among the interior vallies the proportion of beeches and pines is so great that other trees are scarcely noticeable; and surely such woods are at all seasons much less agreeable than that rich and harmonious distribution of oak, ash, elm, birch, and alder, that formerly clothed the sides of Snowdon and Helvellyn; and of which no mean remains still survive at the head of Ulswater. On the Italian side of the Alps, chesnut and walnut-trees grow at a considerable height on the mountains; but, even there, the foliage is not equal in beauty to the 'natural product' of this climate. In fact the sunshine of the South of Europe, so envied when heard of at a distance, is in many respects injurious to rural beauty, particularly as it incites to the cultivation of spots of ground which in colder climates would be left in the hands of nature, favouring at the same time the culture of plants that are more valuable on account of the fruit they produce to gratify the palate, than for affording pleasure to the eye, as materials of landscape. Take, for instance, the Promontory of Bellagio, so fortunate in its command of the three branches of the Lake of Como, yet the ridge of the Promontory itself, being for the most part covered with vines interspersed with olive-trees, accords but ill with the vastness of the green unappropriated mountains, and derogates not a little from the sublimity of those finely contrasted pictures to which it is a fore-ground. The vine, when cultivated upon a large scale, notwithstanding all that may be said of it in poetry,[1] makes but a dull formal appearance in landscape; and the olive-tree (though one is loth to say so) is not more grateful to the eye than our common willow, which it much resembles; but the hoariness of hue, common to both, has in the aquatic plant an

---

[1] Lucretius has charmingly described a scene of this kind.

> 'Inque dies magis in montem succedere sylvas
> Cogebant, infráque locum concedere cultis:
> Prata, lacus, rivos, segetes, vinetaque læta
> Collibus et campis ut haberent, atque olearum
> *Cærula* distinguens inter *plaga* currere posset
> Per tumulos, et convalleis, campósque profusa:
> Ut nunc esse vides vario distincta lepore
> Omnia, quæ pomis intersita dulcibus ornant,
> Arbustisque tenent felicibus obsita circúm.'*

appropriate delicacy, harmonising with the situation in which it most delights. The same may no doubt be said of the olive among the dry rocks of Attica, but I am speaking of it as found in gardens and vineyards in the North of Italy. At Bellagio, what Englishman can resist the temptation of substituting, in his fancy, for these formal treasures of cultivation, the natural variety of one of our parks—its pastured lawns, coverts of hawthorn, of wild-rose, and honey-suckle, and the majesty of forest trees?—such wild graces as the banks of Derwentwater shewed in the time of the Ratcliffes;* and Gowbarrow Park, Lowther, and Rydal do at this day.

As my object is to reconcile a Briton to the scenery of his own country, though not at the expense of truth, I am not afraid of asserting that in many points of view our LAKES, also, are much more interesting than those of the Alps; first, as is implied above, from being more happily proportioned to the other features of the landscape; and next, both as being infinitely more pellucid, and less subject to agitation from the winds.[1] Como, (which may perhaps be styled the King of Lakes, as Lugano is certainly the Queen) is disturbed by a periodical wind blowing *from* the head in the morning, and *towards* it in the afternoon. The magnificent Lake of the four Cantons, especially its noblest division, called the Lake of Uri, is not only much agitated by winds, but in the night time is disturbed from the bottom, as I was told, and indeed as I witnessed, without any apparent commotion in the air; and when at rest, the water is not pure to the eye, but of a heavy green hue—as is that of all the other lakes, apparently according to the degree in which they are fed by melted snows. If the Lake of Geneva furnish an exception, this is probably owing to its vast extent, which allows the water to deposit its impurities. The water of

---

[1] It is remarkable that Como (as is probably the case with other Italian Lakes) is more troubled by storms in summer than in winter. Hence the propriety of the following verses.

> 'Lari! margine ubique confragoso
> Nulli cœlicolum negas sacellum
> Picto pariete saxeoque tecto;
> Hinc miracula multa navitarum
> Audis, nec placido refellis ore,
> Sed nova usque paras, Noto vel Euro
> *Æstivas* quatientibus cavernas,
> Vel surgentis ab Adduæ cubili
> Cæco grandinis imbre provoluto.'   LANDOR.*

the English lakes, on the contrary, being of a crystalline clearness, the reflections of the surrounding hills are frequently so lively, that it is scarcely possible to distinguish the point where the real object terminates, and its unsubstantial duplicate begins.* The lower part of the Lake of Geneva, from its narrowness, must be much less subject to agitation than the higher divisions, and, as the water is clearer than that of the other Swiss Lakes, it will frequently exhibit this appearance, though it is scarcely possible in an equal degree. During two comprehensive tours among the Alps,* I did not observe, except on one of the smaller lakes, between Lugano and Ponte Tresa, a single instance of those beautiful repetitions of surrounding objects on the bosom of the water, which are so frequently seen here: not to speak of the fine dazzling trembling network, breezy motions, and streaks and circles of intermingled smooth and rippled water, which make the surface of our lakes a field of endless variety.* But among the Alps, where every thing tends to the grand and the sublime, in surfaces as well as in forms, if the lakes do not court the placid reflections of land objects, those of first-rate magnitude make compensation, in some degree, by exhibiting those ever-changing fields of green, blue, and purple shadows or lights, (one scarcely knows which to name them) that call to mind a sea-prospect contemplated from a lofty cliff.

The subject of torrents and water-falls has already been touched upon;* but it may be added that in Switzerland, the perpetual accompaniment of snow upon the higher regions takes much from the effect of foaming white streams; while, from their frequency, they obstruct each other's influence upon the mind of the spectator; and, in all cases, the effect of an individual cataract, excepting the great Fall of the Rhine at Schaffhausen, is diminished by the general fury of the stream of which it is a part.

Recurring to the reflections from still water, I will describe a singular phenomenon of this kind of which I was an eye-witness.

Walking by the side of Ulswater upon a calm September morning,* I saw, deep within the bosom of the lake, a magnificent Castle, with towers and battlements, nothing could be more distinct than the whole edifice;—after gazing with delight upon it for some time, as upon a work of enchantment, I could not but regret that my previous knowledge of the place enabled me to account for the appearance. It was in fact the reflection of a pleasure-house called Lyulph's Tower—the towers and battlements magnified and so much changed in shape as not to be immediately recognized. In the meanwhile, the pleasure-house itself was altogether hidden from my view by a body of vapour stretching over it and along the hill-side on which it stands, but not so as to have intercepted its communication with the lake; and hence this novel and most impressive object, which, if I had been a stranger to the spot, would, from its being inexplicable, have long detained the mind in a state of pleasing astonishment.

Appearances of this kind, acting upon the credulity of early ages, may have given birth to, and favoured the belief in, stories of sub-aqueous palaces, gardens, and pleasure-grounds—the brilliant ornaments of Romance.

With this *inverted* scene I will couple a much more extraordinary phenomenon, which will shew how other elegant fancies may have had their origin, less in invention than in the actual processes of nature.

About eleven o'clock on the forenoon of a winter's day, coming suddenly, in company of a friend, into view of the Lake of Grasmere, we were alarmed by the sight of a newly-created Island; the transitory thought of the moment was, that it had been produced by an earthquake or some other convulsion of nature. Recovering from the alarm, which was greater than the reader can possibly sympathize with, but which was shared to its full extent by my companion, we proceeded to examine the object before us. The elevation of this new island exceeded considerably that of the old one, its neighbour; it was likewise larger in circumference, comprehending a space of about five acres; its surface rocky, speckled with snow, and sprinkled over with birch trees; it was divided towards the south from the other island by a narrow frith, and in like manner from the northern shore of the lake; on the east and west it was separated from the shore by a much larger space of smooth water.

Marvellous was the illusion! Comparing the new with the old Island, the surface of which is soft, green, and unvaried, I do not scruple to say that, as an object of sight, it was much the more distinct. 'How little faith,' we exclaimed, 'is due to one sense, unless its evidence be confirmed by some of its fellows! What Stranger could possibly be persuaded that this, which we know to be an unsubstantial mockery, is *really* so; and that there exists only a single Island on this beautiful Lake?' At length the appearance underwent a gradual transmutation; it lost its prominence and passed into a glimmering and dim *inversion*, and then totally disappeared;—leaving behind it a clear open area of ice of the same dimensions. We now perceived that this bed of ice, which was thinly suffused with water, had produced the illusion, by reflecting and refracting (as persons skilled in optics would no doubt easily explain) a rocky and woody section of the opposite mountain named Silver-how.

Having dwelt so much upon the beauty of pure and still water, and pointed out the advantage which the Lakes of the North of England have in this particular over those of the Alps, it would be injustice not to advert to the sublimity that must often be given to Alpine scenes, by the agitations to which those vast bodies of diffused water are there subject. I have witnessed many tremendous thunder-storms among the Alps, and the most glorious effects of light and shadow; but I never happened to be present when any Lake was agitated by those hurricanes which I imagine must often torment them. If the commotions be at all proportionable to the expanse and depth of the waters, and the height of the surrounding mountains, then, if I may judge from what is frequently seen here, the exhibition must be awful and astonishing.—On this day, March 30, 1822, the winds have been acting upon the small Lake of Rydal, as if they had received command to carry its waters from their bed into the sky; the white billows in different quarters disappeared under clouds, or rather drifts, of spray, that were whirled along, and up into the air by scouring winds, charging each other in squadrons in every direction, upon the Lake. The spray, having been hurried aloft till it lost its consistency and whiteness, was driven along the mountain tops like flying showers that vanish in the distance. Frequently an eddying wind scooped the waters out of the basin, and forced them upwards in the very shape of an Icelandic Geyser, or boiling fountain, to the height of several hundred feet.

This small Mere of Rydal, from its position, is subject in a peculiar degree to these commotions. The present season, however, is unusually stormy;—great numbers of fish, two of them not less than 12 pounds weight, were a few days ago cast on the shores of Derwentwater by the force of the waves.

Lest, in the foregoing comparative estimate, I should be suspected of partiality to my native mountains, I will support my general opinion by the authority of Mr. West, whose Guide to the Lakes has been eminently serviceable to the Tourist for nearly 50 years. The Author, a Roman Catholic Clergyman, had passed much time abroad, and was well acquainted with the scenery of the Continent. He thus expresses himself: 'They who intend to make the continental tour should begin here; as it will give, in miniature, an idea of what they are to meet with there, in traversing the Alps and Appenines; to which our northern mountains are not inferior in beauty of line, or variety of summit, number of lakes, and transparency of water; not in colouring of rock, or softness of turf; but in height and extent only. The mountains here are all accessible to the summit, and furnish prospects no less surprising, and with more variety, than the Alps themselves. The tops of the highest Alps are inaccessible, being covered with everlasting snow, which commencing at regular heights above the cultivated tracts, or wooded and verdant sides, form indeed the highest contrast in nature. For there may be seen all the variety of climate in one view. To this, however, we oppose the sight of the ocean, from the summits of all the higher mountains, as it appears intersected with promontories, decorated with islands, and animated with navigation.'—West's *Guide*, p. 5.

EXCURSIONS
TO
THE TOP OF SCAWFELL AND ON
THE BANKS OF ULSWATER

IT was my intention, several years ago, to describe a regular tour through this country, taking the different scenes in the most favourable order; but after some progress had been made in the work it was abandoned* from a conviction, that, if well executed, it would lessen the pleasure of the Traveller by anticipation,* and, if the contrary, it would mislead him. The Reader may not, however, be displeased with the following extract from a letter to a Friend,* giving an account of a visit to a summit of one of the highest of these mountains; of which I am reminded by the observations of Mr. West, and by reviewing what has been said of this district in comparison with the Alps.

Having left Rosthwaite in Borrowdale, on a bright morning in the first week of October, we ascended from Seathwaite to the top of the ridge, called Ash-course,* and thence beheld three distinct views;— on one side, the continuous Vale of Borrowdale, Keswick, and Bassenthwaite,—with Skiddaw, Helvellyn, Saddle-back, and numerous other mountains,—and, in the distance, the Solway Frith and the Mountains of Scotland;—on the other side, and below us, the Langdale Pikes—their own vale below *them*;—Windermere,—and, far beyond Windermere, Ingleborough in Yorkshire. But how shall I speak of the deliciousness of the third prospect! At this time, *that* was most favoured by sunshine and shade. The green Vale of Esk—deep and green, with its glittering serpent stream, lay below us; and, on we looked to the Mountains near the Sea,—Black Comb pre-eminent,—and, still beyond, to the Sea itself, in dazzling brightness. Turning round we saw the Mountains of Wastdale in tumult; to our right, Great Gavel, the loftiest, a distinct, and *huge* form, though the middle of the mountain was, to our eyes, as its base.

We had attained the object of this journey; but our ambition now mounted higher. We saw the summit of Scaw-fell, apparently very near to us; and we shaped our course towards it; but, discovering that it could not be reached without first making a considerable descent, we resolved, instead, to aim at another point of the same mountain, called the *Pikes*, which I have since found has been estimated as higher than the summit bearing the name of Scawfell Head, where the Stone Man* is built.

The sun had never once been overshadowed by a cloud during the whole of our progress from the centre of Borrowdale. On the summit of the Pike,* which we gained after much toil, though without difficulty, there was not a breath of air to stir even the papers containing our refreshment, as they lay spread out upon a rock. The stillness seemed to be not of this world:—we paused, and kept silence to listen; and no sound could be heard: the Scawfell Cataracts were voiceless to us; and there was not an insect to hum in the air. The vales which we had seen from Ash-course lay yet in view; and, side by side with Eskdale, we now saw the sister Vale of Donnerdale terminated by the Duddon Sands. But the majesty of the mountains below, and close to us, is not to be conceived. We now beheld the whole mass of Great Gavel from its base,—the Den of Wastdale at our feet— a gulph immeasurable: Grasmire and the other mountains of Crummock—Ennerdale and its mountains; and the Sea beyond! We sat down to our repast, and gladly would we have tempered our beverage (for there was no spring or well near us) with such a supply of delicious water as we might have procured, had we been on the rival summit of Great Gavel; for on its highest point is a small triangular receptacle in the native rock, which, the shepherds say, is never dry. There we might have slaked our thirst plenteously with a pure and celestial liquid, for the cup or basin, it appears, has no other feeder than the dews of heaven, the showers, the vapours, the hoar frost, and the spotless snow.*

While we were gazing around, 'Look,' I exclaimed, 'at yon ship upon the glittering sea!' 'Is it a ship?' replied our shepherd-guide. 'It can be nothing else,' interposed my companion; 'I cannot be mistaken, I am so accustomed to the appearance of ships at sea.' The Guide dropped the argument; but, before a minute was gone, he quietly said, 'Now look at your ship; it is changed into a horse.' So indeed it was,—a horse with a gallant neck and head. We laughed heartily; and, I hope, when again inclined to be positive, I may remember the ship and the horse upon the glittering sea; and the calm confidence, yet submissiveness, of our wise Man of the Mountains, who certainly had more knowledge of clouds than we, whatever might be our knowledge of ships.

I know not how long we might have remained on the summit of the Pike, without a thought of moving, had not our Guide warned us that we must not linger; for a storm was coming. We looked in vain to espy the signs of it. Mountains, vales, and sea were touched with the clear light of the sun. 'It is there,' said he, pointing to the sea beyond Whitehaven, and there we perceived a light vapour unnoticeable but by a shepherd accustomed to watch all mountain bodings. We gazed around again, and yet again, unwilling to lose the remembrance of what lay before us in that lofty solitude; and then prepared to depart. Meanwhile the air changed to cold, and we saw that tiny vapours swelled into mighty masses of cloud which came boiling over the mountains. Great Gavel, Helvellyn, and Skiddaw, were wrapped in storm; yet Langdale, and the mountains in that quarter, remained all bright in sunshine. Soon the storm reached us; we sheltered under a crag; and almost as rapidly as it had come it passed away, and left us free to observe the struggles of gloom and sunshine in other quarters. Langdale now had its share, and the Pikes of Langdale were decorated by two splendid rainbows. Skiddaw also had his own rainbows. Before we again reached Ash-course every cloud had vanished from every summit.

I ought to have mentioned that round the top of Scawfell-PIKE not a blade of grass is to be seen. Cushions or tufts of moss, parched and brown, appear between the huge blocks and stones that lie in heaps on all sides to a great distance, like skeletons or bones of the earth not needed at the creation, and there left to be covered with never-dying lichens, which the clouds and dews nourish; and adorn with colours of vivid and exquisite beauty. Flowers, the most brilliant feathers, and even gems, scarcely surpass in colouring some of those masses of stone, which no human eye beholds, except the shepherd or traveller be led thither by curiosity: and how seldom must this happen!* For the other eminence is the one visited by the adventurous stranger; and the shepherd has no inducement to ascend the PIKE in quest of his sheep; no food being *there* to tempt them.

We certainly were singularly favoured in the weather; for when we were seated on the summit, our conductor, turning his eyes thoughtfully round, said, 'I do not know that in my whole life, I was ever, at any season of the year, so high upon the mountains on so *calm* a day.' (It was the 7th of October.) Afterwards we had a spectacle of the grandeur of earth and heaven commingled; yet without terror. We knew that the storm would pass away;—for so our prophetic Guide had assured us.

Before we reached Seathwaite in Borrowdale, a few stars had appeared, and we pursued our way down the Vale, to Rosthwaite, by moonlight.

Scawfell and Helvellyn being the two Mountains of this region which will best repay the fatigue of ascending them, the following Verses may be here introduced with propriety. They are from the Author's Miscellaneous Poems.

TO——,

ON HER FIRST ASCENT TO THE SUMMIT OF HELVELLYN.

INMATE of a Mountain Dwelling,
Thou hast clomb aloft, and gazed,
From the watch-towers of Helvellyn;
Awed, delighted, and amazed!

Potent was the spell that bound thee
Not unwilling to obey;
For blue Ether's arms, flung round thee,
Stilled the pantings of dismay.

Lo! the dwindled woods and meadows!
What a vast abyss is there!
Lo! the clouds, the solemn shadows,
And the glistenings—heavenly fair!

And a record of commotion
Which a thousand ridges yield;
Ridge, and gulf, and distant ocean
Gleaming like a silver shield!

—Take thy flight;—possess, inherit
Alps or Andes—they are thine!
With the morning's roseate Spirit,
Sweep their length of snowy line;

Or survey the bright dominions
In the gorgeous colours drest
Flung from off the purple pinions,
Evening spreads throughout the west!

Thine are all the choral fountains
Warbling in each sparry vault
Of the untrodden lunar mountains;
Listen to their songs!—or halt,

To Niphates' top invited,
Whither spiteful Satan steered;
Or descend where the ark alighted,
When the green earth re-appeared:

For the power of hills is on thee,
As was witnessed through thine eye
Then, when old Helvellyn won thee
To confess their majesty!*

Having said so much of *points of view* to which few are likely to ascend, I am induced to subjoin an account of a short excursion through more accessible parts of the country, made at a *time* when it is seldom seen but by the inhabitants. As the journal was written for one acquainted with the general features of the country, only those effects and appearances are dwelt upon, which are produced by the changeableness of the atmosphere, or belong to the season when the excursion was made.

A.D.1805.*—On the 7th of November, on a damp and gloomy morning, we left Grasmere Vale, intending to pass a few days on the banks of Ullswater. A mild and dry autumn had been unusually favourable to the preservation and beauty of foliage; and, far advanced as the season was, the trees on the larger Island of Rydal-mere retained a splendour which did not need the heightening of sunshine. We noticed, as we passed, that the line of the grey rocky shore of that island, shaggy with variegated bushes and shrubs, and spotted and striped with purplish brown heath, indistinguishably blending with its image reflected in the still water, produced a curious resemblance, both in form and colour, to a richly-coated caterpillar, as it might appear through a magnifying glass of extraordinary power. The mists gathered as we went along: but, when we reached the top of Kirkstone, we were glad we had not been discouraged by the apprehension of bad weather. Though not able to see a hundred yards before us, we were more than contented. At such a time, and in such a place, every scattered stone the size of one's head becomes a companion. Near the top of the Pass is the remnant of an old wall, which (magnified, though obscured, by the vapour) might have been taken for a fragment of some monument of ancient grandeur,—yet that same pile of stones we had never before even observed. This situation, it must be allowed, is not favourable to gaiety; but a pleasing hurry of spirits accompanies the surprise occasioned by objects transformed, dilated, or distorted, as they are when seen through such a medium. Many of the fragments of rock on the top and slopes of Kirkstone, and of similar places, are fantastic enough in themselves; but the full effect of such impressions can only be had in a state of weather when they are not likely to be *sought* for. It was not till we had descended considerably that the fields of Hartshope were seen, like a lake tinged by the reflection of sunny clouds: I mistook them for Brothers-water, but, soon after, we saw that Lake gleaming faintly with a steelly brightness,—then, as we continued to descend, appeared the brown oaks, and the birches of lively yellow—and the cottages—and the lowly Hall of Hartshope, with its long roof and ancient chimneys. During great part of our way to Patterdale, we had rain, or rather drizzling vapour; for there was never a drop upon our hair or clothes larger than the smallest pearls upon a lady's ring.

The following morning, incessant rain till 11 o'clock, when the sky began to clear, and we walked along the eastern shore of Ullswater towards the farm of Blowick. The wind blew strong, and drove the clouds forward, on the side of the mountain above our heads;—two storm-stiffened black yew-trees fixed our notice, seen through, or under the edge of, the flying mists,—four or five goats were bounding among the rocks;—the sheep moved about more quietly, or cowered beneath their sheltering places. This is the only part of the country where goats are now found;[1] but this morning, before we had seen these, I was reminded of that picturesque animal by two rams of mountain breed, both with Ammonian horns,* and with beards majestic as that which Michael Angelo has given to his statue of Moses.—But to return; when our path had brought us to that part of the naked common which overlooks the woods and bush-besprinkled fields of Blowick, the lake, clouds, and mists were all in motion to the sound of sweeping winds;—the church and cottages of Patterdale scarcely visible, or seen only by fits between the shifting vapours.* To

---

[1] A.D.1805. These also have disappeared.

the northward the scene was less visionary;—Place Fell steady and bold;—the whole lake driving onward like a great river—waves dancing round the small islands. The house at Blowick was the boundary of our walk; and we returned, lamenting to see a decaying and uncomfortable dwelling in a place where sublimity and beauty seemed to contend with each other. But these regrets were dispelled by a glance on the woods that clothe the opposite steeps of the lake. How exquisite was the mixture of sober and splendid hues! The general colouring of the trees was brown—rather that of ripe hazel nuts; but towards the water, there were yet beds of green, and in the highest parts of the wood, was abundance of yellow foliage, which, gleaming through a vapoury lustre, reminded us of masses of clouds, as you see them gathered together in the west, and touched with the golden light of the setting sun.

After dinner we walked up the Vale: I had never had an idea of its extent and width in passing along the public road on the other side. We followed the path that leads from house to house; two or three times it took us through some of those copses or groves that cover the little hillocks in the middle of the vale, making an intricate and pleasing inter-mixture of lawn and wood. Our fancies could not resist the temptation; and we fixed upon a spot for a cottage, which we began to build:* and finished as easily as castles are raised in the air.—Visited the same spot in the evening. I shall say nothing of the moonlight aspect of the situation which had charmed us so much in the afternoon; but I wish you had been with us when, in returning to our friend's house, we espied his lady's large white dog, lying in the moonshine* upon the round knoll under the old yew-tree in the garden, a romantic image—the dark tree and its dark shadow—and the elegant creature, as fair as a spirit! The torrents murmured softly: the mountains down which they were falling did not, to my sight, furnish a back-ground for this Ossianic picture; but I had a consciousness of the depth of the seclusion, and that mountains were embracing us on all sides; 'I saw not, but I *felt* that they were there.'*

Friday, November 9th.—Rain, as yesterday, till 10 o'clock, when we took a boat to row down the lake. The day improved,—clouds and sunny gleams on the mountains. In the large bay under Place Fell, three fishermen were dragging a net,—a picturesque group beneath the high and bare crags! A raven was seen aloft; not hovering like the kite, for that is not the habit of the bird; but passing on with a straight-forward perseverance, and timing the motion of its wings to its own croaking. The waters were agitated; and the iron tone of the raven's voice, which strikes upon the ear at all times as the more dolorous from its regularity, was in fine keeping with the wild scene before our eyes. This carnivorous fowl is a great enemy to the lambs of these solitudes; I recollect frequently seeing, when a boy, bunches of unfledged ravens suspended from the churchyard gates of H———, for which a reward of *so* much a head was given to the adventurous destroyer.*—The fishermen drew their net ashore, and hundreds of fish were leaping in their prison. They were all of the kind called skellies, a sort of fresh-water herring, shoals of which may sometimes be seen dimpling or rippling the surface of the lake in calm weather. This species is not found, I believe, in any other of these lakes; nor, as far as I know, is the chevin, that *spiritless* fish, (though I am loth to call it so, for it was a prime favourite with Isaac Walton,) which must frequent Ullswater, as I have seen a large shoal passing into the lake from the river Eamont. *Here* are no pike, and the char are smaller than those of the other lakes, and of inferior quality; but the grey trout attains a very large size, sometimes weighing above twenty pounds. This lordly creature seems to know that 'retiredness is a piece of majesty';* for it is scarcely ever caught, or even seen, except when it quits the depths of the lake in the spawning season, and runs up into the streams, where it is too often destroyed in disregard of the law of the land and of nature.

Quitted the boat in the bay of Sandwyke, and pursued our way towards Martindale along a pleasant path—at first through a coppice, bordering the lake, then through green fields—and came to the village, (if village it may be called, for the houses are few, and separated from each other,) a sequestered spot, shut out from the view of the lake. Crossed the one-arched bridge, below the chapel, with its 'bare ring of mossy wall,'* and single yew-tree. At the last house in the dale we were greeted by the master, who was sitting at his door, with a flock of sheep collected round him, for the purpose of smearing them with tar (according to the custom of the season) for protection against the winter's cold. He invited us to enter, and view a room built by Mr. Hasell for the accommodation of his friends at the annual chase of red deer in his forests at the head of these dales. The room is fitted up in the sportsman's style, with a cupboard for bottles and glasses, with strong chairs, and a dining-table; and ornamented with the horns of the stags caught at these hunts for a succession of years—the length of the last race each had run being recorded under his spreading antlers. The good woman treated us with oaten cake, new and crisp; and after this welcome refreshment and rest, we proceeded on our return to Patterdale by a short cut over the mountains. On leaving the fields of Sandwyke, while ascending by a gentle slope along the valley of Martindale, we had occasion to observe that in thinly-peopled glens of this character the general want of wood gives a peculiar interest to the scattered cottages embowered in sycamore.* Towards its head, this valley splits into two parts; and in one of these (that to the left) there is no house, nor any building to be seen but a cattle-shed on the side of a hill, which is sprinkled over with trees, evidently the remains of an extensive forest. Near the entrance of the other division stands the house where we were entertained, and beyond the enclosures of that farm there are no other. A few old trees remain, relics of the forest, a little stream hastens, though with serpentine windings, through the uncultivated hollow, where many cattle were pasturing. The cattle of this country are generally white, or light-coloured; but these were dark brown, or black, which heightened the resemblance this scene bears to many parts of the Highlands of Scotland.—While we paused to rest upon the hill-side, though well contented with the quiet every-day sounds—the lowing of cattle, bleating of sheep, and the very gentle murmuring of the valley stream, we could not but think what a grand effect the music of the bugle-horn would have among these mountains. It is still heard once every year, at the chase I have spoken of; a day of festivity for the inhabitants of this district except the poor deer, the most ancient of them all. Our ascent even to the top was very easy; when it was accomplished we had exceedingly fine views, some of the lofty Fells being resplendent with sunshine, and others partly shrouded by clouds. Ullswater, bordered by black steeps, was of dazzling brightness; the plain beyond Penrith smooth and bright, or rather gleamy, as the sea or sea sands. Looked down into Boardale, which, like Stybarrow, has been named from the wild swine that formerly abounded here; but it has now no sylvan covert, being smooth and bare, a long, narrow, deep, cradle-shaped glen, lying so sheltered that one would be pleased to see it planted by human hands, there being a sufficiency of soil; and the trees would be sheltered almost like shrubs in a green-house.*—After having walked some way along the top of the hill, came in view of Glenriddin and the mountains at the head of Grisdale.—Before we began to descend, turned aside to a small ruin, called at this day the chapel,* where it is said the inhabitants of Martindale and Patterdale were accustomed to assemble for worship. There are now no traces from which you could infer for what use the building had been erected; the loose stones and the few which yet continue piled up resemble those which lie elsewhere on the mountain; but the shape of the building having been oblong, its remains differ from those of a common sheep-fold; and it has stood east and west. Scarcely did the Druids, when they fled to these fastnesses, perform their rites in any situation more exposed to disturbance from the elements. One cannot pass by without being reminded that the rustic psalmody must have had the accompaniment of many a wildly-whistling blast; and what dismal storms must have often drowned the voice of the preacher! As we descend, Patterdale opens upon the eye in grand simplicity, screened by mountains, and proceeding from two heads, Deepdale and Hartshope, where lies the little lake of Brotherswater, named in old maps Broaderwater, and probably rightly so; for Bassenthwaite-mere at this day, is familiarly called Broadwater; but the change in the appellation of this small lake or pool (if it be a corruption) may have been assisted by some melancholy accident similar to what happened about twenty years ago, when two brothers were drowned there,* having gone out to take their holiday pleasure upon the ice on a new-year's day.

A rough and precipitous peat track brought us down to our friend's house.—Another fine moonlight night; but a thick fog rising from the neighbouring river, enveloped the rocky and wood-crested knoll on which our fancy-cottage had been erected; and, under the damp cast upon my feelings, I consoled myself with moralising on the folly of hasty decisions in matters of importance, and the necessity of having at least one year's knowledge of a place before you realise airy suggestions in solid stone.

Saturday, November 10th. At the breakfast-table tidings reached us of the death of Lord Nelson, and of the victory at Trafalgar.* Sequestered as we were from the sympathy of a crowd, we were shocked to hear that the bells had been ringing joyously at Penrith to celebrate the triumph. In the rebellion of the year 1745, people fled with their valuables from the open country to Patterdale, as a place of refuge secure from the incursions of strangers. At that time, news such as we had heard might have been long in penetrating so far into the recesses of the mountains; but now, as you know, the approach is easy, and the communication, in summer time, almost hourly: nor is this strange, for travellers after pleasure are become not less active, and more numerous than those who formerly left their homes for purposes of gain. The priest on the banks of the remotest stream of Lapland will talk familiarly of Buonaparte's last conquests, and discuss the progress of the French revolution, having acquired much of his information from adventurers impelled by curiosity alone.*

The morning was clear and cheerful after a night of sharp frost. At 10 o'clock we took our way on foot towards Pooley Bridge, on the same side of the lake we had coasted in a boat the day before.—Looked backwards to the south from our favourite station above Blowick. The dazzling sunbeams striking upon the church and village, while the earth was steaming with exhalations not traceable in other quarters, rendered their forms even more indistinct than the partial and flitting veil of unillumined vapour had done two days before. The grass on which we trod, and the trees in every thicket were dripping with melted hoar-frost.* We observed the lemon-coloured leaves of the birches, as the breeze turned them to the sun, sparkle, or rather *flash*, like diamonds, and the leafless purple twigs were tipped with globes of shining crystal.*

The day continued delightful, and unclouded to the end. I will not describe the country which we slowly travelled through, nor relate our adventures: and will only add, that on the afternoon of the 13th we returned along the banks of Ullswater by the usual road. The lake lay in deep repose after the agitations of a wet and stormy morning. The trees in Gowbarrow park were in that state when what is gained by the disclosure of their bark and branches compensates, almost, for the loss of foliage, exhibiting the variety which characterises the point of time between autumn and winter. The hawthorns were leafless; their round heads covered with rich red berries, and adorned with arches of green brambles, and eglantines hung with glossy hips; and the grey trunks of some of the ancient oaks, which in the summer season might have been regarded only for their venerable majesty, now attracted notice by a pretty embellishment of green mosses and fern intermixed with russet leaves retained by those slender outstarting twigs which the veteran tree would not have tolerated in his strength. The smooth silver branches of the ashes were bare; most of the alders as green as the Devonshire cottage-myrtle that weathers the snows of Christmas.—Will you accept it as some apology for my having dwelt so long on the woodland ornaments of these scenes—that artists speak of the trees on the banks of Ullswater, and especially along the bays of Stybarrow crags, as having a peculiar character of picturesque intricacy in their stems and branches, which their rocky stations and the mountain winds have combined to give them.

At the end of Gowbarrow park a large herd of deer were either moving slowly or standing still among the fern. I was sorry when a chance-companion, who had joined us by the way, startled them with a whistle, disturbing an image of grave simplicity and thoughtful enjoyment; for I could have fancied that those natives of this wild and beautiful region were partaking with us a sensation of the solemnity of the closing day. The sun had been set some time; and we could perceive that the light was fading away from the coves of Helvellyn, but the lake, under a luminous sky, was more brilliant than before.

After tea at Patterdale, set out again:—a fine evening; the seven stars close to the mountain-top; all the stars seemed brighter than usual. The steeps were reflected in Brotherswater, and, above the lake, appeared like enormous black perpendicular walls. The Kirkstone torrents had been swoln by the rains, and now filled the mountain pass with their roaring, which added greatly to the solemnity of our walk. Behind us, when we had climbed to a great height, we saw one light, very distinct, in the vale, like a large red star—a solitary one in the gloomy region. The cheerfulness of the scene was in the sky above us.

Reached home a little before midnight. The following verses (from the Author's Miscellaneous Poems,) after what has just been read may be acceptable to the reader, by way of conclusion to this little Volume.

ODE

THE PASS OF KIRKSTONE

1

WITHIN the mind strong fancies work,
A deep delight the bosom thrills,
Oft as I pass along the fork
Of these fraternal hills:
Where, save the rugged road, we find
No appanage of human kind;
Nor hint of man, if stone or rock
Seem not his handy-work to mock
By something cognizably shaped;
Mockery—or model roughly hewn,
And left as if by earthquake strewn,
Or from the Flood escaped:
Altars for Druid service fit;
(But where no fire was ever lit,
Unless the glow-worm to the skies
Thence offer nightly sacrifice;)
Wrinkled Egyptian monument;
Green moss-grown tower; or hoary tent;
Tents of a camp that never shall be raised;
On which four thousand years have gazed!

2

Ye plough-shares sparkling on the slopes!
Ye snow-white lambs that trip
Imprisoned 'mid the formal props
Of restless ownership!
Ye trees, that may to-morrow fall
To feed the insatiate Prodigal!
Lawns, houses, chattels, groves, and fields,
All that the fertile valley shields;
Wages of folly—baits of crime,—
Of life's uneasy game the stake,
Playthings that keep the eyes awake
Of drowsy, dotard Time;
O care! O guilt!—O vales and plains,

Here, 'mid his own unvexed domains,
A Genius dwells, that can subdue
At once all memory of You,—
Most potent when mists veil the sky,
Mists that distort and magnify;
While the coarse rushes, to the sweeping breeze,
Sigh forth their ancient melodies!

3

List to those shriller notes!—*that* march
Perchance was on the blast,
When through this Height's inverted arch,
Rome's earliest legion passed!
—They saw, adventurously impelled,
And older eyes than theirs beheld,
This block—and yon, whose Church-like frame
Gives to the savage Pass its name.
Aspiring Road! that lov'st to hide
Thy daring in a vapoury bourn,
Not seldom may the hour return
When thou shalt be my Guide:
And I (as often we find cause,
When life is at a weary pause,
And we have panted up the hill
Of duty with reluctant will)
Be thankful, even though tired and faint,
For the rich bounties of Constraint;
Whence oft invigorating transports flow
That Choice lacked courage to bestow!

4

My Soul was grateful for delight
That wore a threatening brow;
A veil is lifted—can she slight
The scene that opens now?
Though habitation none appear,
The greenness tells, man must be there;
The shelter—that the perspective
Is of the clime in which we live;
Where Toil pursues his daily round;
Where Pity sheds sweet tears, and Love,
In woodbine bower or birchen grove,

Inflicts his tender wound.
—Who comes not hither ne'er shall know
How beautiful the world below;
Nor can he guess how lightly leaps
The brook adown the rocky steeps.
Farewell, thou desolate Domain!
Hope, pointing to the cultured Plain,
Carols like a shepherd boy;
And who is she?—Can that be Joy!
Who, with a sun-beam for her guide,
Smoothly skims the meadows wide;
While Faith, from yonder opening cloud,
To hill and vale proclaims aloud,
'Whate'er the weak may dread, the wicked dare,
Thy lot, O man, is good, thy portion fair!'*

The Publishers, with permission of the Author,
have added the following

ITINERARY OF THE LAKES,

FOR THE USE OF TOURISTS

STAGES	Miles
Lancaster to Kendal, by Kirk by Lonsdale	30
Lancaster to Kendal, by Burton	22
Lancaster to Kendal, by Milnthorpe	21
Lancaster to Ulverston, over Sands	21
Lancaster to Ulverston, by Levens Bridge	35½
Ulverston to Hawkshead, by Coniston Water Head	19
Ulverston to Bowness, by Newby Bridge	17
Hawkshead to Ambleside	5
Hawkshead to Bowness	6
Kendal to Ambleside	14
Kendal to Ambleside, by Bowness	15
From and back to Ambleside round the two Langdales	18
Ambleside to Ullswater	10
Ambleside to Keswick	16¼
Keswick to Borrowdale, and round the Lake	12
Keswick to Borrowdale and Buttermere	23
Keswick to Wastdale and Calder Bridge	27
Calder Bridge to Buttermere and Keswick	29
Keswick, round Bassenthwaite Lake	18
Keswick to Patterdale, Pooley Bridge, and	38
Keswick to Pooley Bridge and Penrith	24
Keswick to Penrith	17½
Whitehaven to Keswick	27
Workington to Keswick	21
Excursion from Penrith to Hawes Water	27
Carlisle to Penrith	18
Penrith to Kendal	26

Inns and Public Houses, when not mentioned, are marked thus. ★

LANCASTER to KENDAL, by KIRKBY LONSDALE, 30 m.

Miles		Miles	Miles		Miles
5	Caton	5	2	Tunstall	13
2	Claughton	7	2	Burrow	15
2	Hornby★	9	2	Kirkby Lonsdale	17
2	Melling	11	13	Kendal	30

INNS.—*Lancaster*, King's Arms, Commercial Inn, Royal Oak.
INNS.—*Kirkby Lonsdale*, Rose and Crown, Green Dragon.

LANCASTER to KENDAL, by BURTON, 21¾ m.

10¾	Burton	10¾	½	End Moor★	16
4¾	Crooklands★	15½	5¾	Kendal	21¾

INNS.—*Kendal*, King's Arms, Commercial Inn. *Burton*, Royal Oak, King's Arms.

LANCASTER to KENDAL, by MILNTHORPE, 21¼ m.

2¾	Slyne★	2¾	4	Hale★	12
1¼	Bolton-le-Sands★	4	½	Beethom★	12½
2	Carnforth★	6	1¼	Milnthorpe	13¾
2	Junction of the Milnthorpe and Burton roads	8	1¼	Heversham★	15
			1½	Levens-bridge	16½
			4¾	Kendal	21¼

INN.—*Milnthorpe*, Cross Keys.

LANCASTER to ULVERSTON, OVER SANDS, 21 m.

3½	Hest Bank★	3½	1¼	Flookburgh★	15
¼	Lancaster Sands	3¾	¾	Cark	15¾
9	Kent's Bank	12¾	¼	Leven Sands	16
1	Lower Allithwaite	13¾	5	Ulverston	21

INNS.—*Ulverston*, Sun Inn, Bradyll's Arms.

LANCASTER to ULVERSTON, by LEVENS BRIDGE, 35½ m.

12	Hale★	12	3	Lindal★	23½
½	Beethom★	12½	2	Newton★	25½
1¼	Milnthorpe	13¾	2	Newby-Bridge★	27½
1¼	Heversham★	15	2	Low Wood	29½
1¼	Levens-bridge	16½	3	Greenodd	32½
4	Witherslack★	20½	3	Ulverston	35½

ULVERSTON to HAWKSHEAD, by CONISTON WATER-HEAD, 19 m.

6	Lowick-bridge	6	8	Coniston Water-Head★	16
2	Nibthwaite	8	3	Hawkshead	19

INN.—*Hawkshead*, Red Lion.

ULVERSTON to BOWNESS, by NEWBY BRIDGE, 16 m.

3	Green Odd	3	2	Newby-bridge	8
3	Low Wood	6	8	Bowness	16

INNS.—*Bowness*, White Lion, Crown Inn.

HAWKSHEAD to AMBLESIDE, 5 m.

HAWKSHEAD to BOWNESS, 5½ m.

2	Sawrey	2	1½	Bowness	5½
2	Windermere Ferry★	4			

KENDAL to AMBLESIDE, 13½ m.

5	Staveley★	5	1½	Troutbeck-bridge★	10
1½	Ings Chapel	6½	2	Low Wood Inn	12
2	Orrest-head	8½	1½	Ambleside	13½

INNS.—*Ambleside*, Salutation Hotel, Commercial Inn.

KENDAL to AMBLESIDE, by BOWNESS, 15 m.

4	Crook★	4	2½	Troutbeck-bridge	11½
2	Gilpin Bridge★	6	2	Low Wood Inn	13½
3	Bowness	9	1½	Ambleside	15

A CIRCUIT from and back to AMBLESIDE by LITTLE and GREAT LANGDALE, 18 m.

3	Skelwith Bridge★	3	2	Langdale Chapel Stile★	13
2	Colwith Cascade	5			
3	Blea Tarn	8	5	By High Close and	18
3	Dungeon Ghyll	11		Rydal to Ambleside	

AMBLESIDE to ULLSWATER, 10 m.

4	Top of Kirkstone	4	3	Inn at Patterdale	10
3	Kirkstone Foot	7			

AMBLESIDE to KESWICK, 16¼ m.

1½	Rydal	1½	4	Smalthwaite-bridge	12¼
3½	Swan, Grasmere★	5	3	Castlerigg	15¼
2	Dunmail Raise	7	1	Keswick	16¼
1¼	Nag's Head, Wythburn	8¼			

EXCURSIONS FROM KESWICK

INNS.—*Keswick*, Royal Oak, Queen's Head.

To BORROWDALE, and ROUND THE LAKE, 12 m.

2	Barrow-house	2	1	Return to Grange	6
1	Lodore	3	4½	Portinscale	10½
1	Grange	4	1½	Keswick	12
1	Bowder Stone	5			

To BORROWDALE and BUTTERMERE

5	Bowder Stone	5	2	Buttermere★	14
1	Rosthwaite	6	9	Keswick, by Newlands	23
2	Seatoller	8			
4	Gatesgarth	12			

TWO DAYS' EXCURSION TO WASTDALE, ENNER-DALE, and LOWES-WATER

FIRST DAY

6	Rosthwaite	6	6	Strands*, Nether Wastdale	20
2	Seatoller	8			
1	Seathwaite	9	4	Gosforth*	24
3	Sty-head	12	3	Calder Bridge*	27
2	Wastdale-head	14			

SECOND DAY

7	Ennerdale Bridge	7	2	Scale-hill*	16
3	Lamplugh Cross	10	4	Buttermere*	20
4	Lowes-water	14	9	Keswick	29

KESWICK ROUND BASSENTHWAITE WATER

8	Peel Wyke*	8	3	Bassenthwaite Sand-bed	13
1	Ouse Bridge	9			
1	Castle Inn	10	5	Keswick	18

KESWICK to PATTERDALE, and by POOLEY BRIDGE to PENRITH

10	Springfield*	10	10	Pooley Bridge* through Gowbarrow Park	32
7	Gowbarrow Park	17			
5	Patterdale*	22	6	Penrith	38

INNS.—*Penrith*, Crown Inn, The George.

KESWICK to POOLEY BRIDGE and PENRITH

12	Penruddock*	12	3	Pooley Bridge	18
3	Dacre*	15	6	Penrith	24

KESWICK to PENRITH, 17½ m.

4	Threlkeld*	4	3½	Stainton*	15
7½	Penruddock	2½	2½	Penrith	17½

WHITEHAVEN to KESWICK, 27 m.

2	Moresby	2	5	Cockermouth	14
2	Distington	4	2½	Embleton	16½
2	Winscales	6	6½	Thornthwaite	23
3	Little Clifton	9	4	Keswick	27

INNS.—*Whitehaven*, Black Lion, Golden Lion, The Globe.
INNS.—*Cockermouth*, The Globe, The Sun.

WORKINGTON to KESWICK, 21 m.

The road joins that from Whitehaven to Keswick 4 miles from Workington.

INNS.—*Workington*, Green Dragon, New Crown, King's Arms.

EXCURSION from PENRITH to HAWESWATER

5	Lowther, or Askham*		5	Over Moor Dovack to Pooley	21
7	By Bampton* to Haweswater	12	6	By Dalemain to Penrith	27
4	Return by Butterswick	16			

CARLISLE to PENRITH, 18 m.

2½	Carlton*	2½	2	Plumpton*	13
7	Low Hesket*	9½	5	Penrith	18
1½	High Hesket*	11			

INNS.—*Carlisle*, The Bush, Coffee House, King's Arms.

PENRITH to KENDAL, 26 m.

1	Eamont Bridge*	1	6¾	Hawse Foot*	17
2½	Clifton*	2½	4	Plough Inn*	21
2	Hackthorpe*	4½	2½	Skelsmergh Stocks*	23½
5¾	Shap	10¼	2½	Kendal	26

INNS.—*Shap*, Greyhound, King's Arms.

HERE ENDS THE FIFTH EDITION OF THE GUIDE

APPENDIX I

SECTION II OF *SELECT VIEWS IN CUMBERLAND, WESTMORELAND, AND LANCASHIRE* (1810)

APPENDIX I reproduces Section II of *Select Views* (1810), which roughly corresponds to 'Directions and Information for the Tourist' in the 1835 *Guide*, but is considerably different. The text is followed by a list of Joseph Wilkinson's 48 plates and a selection of the plates.

It is obvious that the point, from which a Stranger should begin this Tour, and the order in which it will be convenient to him to see the different Vales will depend upon this circumstance; viz: from what quarter of the Island he comes. If from Scotland, or by the way of Stainmoor, it will suit him to start from Penrith, taking the scenery of Lowther in his way to Hawes-water. He will next visit Ullswater, &c. reversing the order which I shall point out as being in itself the best. Mr. West has judiciously directed those to whom it is convenient to proceed from Lancaster over the Sands; to take Furness Abbey in their way, if so inclined; and then to advance by the Lake of Coniston. This is unquestionably the most favourable approach. The beautiful Lake of Coniston will thus be traced upwards from its outlet,* the only way in which it can be seen, for the first time, without an entire yielding up of its most delightful appearances. And further, the Stranger, from the moment he sets his foot upon the Sands, seems to leave the turmoil and the traffic of the world behind him; and crossing the majestic Plain from which the Sea has retired, he beholds, rising apparently from its base, that cluster of Mountains, among the recesses of which he is going to wander, and into which, by the Vale of Coniston, he is gradually and peacefully introduced. The Lake and Vale of Coniston, approached in this manner, improve in appearance with every step. And I may here make this general remark, which, indeed the Reader may have deduced from the representation of the Country, given in the Introduction,* that, wherever it is possible, these Lakes and Vallies should be approached from the foot; otherwise most things will come upon the Spectator to great disadvantage. This general rule applies, though not with equal force to all the Lakes, with the single exception of Lowes-water, which, lying in a direction opposite to the rest, has its most favourable aspects determined accordingly.

At the head of Coniston close to the water side is a small and comfortable Inn, which I would advise the Traveller, who is not part of a large company, and who does not look for a parade of accommodation, to make his head-quarters for two days. The first of these days, if the weather permit, may be agreeably passed in an excursion to the Vale of Duddon, or

Donnerdale, as part of it is called, and which name may with propriety be given to the whole. It lies over the high hill which bounds the Vale of Coniston on the West. This Valley is very rarely visited; but I recommend it with confidence to the notice of the Traveller of taste and feeling. It will be best approached by a road,* ascending from near the church of Coniston, which leads to that part of Donnerdale called Seathwaite. The road is so long and steep that the Traveller will be obliged to lead his horse a considerable part of it. The ascent and descent cannot I think be less than five miles; but, nothing can be found more beautiful than the scene, into which he will be received at the bottom of the hill on the other side. This little circular Valley is a collateral compartment of the long winding Vale, through which flows the stream of Duddon; and its Brook finds its way to the River. Advancing, you will come to the lowly Chapel of Seathwaite,* and a field or two beyond, is a Farm-house,* where, though there be no sign-board, or outward mark of an Inn, the Traveller who can content himself with homely diet may be accommodated.—Having satisfied himself with strolling about Seathwaite, he will proceed down Donnerdale to Ulpha Kirk; and from this Church-yard he will have as grand a combination of mountain lines and forms as perhaps this country furnishes. The whole scene is inspirited by the sound and sight of the River rolling immediately below the steep ground upon the top of which the Church stands.* From Ulpha Kirk proceed down the Vale towards Broughton. The same character of mingled wildness and cultivation is still preserved. Rocky grounds, which must for ever forbid the entrance of the plough, here and there, interrupt the cultivation; and in part or wholly fill up the bottom or sides of the Vale.—This beautiful Vale does not gradually disappear in a flat Plain, but terminates abruptly in a prospect of the Sands of Duddon, and of the Irish Sea. These are seen in conjunction with its River, and deep recesses of wood. On this account, and for the sake of descending upon Seathwaite so advantageously, I have recommended in opposition to the general rule, that it should be approached from the upper part, rather than from its outlet.* From Broughton return to Coniston by the nearest road. The morning of the next day may be employed in sailing upon, and looking about the higher part of the Lake, and in strolling upon its Banks; and the other half in an excursion to the Valley of Yewdale (a branch of the Vale of Coniston) and round the sequestered Valley of Tilberthwaite, which may be considered as a remoter apartment of the Valley of Yewdale. This excursion may be about five miles, and may be taken either on foot or horse-back; but not in a carriage. From the Valley of Yewdale having mounted to that of Tilberthwaite, with the Brook upon the right hand, pursue the road till it leads to the furthest of two Cottages; there, ask the way through the fields to an house called Holm-ground. If, on horse-back, alight there; and from a rocky and woody hill, behind the house you will look down upon this wild, beautiful, and singularly secluded Valley. From Holm-ground return to the Inn at Coniston. Next day proceed to Hawkshead; and thence by the side of Estwaite looking back a little while after the road has left the Lake side upon a fine view (which will be found among these Etchings) of the Lake of Estwaite.* Thence, through the two Villages of Sawrey, you come to the Ferry-house upon Windermere where are good accommodations for the night.

The Tourist has now reached Windermere, and has been introduced in his road to some sequestered spots not exemplified in these Etchings,* but, which, if he wishes to have a complete knowledge of the various features of this Country, he will be glad to have visited. Every thing that is of conse-quence has been taken in its best order, except that the first burst of the Vale of Windermere, though very interesting from this approach, is much inferior to that which would have come upon him had he descended by the road from Kendal. Before the Traveller, whom I have thus far accompanied, enters the Peninsula, at the extremity of which the Ferry House stands, it will be adviseable to ascend to a Pleasure-house belonging to J.C. Curwen, Esq.* which he will see upon the side of the rocks on his left hand.—There is a gate, and a person, attending at a little Lodge, or Cot adjoining, who will conduct him. From this point he will look down upon the cluster of Islands in the central part of the Lake, upon Bowness, Rayrigg, and the Mountains of Troutbeck; and will have a prospect of the lower division of this expanse of water to its extremity. The upper part is hidden. The Pleasure house is happily situated, and is well in its kind, but, without intending any harsh reflections on the contriver, from whom it was purchased by its present Proprietor, it may be said that he, who remembers the spot on which this building stands, and the immediate surrounding grounds as they were less than thirty years ago, will sigh for the coming of that day when Art, through every rank of society, shall be taught to have more reverence for Nature. This scene is, in its natural constitution, far too beautiful to require any exotic or obtrusive embellishments, either of planting or architecture. With Winandermere a large majority of Visitants begin this Tour. The ordinary course is from Kendal, by the nearest road to Bowness; but I would recommend it to all persons, whatever may be their mode of conveyance, or however large their party, when they shall have reached the Turnpike-house, about a mile beyond Kendal, not to take, as is commonly done, the road which leads directly to Bowness; but that through Stavely; inasmuch as the break of prospect from Orrest-head, where the road brings you to the first sight of Windermere,* in itself one of the finest things in the Tour, is much grander than as it appears from the other road. This for two reasons; first, that you are between two and three miles nearer the sublime mountains and large expanse of water at the head of the Lake;

and secondly that the new houses and plantations, and the number of trim and artificial objects with which the neighbourhood of Bowness is crowded, are so far removed from this point, as not to be individually offensive, as they melt into the general mass of the Landscape. At the bottom of the hill, you find a Guide-post; and, turning, abruptly to the left, will immediately come in sight of the same general prospect which has been seen above, from a point, which, as it is comparatively low, necessarily changes the character of the scene. Thence on, through the close woods of Rayrigg, to the bustling Inn of Bowness.*

I will not call upon the Reader to waste his time upon descriptions of things, which every one makes a point of seeing, and of such as lie open to the notice of the most inattentive Traveller. This, with respect to a country now so well known, would be useless in itself; and would be especially improper in a publication of this kind, the main purport of which is, to exhibit scenes which lie apart from the beaten course of observation.— Accordingly I shall chiefly expatiate upon those retired spots, which have furnished subjects for the majority of these Etchings, or upon others of the same character; and when I treat of the more frequent scenes, I shall attempt little more than to point out qualities by which they are character-ized, which may easily escape the notice of the cursory Spectator. The appearance of the neighbourhood of Bowness, within the last five and thirty years, has undergone many changes, and most of these for the worse, for want of due attention to those principles of taste, and those rules for planting and building in a country of this kind, which have been discussed at large in the Introduction.* The Islands of Windermere are beautifully shaped and intermingled. Upon the largest are a few fine old trees; but a great part of this delightful spot, when it first fell into the Improver's hand, was struck over with trees that are here out of place; and, had the present public-spirited Proprietor sufficient leisure amidst his important avocations to examine the principles which have been enforced in these pages, he would probably be induced to weed these foreigners out by little and little, and introduce more appropriate trees in their stead; such as would be pleasing to look at in their youth, and in maturity and old age might succeed to those venerable natives which the axe has spared. The embankment also, which has been raised round this Island for the sake of preserving the land, could only, it should seem, have been necessary in a few exposed points; and the artificial appearance which this has given to the whole spot is much to be regretted; not to speak of the infinite varieties of minute beauty which it must have destroyed. Could not the margin of this noble Island be given back to Nature? Winds and Waves work with a careless and graceful hand; and any thing which they take away would be amply compensated by the additional spirit, dignity and loveliness which these agents and the other powers of Nature would soon communicate to what was left behind.*

Windermere ought to be seen both from its shores and from its surface. None of the other Lakes unfold so many fresh beauties to him who sails upon them. This is owing to its greater size, to its Islands, and to a circumstance in which this Lake differs from all the rest, viz. that of having two Vales at its head, with their accompanying mountains of nearly equal dignity. Nor can the whole grandeur of these two terminations be seen at the same time from any one point, except from the bosom of the Lake. The Islands may be explored at any time of the day; but one bright unruffled evening at least, must, if possible, be set apart for the splendour, the stillness and solemnity of a three hours voyage upon the higher division of the Lake, not omitting, towards the end of the excursion, to quit the expanse of water, and peep into the close and calm River at the head; which, in its quiet character, at such a time, appears rather like an overflow of the peaceful Lake itself than to have any more immediate connection with the rough mountains from which it has descended, or the turbulent Torrents of which it is composed. Many persons content themselves with what they see of Windermere in their progress in a boat from Bowness to the head of the Lake, walking thence to Ambleside; but this is doing things by halves. The whole road from Bowness is rich in diversity of pleasing or grand scenery; there is scarcely a field on the road side which, if it were entered, would not give to the Landscape some additional charm. Low-wood Inn, a mile from the head of Windermere is a pleasant halting-place; and the fields above it, and the lane which leads to the Troutbeck, present beautiful views towards each extremity of the Lake. From this place, and still more conveniently from Ambleside, rides on horse-back or in carriages may be taken in almost every direction, and the interesting walks are inexhaustible.

Ambleside, &c.

This Town or Market-village was formerly perhaps more rich in picturesque beauty, arising from a combination of rustic architecture and natural scenery than any small Town or Village in Great Britain. Many of the ancient buildings with their porches, projections, round chimnies* and galleries have been displaced to make way for the docked, featureless, and memberless edifices of modern architecture; which look as if fresh brought upon wheels from the Foundry, where they had been cast. Yet this Town, if carefully noticed, will still be found to retain such store of picturesque materials as will secure the praise of what it once was from any suspicion of partiality. The Brook,* which divides the Town ought to be explored along its channel; if the state of the stream will permit. Below the Bridge is a Mill, and also an old Summer-house, with other old buildings, ivied Trunks of

Trees, and mossy Stones, which have furnished subjects for many a pic-
ture; and above the Bridge, though there are no Buildings, every step is
interesting till the curious Traveller is stopped by the huge breastwork of
Stock-gill Force. Within a quarter of a mile of Ambleside is a scene called
the Nook, which deserves to be explored. It is to be found in Scandle Gill,
the channel of the first Brook that comes down Scandle Fell to the North
of Ambleside. I need not describe the scene; its principal feature is a Bridge
thrown over the Torrent. From this Bridge I wish it were in my power to
recommend it to the Traveller to proceed northwards, along the slope of
the hill-side, till he reaches the Park of Rydale; but this would be a tres-
pass;* for there is no path, and high and envious stone walls interpose. We
must therefore give up the best approach to some of the most glorious
scenes in the world; this may be yet said, though not without painful regret
for the havoc which has been made among them. Some hundreds of oaks
are gone,

> 'Whose boughs were mossed with age,'
> 'And high tops bald with dry antiquity,'*

a majestic Forest covering a mountain side! into the recesses of which
penetrated like a vision, Landscapes of rivers, broad waters, vallies, rocks
and mountains:—The Lake of Rydale on the Northwest, with its Islands
and rocky steeps, circular and deeply embosomed; and to the South the
long Valley of Ambleside and the gleaming Lake of Windermere. The
noblest of these trees have been sacrificed; but the side of the hill, though
thinned, is not wholly laid bare; and the Herons and Rooks that hover
round this choice retreat have yet a remnant of their ancient roosting-place.
The unfrequented spots, of which I have been speaking may be visited,
with permission from the Mansion, after the Water-fall* has been seen.

Of places at a distance from Ambleside, but commodiously visited from
that Village, Coniston may be first mentioned; though this Lake as I said
before, will thus be approached to great disadvantage.—Next comes Great
Langdale, a Vale which should on no account be missed by him who has
a true enjoyment of grand separate Forms composing a sublime Unity, aus-
tere but reconciled and rendered attractive to the affections by the deep
serenity that is spread over every thing. There is no good carriage road
through this Vale; nor ought that to be regretted; for it would impair its
solemnity; but the road is tolerable for about the distance of three miles
from Ambleside, namely along the Vale of Brathay, and above the western
banks of Loughrigg Tarn, and still further, to the entrance of Langdale
itself; but the small and peaceful Valley of Loughrigg is seen to much
greater advantage from the eastern side. When therefore you have quitted
the River Brathay enquire at the first house for the foot road, which will

conduct you round the lower extremity of the Tarn, and so on to its head, where, at a little distance from the Tarn the path again leads to the publick road and about a mile further conducts you to Langdale Chapel.—A little way beyond this sequestered and simple place of worship is a narrow passage on the right leading into a slate-quarry which has been finely excavated. Pursuing this road a few hundred yards further, you come in view of the noblest reach of this Vale, which I shall not attempt to describe. Under the Precipice adjoining to the Pikes lies invisibly Stickle Tarn, and thence descends a conspicuous Torrent down the breast of the Mountain. Near this Torrent is Dungeon Gill Force, which cannot be found without a Guide, who may be taken up at one of the Cottages at the foot of the Mountain.

> 'Into the chasm a mighty block
> Hath fallen, and made a bridge of rock;
> The gulph is deep below,
> And in a bason black and small
> Receives a lofty Waterfall.'*

At the head of Langdale is a passage over the Borrowdale; but this ought on no account to be taken by a person who has not seen the main features of the country from their best approaches.—If the Traveller has been zealous enough to advance as far as Dungeon-gill Force, let him enquire for Blea Tarn; he may return by that circuit to Ambleside. Blea Tarn is not an object of any beauty in itself, but it is situated in a small, deep circular Valley of peculiar character; for it contains only one Dwelling-house and two or three cultivated fields.* Passing down this Valley, fail not to look back now and then, and you will see Langdale Pikes, from behind the rocky steeps that form its north-eastern boundary, lifting themselves, as if on tip-toe, to pry into it. Quitting the Valley you will descend into little Langdale, and thence may proceed by Colwith Force and Bridge. Leaving Skelwith-Bridge on your left, ascend with the road to Skelwith; and from a field on the northern side of that small cluster of houses, you will look down upon a grand view of the River Brathay, Elter-water and the mountains of Langdale, &c.* Thence proceed occasionally looking down the Brathay on the side of the River opposite to that by which you had ascended in your way to Loughrigg Tarn. The whole of this excursion may be as much as 18 miles, and would require a long morning to be devoted to the accomplishment. I will now mention only one more ride or walk from Ambleside. Go to the Bridge over the Rothay (of which a view is given in the Etchings), between Ambleside and Clappersgate.* When you have crossed the Bridge, turn to a Gate on the right hand, and proceed with the road up the Valley of Ambleside, till you come opposite to the Village of Rydale;* do not cross over to Rydale, but keep close to the Mountain on your left hand, with the River at a little distance on your right, till you come in view of Rydale Lake. Advance with the Lake on your right till you quit the Vale of Rydale, and come in view of Grasmere. Follow the road, which will conduct you round along the lower extremity of the Lake of Grasmere, till you reach the Church; thence into the main road back to Ambleside, looking behind you frequently.*

The two hours before sun-set are the most favourable time of the day for seeing the lower division of Wytheburne Lake, but it is advisable to choose the earlier part of this time, in order that the Traveller may be enabled to descend into the Vale of Keswick while the sun-beams are upon it.* That this first impression of that Vale should be received under the most favourable circumstances, is very desirable; and therefore I do not recommend, as I should otherwise have done, that the Traveller, who has been guided by my directions thus far, should lengthen his journey to Keswick still further, and follow the stream that issues out of Wytheburn Lake till it enters St. John's Vale, which he may do if he be on foot, keeping to the side of it almost all the way; and, if on horseback, he may return to it by a small circuit, after having crossed Shoulthwaite Moss. I should have directed the Traveller in this case to proceed a mile and a half down St. John's Vale, and then to cross Naddle Fell, by St. John's Chapel, which would bring him into the road between Ambleside and Keswick, something better than two miles short of the latter place. This may easily be done, taking the lower division of Wytheburn earlier in the afternoon than the time which I have recommended as the best.

We have now reached Keswick.* I shall not attempt a general description of this celebrated Vale, because this has already been admirably performed by Dr. Brown, and by the Poet Gray; and the place is at this time very generally well known. As the Views in this work have been taken almost exclusively from retired spots in the *Ghylls*, or Gills, and smaller Vallies that branch off from the trunk of the Vale, it will be more appropriate to this publication, and will better suit its narrow limits, to say a few words upon them. And to begin with one of the smallest, Applethwaite (for Views of which see Nos. 22, 23, and 24). This is a hamlet of six of seven houses, hidden in a small recess at the foot of Skiddaw, and adorned by a little Brook, which, having descended from a great height in a silver line down the steep blue side of the Mountain, trickles past the doors of the Cottages. This concealed spot is very interesting as you approach from the bottom, with your face towards the green and blue mass of Skiddaw;* and is not less pleasing when, having advanced by a gentle slope for some space, you turn your head and look out from this chink or fissure, which is sprinkled with little orchards and trees, and behold the whole splendour of the upper and middle part of the Vale of Keswick, with its Lakes and Mountains spread before your eyes.* A small Spinning-mill has lately been erected here, and some of the old Cottages, with their picturesque appendages, are fallen into decay. This is to be regretted; for, these blemishes excepted, the scene is a rare and almost singular combination of minute and sequestered beauty, with splendid and extensive prospects. On the opposite side of the Vale of Keswick lie the Valley of Newlands, and the Village of Braithwaite, with its stream descending from a cove of the Mountain. From both these spots I have given Views,* from which an idea of their features may be collected. Braithwaite lies at the foot of Whenlater, in the road to Lorton and Cockermouth; and through Newlands passes the nearest road to Buttermere. Returning to the eastern side of the Vale of Keswick, we find the narrow and retired Valley of Watenlath, enclosed on each side and at the head by craggy Mountains. In the Mountains at the head, the stream rises, which forms the Cascade of Lodore. This, after flowing a short way through a pastoral tract, falls into a small Lake or Tarn, which lies midway in the long Valley of Watenlath. At the point where the stream issues out of the Tarn, is a beautiful Bridge of one arch, and close beside the Bridge is a little Hamlet, a cluster of grey Cottages. There are no other dwellings in the Valley; and a more secluded spot than this Hamlet cannot well be conceived; yet ascend a very little up the hill above it, and you have a most magnificent prospect of the Vale of Keswick, as far as Skiddaw; and, pursuing the Valley of Watenlath to its head, if you look back, the view of the little Valley itself, with its Lake, Bridge, and Cottages, is combined with that of the majestic Vale beyond, so that each seems to be a part of the other. But the most considerable of the Dales which communicate with the Vale of Keswick by the Rivers which flow through them, are Borrowdale and St. John's. Of St. John's we have already spoken; and Borrowdale is in fact the head of the Vale of Keswick. It would be an endless task to attempt, by verbal descriptions, to guide the traveller among the infinite variety of beautiful or interesting objects which are found in the different reaches of the broad Valley itself, nor less so to attempt to lead him through its little recesses, its nooks, and tributary glens. I must content myself with saying, that this Valley surpasses all the others in variety. Rocks and Woods are intermingled on the hill-sides with profuse wildness; and on the plain below (for the area of the Valley, through all its windings is generally a level plain, out of which the Mountains rise as from their base,) the single Cottages and clusters of Houses are numerous; not glaringly spread before the eye, but unobtrusive as the rocks themselves, and mostly coloured like them.* There is scarcely a Cottage that has not its own tuft of trees. The Yew-tree has been a favourite with the former Inhabitants of Borrowdale; for many fine old Yew-trees yet remain near the Cottages, probably first planted for an ornament to their gardens, and now preserved as a shelter, and for the sake of their venerable appearance. But the noblest Yew-trees to be found here, are a cluster of three, with a fourth a little detached,* which do not stand in connection with any houses; they are in that part of Borrowdale which is called Seathwaite, immediately under the entrance into the Lead-mines. Nothing of the kind can be conceived more solemn and impressive than the small gloomy grove formed by these trees.

The lower part of the Vale of Keswick is occupied by the Lake of Bassenthwaite; and he who coasts its western shore, will be well and variously recompensed; and in particular by the appearance of Skiddaw, rising immediately from the opposite side of the Lake. Following this road, we cross the lower extremity of Embleton Vale. Embleton may be mentioned as the last of the Vallies collateral to the main Vale of Keswick. It unfolds on the west, near the foot of Bassenthwaite Lake, a scene of humble and gentle character; but deriving animated beauty from the Lake, and striking majesty from the Mountain of Skiddaw, which is on this side broken and rugged, and of an aspect which is forcibly contrasted with that with which it looks upon Derwent Lake. The view of the whole vista of the Vale of Keswick from Armathwaite and Ouze Bridge is magnificent; and the scenes upon the River Derwent, as far as the grand ruins of Cockermouth Castle, are soft and varied, and well worthy of the notice of the Pedestrian, who has leisure to go in search of them.

From the Vale of Keswick, of which there is no need to say any thing more, the Tourist usually proceeds to Buttermere, to which there are three roads; the one through part of Borrowdale, which brings him down into the Vale of Buttermere, at its head; but Borrowdale I suppose to have been already explored, a strong reason against choosing this approach. Yet in justice to this road I must add, that the descent into Gatesgarth, immediately under Honister Crag, causes one of the sublimest impressions which this country can produce. The second road leads through Newlands. The descent into Buttermere by this way is solitary and grand; but the Vale of Newlands itself I suppose also to have been visited in the Tour round the Lake of Keswick (which no person of taste ought to omit), or in other rambles. It follows, then, that the third is the road which I would recommend, namely, the carriage road, which leads over Whinlater, through part of the Vale of Lorton, to the outlet of Crummock-water. Here was formerly an inn, kept at a house called Scale Hill, an accommodation which I believe no longer exists. It would, however, be ill-judged not to turn aside to Scale Hill; the carriage or horses might be sent forward by the high-road, and ordered to wait till the Traveller rejoined them by the footpath, which leads through the woods along the side of Crummock. This path presents noble scenes, looking up the Lake towards Buttermere. If the Traveller be desirous of visiting Lowes-water, instead of proceeding directly along this path, he must cross the Bridge over the Cocker, near Scale Hill, to which he must return after a walk or ride of three or four miles. I am not sure that the circuit of this Lake can be made on horseback; but every path and field in the neighbourhood would well repay the active exertions of the Pedestrian. Nor will the most hasty Visitant fail to notice with pleasure, that community of attractive and substantial houses which are dispersed over the fertile inclosures at the foot of those rugged Mountains, and form a most impressive contrast with the humble and rude dwellings which are usually found at the head of these far-winding Dales. It must be mentioned also, that there is scarcely any thing finer than the view from a boat in the centre of Crummock-water. The scene is deep, and solemn, and lonely; and in no other spot is the majesty of the Mountains so irresistibly felt as an omnipresence, or so passively submitted to as a spirit incumbent upon the imagination. Near the head of Crummock-water, on the right, is Scale Force, a Waterfall worthy of being visited, both for its own sake, and for the sublime View across the Lake, looking back in your ascent towards the Chasm. The Fall is perpendicular from an immense height, a slender stream faintly illuminating a gloomy fissure. This spot is never seen to a more advantage than when it happens, that, while you are looking up through the Chasm towards the summit of the lofty Waterfall, large fleecy clouds, of dazzling brightness, suddenly ascend into view, and disappear silently upon the wind. The Village of Buttermere lies a mile and a half higher up the Vale, and of the intermediate country I have nothing to say. It would be advisable, if time permit, that you should go as far up the Vale as Honister Crag; and if in horseback, or on foot, you may return to Keswick by Newlands.

The rest of the scenes in this part of the country of which I have given views, namely, those of Ennerdale and Westdale, cannot, without a good deal of trouble, be approached in a carriage. For Foot-travellers, and for those who are not afraid of leading their horses through difficult ways, there is a road from Buttermere directly over the mountains to Ennerdale; there is also another road from the head of Buttermere to the head of Westdale, without going into Borrowdale; but both Ennerdale and Westdale are *best* seen by making a considerable circuit; namely, by retracing our steps to Scale Hill, and thence by Lowes-water and Lamplugh to Ennerdale. The first burst of Ennerdale from an eminence is very noble, and the mind is more alive to the impression, because we have quitted for a while the heart of the mountains, and been led through a tamer country. Ennerdale is bold and savage in its general aspect, though not destitute, towards the higher part of the Lake, of fertile and beautiful spots. From Ennerdale-Bridge to Calder-Bridge, the road leads over Cold Fell. The distance is six miles, a desolate tract, with the exception of the last half mile, through a narrow and well-wooded Valley, in which is a small, but beautiful fragment of Calder Abbey. The village lying close to Calder-Bridge has good inns, and the bed of the River about the Bridge is rocky and spirited. We are here in a plain country near to the sea, and therefore better prepared to enjoy the mountain sublimities of Westdale, which soon begin to shew themselves, and grow upon us at every step, till we reach the margin of the Lake. This Water (for the Lakes are generally called *Waters* by the country people) is not so much as four miles in length, and becomes very narrow for the space of half a mile towards its outlet. On one side it is bordered by a continued straight line of high and almost perpendicular steeps, rising immediately from the Lake, without any bays or indentings. This is a very striking feature; for these steeps, or *screes* (as places of this kind are named), are not more distinguished by their height and extent, than by the beautiful colours with which the pulverized rock, for ever crumbling down their sides, overspreads them. The surface has the apparent softness of the dove's neck, and (as was before mentioned, in reference to spots of this kind,) resembles a dove's neck strongly in its hues, and in the manner in which they are intermingled. On the other side, Wast-water is bordered by knotty and projecting rocky mountains, which, retiring in one place, admit the interposition of a few green fields between them and the Lake, with a solitary farm-house. From the termination of the Screes rises Scaw Fell, deemed higher than Skiddaw, or Helvellyn, or any of the Mountains. The summit, as seen from Westdale, is bold and abrupt, and if you should quit the Valley and ascend towards it, it appears, from the Cove beneath, like the shattered walls or towers of an enormous edifice. Upon the summit of one of those towers is a fragment of rock that looks like an eagle, or a large owl, on that commanding eminence, stationary through all seasons. The Views which I have given are from the shore about the middle of Wast-water, from a point where the Vale appears to be terminated by three large conical Mountains, Yewbarrow on the left, Great Gavel in the centre, and Lingmoor on the right.* About two miles further is the Division of Westdale Head, with its lowly Chapel. This place formerly consisted of twenty tenements. It is now reduced to six. This Valley has been described in the Introduction,* as seen from the summit of Great Gavel; but the Traveller will be pleased with a nearer view of these pastoral dwellings, which in the inside are as comfortable as their outside is beautiful and picturesque. A hospitable people live here, and do not repine at the distance and the barriers which separate them from the noisy world. Give them more sunshine and a richer soil, and they would have little to complain of. The Stranger will observe here and elsewhere large heaps of stones, like Sepulchral Barrows, which have been collected from the fields and thrown together by the labours of many generations.* From the summits either of Great Gavel, or Scaw Fell, there are sublime prospects. Great Gavel may be proud of the Vallies which it looks down into, and Scaw Fell of the dark multitudinous Mountains, rising ridge above ridge, which it commands on the one side, and of the extent of sea and sand spreading in a level plain on the other. The ascent of Scaw Fell is easy, that of Great Gavel laborious. I cannot deny myself the pleasure of adding, that on the highest point of Great Gavel is a small triangular receptacle of water in a rock. It is not a spring; yet the shepherds say it is never dry; certainly when I was there, during a season of drought, it was well supplied with water. Here the Traveller may slake his thirst plenteously with a pure and celestial beverage; for it appears that this cup or bason has no other feeder than the dews of heaven, the showers, the vapours, the hoar frost, and the spotless snow.* From Wastdale return to Keswick by Stye-Head and Borrowdale. Take a look backwards upon Wastdale, from the last point where it is visible. The long strait vista of the Vale, and the sea beyond, apparent between the Mountains, form a grand whole. A few steps further bring you to Stye-Head Tarn (for which see No. 43).* By the side of the Tarn, an eagle (I believe of the ospray species) was killed last spring. Though large, it was very light, and seemed exhausted by hunger. The stream which flows into this Tarn comes from another, called Sprinkling Tarn, famous among anglers for the finest trouts in the country. In rainy seasons there is a magnificent waterfall formed by the stream which issues from Stye-Head Tarn. You have it on your left as you descend into Seathwaite division of Borrowdale. About a mile further down upon the left is that cluster of yew-trees recommended to notice; thence through a succession of magnificent scenes to Keswick.

It remains that we should speak of Ullswater.* There are two roads by which this Lake may be visited from Keswick. That which is adapted for Travellers on horseback, or on foot, crosses the lower part of St. John's Vale, and brings you down through the Valley and scattered Village of Matterdale into Gowbarrow Park, unfolding at once a magnificent view of the two higher reaches of the Lake. Airey Force thunders down the *Ghyll*, or Gill, on the left, at a small distance from the road; but you are separated from it by the Park-wall. In a carriage, Ullswater is best approached from Penrith. A mile and a half brings you to the winding Vale of Emont, and the prospects increase in interest till you reach Patterdale; but the first four miles along Ullswater by this road are comparatively tame, and in order to see the lower part of the Lake to advantage, it is absolutely necessary to go round by Poolly-Bridge, and to ride at least three miles along the Westmoreland side of the Water, towards Martindale. The Views from this quarter, especially if you ascend from the road into the fields, are magnificent; yet I only mention this that the transient Traveller may know what exists; for it will be very inconvenient for him to go in search of them. The person who takes this course of three or four miles, which I am now recommending, *on foot*, should take care to have a boat in readiness at the end of his walk, to carry him right across to the Cumberland side, along which he may pursue his way upwards to Patterdale.

Having conducted the Traveller hither, I shall treat no further of the body of this celebrated Vale; but, for the same reasons which governed me when I was speaking of Keswick, I shall confine myself to the Glens and Vallies which branch off from it.

At Dalemain, about three miles from Penrith, a Stream is crossed, called Dacre, which, rising in the moorish country about Penruddock, flows down a soft sequestered Valley, passing by the ancient mansions of Hutton John and Dacre Castle. The former is pleasantly situated, though of a character somewhat gloomy and monastic; and from some of the fields near Dalemain, Dacre Castle, backed by the jagged summit of Saddleback, and with the Valley and Stream in front of it, forms a grand picture. There is no other stream that conducts us to any glen or valley worthy of being mentioned, till you reach the one which leads you up to Airey Force, and then into Matterdale, before spoken of. Matterdale, though a wild and interesting spot, has no peculiar features that would make it worth the Stranger's while to go in search of them; but in Gowbarrow Park the lover of Nature might wish to linger for hours. Here is a powerful Brook, which dashes among rocks through a deep glen, hung on every side with a rich and happy intermixture of native wood; here are beds of luxuriant fern, aged hawthorns, and hollies decked with honeysuckles; and fallow-deer glancing and bounding over the lawns and through the thickets. These are the attractions of the retired views, or constitute a fore-ground to ever-varying pictures of the majestic Lake, forced to take a winding course by bold promontories, and environed by mountains of sublime form, towering above each other. Having passed under a plantation of larches, we reach, at the outlet of Gowbarrow Park, a third Stream, which flows through a little recess called Glencoin, in which lurks a single house, yet visible from the road. Let the Artist and leisurely Traveller turn aside to it, for the buildings and the objects around them are both romantic and exquisitely picturesque. Having passed under the steeps of Styebarrow Crag, and the remains of its native woods, you cross, at Glenridding-Bridge, a fourth Stream, which, if followed up, would lead to Red Tarn and the recesses of Helvellyn. The opening on the side of Ullswater Vale, down which the Stream flows, is adorned with fertile fields, cottages, and natural groves, which agreeably coalesce with the transverse views of the Lake; and the Stream, if followed up after the enclosures are left behind, will lead along bold water-breaks and waterfalls to a silent Tarn in the recesses of Helvellyn. This desolate spot was formerly haunted by eagles, that built in the precipice which forms its western barrier. These birds used to wheel and hover round the head of the solitary angler. It also now derives a melancholy interest from the fate of a young man, a stranger, who perished here a few years ago, by falling down the rocks in his attempt to cross over to Grasmere. His remains were discovered by means of a faithful dog, which had lingered here for the space of three months, self supported, and probably retaining to the last an attachment to the skeleton of its dead master. But to return to the road which we have left in the main Vale of Ullswater.—At the head of the Lake (being now in Patterdale) we cross a fifth Stream, Grisdale Beck; this conducts through a woody steep, where may be seen some unusually large ancient hollies, up to the level area of the Valley of Grisdale; hence there is a path for Foot-travellers, and along which a horse may be led, but not without difficulty, to Grasmere. I know not any where a more sublime combination of mountain forms than those which appear in front, as we ascend along the bed of this Valley; and the impression increases with every step till the path grows steep; and as we climb almost immediately under the projecting masses of Helvellyn, the mind is overcome with a sensation, which in some would amount to personal fear, and cannot but be awful even to those who are most familiar with the images of duration, and power, and other kindred influences, by which mountainous countries controul or exalt the imaginations of men. It is not uninteresting to know, that in the last house but one of this Valley, separated, as it might seem, from all the ambition and troubles of the world, from its wars and commotions, was born the youth, who, in Spain, took prisoner the Colonel of the Imperial Guard of Buonaparte. This favourite of the tyrant fled from the assault of our British mountaineer, with his two attendants who escaped; but he himself was not so fortunate.* Having retraced the banks of this stream to Patterdale, and pursued our way up the main Dale, the next considerable stream which we cross, would, if ascended in the same manner, conduct us into Deepdale, the character of which Valley may be conjectured by its name. It is terminated by a cove, a craggy and gloomy abyss, with precipitous sides; a faithful receptacle of the snows, which are carried into it, by the west wind, from the summit of Fairfield. Lastly, having gone along the western side of Brothers-water and passed Hartsop Hall, we are brought soon after to a stream which issues from a cove richly decorated with native wood. This spot is, I believe, never explored by Travellers; but whether from these sylvan and rocky recesses you look back on the gleaming surface of Brothers-water, or forward to the precipitous sides and lofty ridges of the mountains, you will be equally pleased with the beauty, the grandeur, and the wildness of the scenery.

We have thus noticed no less than seven Glens, or Vallies, which branch off from the western side of the long Vale which we have been ascending.

The opposite side has only two streams of any importance, one of which flows by the Village of Hartsop, near the foot of Brothers-water, and the other, coming down Martindale, enters Ullswater at Sandwyke, opposite to Gowbarrow Park. Of Martindale I shall say a few words, but I must first return to our head-quarters at the Village of Patterdale. No persons, but such as come to this place merely to pass through it, should fail to walk a mile and a half down the side of the Lake opposite to that on which the highroad lies; they should proceed beyond the point where the inclosures terminate. I have already had too frequent reason to lament the changes which have been made in the face of this country; and scarcely any where has a more grievous loss been sustained than upon the Farm of Blowick, the only enclosed land which on this side borders the higher part of the Lake. The axe has indiscriminately leveled a rich wood of birches and oaks, which, two or three years ago, varied this favoured spot into a thousand pictures. It has yet its land-locked bays and promontories; but now those beautiful woods are gone, which clothed its lawns and *perfected* its seclusion. Who, then, will not regret that those scenes, which might formerly have been compared to an inexhaustible volume, are now spread before the eye in a single sheet, magnificent indeed, but seemingly perused in a moment? From Blowick, a narrow track, by which a horse may be led, but with difficulty, conducts along the cragged side of Place Fell, richly adorned with juniper, and sprinkled over with birches, to the Village of Sandwyke; a few straggling houses, which, with the small estates attached to them, occupy an opening opposite to Lyulph's Tower and Gowbarrow Park.* This stream flows down Martindale, a Valley deficient in richness, but interesting from its seclusion. In Vales of this character the general want of wood gives a peculiar interest to the scattered cottages, embowered in sycamores; and few of the Mountain Chapels are more striking than this of Martindale, standing as it does in the centre of the Valley, with one dark yew-tree, and enclosed by 'a bare ring of mossy wall.' The name of Boardale, a bare, deep, and houseless Valley, which communicates with Martindale, shews that the wild swine were once numerous in that nook; and Martindale Forest is yet one of the few spots in England ranged over by red deer. These are the descendants of the aboriginal herds.* In Martindale, the road loses sight of the Lake, and leads over a steep hill, bringing you again into view of Ullswater. Its lowest reach, four miles in length, is before you; and the View is terminated by the long ridge of Cross Fell at a distance. Immediately under the eye is a deep-indented bay, with a plot of fertile land by the side of it, traversed by a small brook, and rendered cheerful by two or three substantial houses of a more ornamental and shewy appearance than is usual in these wild spots. Poolly-Bridge, at the foot of the Lake, to which we have again returned, has a good inn; and from this place Hawes-water, which has furnished me with the subject of an Etching,* may be conveniently visited. Of Hawes-water I shall only say, that it is a lesser Ullswater, with this advantage, that it remains undefiled by the intrusion of bad taste.

Lowther Castle is about four miles from Poolley-Bridge, and if during this Tour the Stranger has complained, as he will have reason to do, of a want of majestic trees, he may be abundantly recompensed for his loss in the far-spreading woods which surround that mansion.

I must now express my hope,* that the Reader of the foregoing pages will not blame me for having led him through unfrequented paths so much out of the common road. In this I have acted in conformity to the spirit of the Etchings, which are chiefly taken from sequestered scenes; and these must become every day more attractive in the eyes of the man of taste, unless juster notions and more appropriate feelings should find their way into the minds of those who, either from vanity, want of judgment, or some other cause, are rapidly taking away the native beauties of such parts of this Country as are most frequented, or most easy of access; and who are disfiguring the Vales, and the Borders of the Lakes, by an accumulation of unsightly buildings and discordant objects.

THE END

LIST OF WILKINSON'S PLATES IN THE ORDER GIVEN
IN THE TABLE OF CONTENTS, WITH ORIGINAL SPELLING
AND PUBLICATION DATES

The titles on the plates sometimes differ slightly from the contents list. The asterisks indicate the plates referred to in Wordsworth's text; bold type indicates those reproduced in the present edition.

*14. **Dec. 1, Brathy Bridge, near Ambleside**.

15. Nov. 1, Cottage near Rydal.

16. Oct. 1, Dunmail-raise Gap on the Ambleside Road.

17. Feb. 1, Thirle-mere, or Leathes Water.

18. June 1, View on the Ambleside Road, near Bridge-foot, with part of St. John's Vale.

19. May 1, Legbethwaite Mill, St. John's Vale.

20. March 1, View in St. John's Vale, with Green Crag, &c.

21. Apr. 1, View in St. John's Vale, near Wanthwaite.

*22. Jan. 1, Derwent Water from Applethwaite.

*23. **June 1, Part of Skiddaw from Applethwaite Gill.**

*24. Feb. 1, Cottages in Applethwaite, looking from Skiddaw.

*25. Apr. 1, Cottages at Braithwaite.

*26. Jan. 1, Cottages at Braithwaite.

27. May 1, Scale, or Skell-Gill Farm-house, above Portinscale.

*28. June 1, Stony-croft Bridge, Vale of Newlands.

*29. Mar. 1, Cottage in the Vale of Newlands, near Stare Bridge.

*30. Feb. 1, Cottage in the Vale of Newlands, with Robinson's Crag.

*31. Dec. 1, Cottage in the Vale of Newlands, between Keswick and Buttermere.

*32. Feb. 1, View in the Vale of Newlands.

33. Mar. 1, View on the Grange River, Borrowdale, looking towards Derwent Water.

34. Mar. 1, View on the Grange River, Borrowdale.

35. May 1, View near Seatoller, Borrowdale.

36. Nov. 1, View above Seatoller.

37. July 1, Smelting-Mill near Thornthwaite, on the western Side Bassenthwaite Lake.

38. July 1, Bassenthwaite Lake from Embleton Vale.

39. Oct. 1, Cottages in the Vale of Lorton.

*40. Jan 1, Ennerdale Broad Water.

*41. **June 1, Wast Water, looking up to Wastdale Head.**

*42. Apr. 1, View on the Banks of Wast Water.

*43. **Apr. 1, Stye-Head Tarn, with Aron or Great End, above Borrowdale.**

44. **Oct. 1, Lyulph's Tower, Ullswater.**

45. Jan. 1, View near Brothers Water.

46. Dec. 1, View on Kirkston, between Ambleside and Patterdale.

*47. Aug. 1, Hawes Water.

48. Aug. 1, Lanercost Priory.

FIGURE 1. Penny Bridge, between Ulverstone and Coniston, with the Tide in (Plate No. 3).

Estwaite water from below Bellemount

FIGURE 2. Estwaite Water from below Bellemount (Plate No. 8).

FIGURE 3. Elter Water (Plate No. 13).

FIGURE 4. Brathy Bridge, near Ambleside (Plate No. 14).

Part of Skiddaw from Applethwaite Gill

FIGURE 5. Part of Skiddaw from Applethwaite Gill (Plate No. 23).

Wast water, looking up to Wastdale Head.

FIGURE 6. Wast Water, looking up to Wastdale Head (Plate No. 41).

Stye-head Tarn, with Aron, or Great End, above Borrowdale.

FIGURE 7. Stye-Head Tarn, with Aron or Great End, above Borrowdale (Plate No. 43).

FIGURE 8. Lyulph's Tower, Ullswater (Plate No. 44).

APPENDIX II

KENDAL AND WINDERMERE RAILWAY.
TWO LETTERS
RE-PRINTED FROM THE *MORNING POST*

REVISED, WITH ADDITIONS.

LONDON:
WHITTAKER AND CO., AVE MARIA LANE, AND EDWARD
MOXON, DOVER STREET.
R. BRANTHWAITE AND SON, KENDAL.

Sonnet on the Projected Kendal and Windermere Railway

Is then no nook of English ground secure
From rash assault? Schemes of retirement sown
In youth, and mid the busy world kept pure
As when their earliest flowers of hope were blown,
Must perish;—how can they this blight endure?
And must he too the ruthless change bemoan
Who scorns a false utilitarian lure
Mid his paternal fields at random thrown?
Baffle the threat, bright Scene, from Orrest-head
Given to the pausing traveller's rapturous glance:
Plead for thy peace, thou beautiful romance
Of nature; and, if human hearts be dead,
Speak, passing winds; ye torrents, with your strong
And constant voice, protest against the wrong.

WILLIAM WORDSWORTH.

RYDAL MOUNT,
October 12th, 1844.

The degree and kind of attachment which many of the yeomanry feel to their small inheritances can scarcely be overrated. Near the house of one of them stands a magnificent tree, which a neighbour of the owner advised him to fell for profit's sake. 'Fell it,' exclaimed the yeoman, 'I had rather fall on my knees and worship it.' It happens, I believe, that the intended railway would pass through this little property, and I hope that an apology for the answer will not be thought necessary by one who enters into the strength of the feeling.   W. W.

Kendal and Windermere Railway

NO. I

TO THE EDITOR OF THE MORNING POST

Sɪʀ—Some little time ago you did me the favour of inserting a sonnet expressive of the regret and indignation which, in common with others all over these Islands, I felt at the proposal of a railway to extend from Kendal to Low Wood, near the head of Windermere. The project was so offensive to a large majority of the proprietors* through whose lands the line, after it came in view of the Lake, was to pass, that, for this reason, and the avowed one of the heavy expense without which the difficulties in the way could not be overcome, it has been partially abandoned, and the terminus is now announced to be at a spot within a mile of Bowness.* But as no guarantee can be given that the project will not hereafter be revived, and an attempt made to carry the line forward through the vales of Ambleside and Grasmere,* and as in one main particular the case remains essentially the same, allow me to address you upon certain points which merit more consideration than the favourers of the scheme have yet given them. The matter, though seemingly local, is really one in which all persons of taste must be interested, and, therefore, I hope to be excused if I venture to treat it at some length.

I shall barely touch upon the statistics of the question, leaving these to the two adverse parties, who will lay their several statements before the Board of Trade, which may possibly be induced to refer the matter to the House of Commons; and, contemplating that possibility, I hope that the observations I have to make may not be altogether without influence upon the public, and upon individuals whose duty it may be to decide in their place whether the proposed measure shall be referred to a Committee of the House. Were the case before us an ordinary one, I should reject such an attempt as presumptuous and futile; but it is not only different from all others, but, in truth, peculiar.

In this district the manufactures are trifling; mines it has none, and its quarries are either wrought out or superseded; the soil is light, and the cultivateable parts of the country are very limited; so that it has little to send out, and little has it also to receive. Summer Tourists, (and the very word precludes the notion of a railway)* it has in abundance; but the inhabitants are so few and their intercourse with other places so infrequent, that one daily coach, which could not be kept going but through its connection with the Post-office, suffices for three-fourths of the year along the line of country as far as Keswick. The staple of the district is, in fact, its beauty and its character of seclusion and retirement;* and to these topics and to others connected with them my remarks shall be confined.

The projectors have induced many to favour their schemes by declaring that one of their main objects is to place the beauties of the Lake district within easier reach of those who cannot afford to pay for ordinary conveyances. Look at the facts. Railways are completed, which, joined with others in rapid progress, will bring travellers who prefer approaching by Ullswater to within four miles of that lake. The Lancaster and Carlisle Railway will approach the town of Kendal, about eight or nine miles from eminences that command the whole vale of Windermere. The Lakes are therefore at present of very easy access for *all* persons;* but if they be not made still more so, the poor, it is said, will be wronged. Before this be admitted let the question be fairly looked into, and its different bearings examined. No one can assert that, if this intended mode of approach be not effected, anything will be taken away that is actually possessed. The wrong, if any, must lie in the unwarrantable obstruction of an attainable benefit. First, then, let us consider the probable amount of that benefit.

Elaborate gardens, with topiary works,* were in high request, even among our remote ancestors, but the relish for choice and picturesque natural *scenery* (a poor and mean word which requires an apology, but will be generally understood) is quite of recent origin.* Our earlier travellers—Ray, the naturalist, one of the first men of his age—Bishop Burnet, and others who had crossed the Alps, or lived some time in Switzerland, are silent upon the sublimity and beauty of those regions; and Burnet even uses these words, speaking of the Grisons—'When they have made up estates elsewhere they are glad to leave Italy and the best parts of Germany, and to come and live among those mountains of which the very sight is enough to fill a man with horror.' The accomplished Evelyn, giving an account of his journey from Italy through the Alps, dilates upon the terrible, the melancholy, and the uncomfortable; but, till he comes to the fruitful country in the neighbourhood of Geneva, not a syllable of delight or praise. In the Sacra Telluris Theoria of the other Burnet* there is a passage—omitted, however, in his own English translation of the work—in which he gives utterance to his sensations, when, from a particular spot he beheld a tract of the Alps rising before him on the one hand, and on the other the Mediterranean Sea spread beneath him. Nothing can be worthier of the magnificent appearances he describes than his language. In a noble strain also does the Poet Gray address, in a Latin Ode, the *Religio loci* at the Grande Chartruise. But before his time, with the exception of the passage from Thomas Burnet just alluded to, there is not, I believe, a single English traveller whose published writings would disprove the assertion, that, where precipitous rocks and mountains are mentioned at all, they are spoken of as objects of dislike and fear, and not of admiration. Even Gray himself, describing, in his Journal, the steeps at the entrance of Borrowdale, expresses his terror in the language of Dante:—'Let us not speak of them, but look and pass on.'* In my youth, I lived some time in the vale of Keswick,* under the roof of a shrewd and sensible woman, who more than once exclaimed in my hearing, 'Bless me! folk are always talking about prospects: when I was young there was never sic a thing neamed.' In fact, our ancestors, as everywhere appears, in choosing the site of their houses, looked only at shelter and convenience, especially of water, and often would place a barn or any other out-house directly in front of their habitations, however beautiful the landscape which their windows might otherwise have commanded. The first house that was built in the Lake district for the sake of the beauty of the country was the work of a Mr. English, who had travelled in Italy, and chose for his site, some eighty years ago, the great island of Windermere; but it was sold before his building was finished, and he showed how little he was capable of appreciating the character of the situation by setting up a length of high garden-wall, as exclusive as it was ugly, almost close to the house. The nuisance was swept away when the late Mr. Curwen became the owner of this favoured spot. Mr. English was followed by Mr. Pocklington, a native of Nottinghamshire, who played strange pranks by his buildings and plantations upon Vicar's Island, in Derwentwater, which his admiration, such as it was, of the country, and probably a wish to be a leader in a new fashion, had tempted him to purchase.* But what has all this to do with the subject?—Why, to show that a vivid perception of romantic scenery is neither inherent in mankind, nor a necessary consequence of even a comprehensive education. It is benignly ordained that green fields, clear blue skies, running streams of pure water, rich groves and woods, orchards, and all the ordinary varieties of rural nature, should find an easy way to the affections of all men, and more or less so from early childhood till the senses are impaired by old age and the sources of mere earthly enjoyment have in a great measure failed. But a taste beyond this, however desirable it may be that every one should possess it, is not to be implanted at once; it must be gradually developed both in nations and individuals. Rocks and mountains, torrents and wide-spread waters, and all those features of nature which go to the composition of such scenes as this part of England is distinguished for, cannot, in their finer relations to the human mind, be comprehended, or even very imperfectly conceived, without processes of culture or opportunities of observation in some degree habitual.* In the eye of thousands and tens of thousands, a rich meadow, with fat cattle grazing upon it, or the sight of what they would call a heavy crop of corn, is worth all that the Alps and Pyrenees in their utmost grandeur and beauty could show to them; and, notwithstanding the grateful influence, as we have observed, of ordinary nature and the productions of the fields, it is noticeable what trifling conventional prepossessions will, in common minds, not only preclude pleasure from the sight of natural beauty, but will even turn it into an object of disgust. 'If I had to do with this garden,' said a respectable person, one of my neighbours, 'I would sweep away all the black and dirty stuff from that wall.' The wall was backed by a bank of earth, and was exquisitely decorated with ivy, flowers, moss, and ferns, such as grow of themselves in like places; but the mere notion of fitness associated with a trim garden-wall prevented, in this instance, all sense of the spontaneous bounty and delicate care of nature.* In the midst of a small pleasure-ground, immediately below my house, rises a detached rock, equally remarkable for the beauty of its form, the ancient oaks that grow out of it, and the flowers and shrubs which adorn it. 'What a nice place would this be,' said a Manchester tradesman, pointing to the rock, 'if that ugly lump were but out of the way.' Men as little advanced in the pleasure which such objects give to others are so far from being rare, that they may be said fairly to represent a large majority of mankind. This is a fact, and none but the deceiver and the willingly deceived can be offended by its being stated. But as a more susceptible taste is undoubtedly a great acqui-sition, and has been spreading among us for some years, the question is, what means are most likely to be beneficial in extending its operation? Surely that good is not to be obtained by transferring at once uneducated persons in large bodies to particular spots, where the combinations of nat-ural objects are such as would afford the greatest pleasure to those who have been in the habit of observing and studying the peculiar character of such scenes, and how they differ one from another. Instead of tempting artisans and labourers, and the humbler classes of shopkeepers, to ramble to a distance, let us rather look with lively sympathy upon persons in that condition, when, upon a holiday, or on the Sunday, after having attended divine worship, they make little excursions with their wives and children among neighbouring fields, whither the whole of each family might stroll, or be conveyed at much less cost than would be required to take a single individual of the number to the shores of Windermere by the cheapest conveyance. It is in some such way as this only, that persons who must labour daily with their hands for bread in large towns, or are subject to confinement through the week, can be trained to a profitable intercourse with nature where she is the most distinguished by the majesty and sublim-ity of her forms.

For further illustration of the subject, turn to what we know of a man of extraordinary genius, who was bred to hard labour in agricultural employ-ments, Burns, the poet. When he had become distinguished by the publi-cation of a volume of verses, and was enabled to travel by the profit his poems brought him, he made a tour, in the course of which, as his compan-ion, Dr. Adair, tells us, he visited scenes inferior to none in Scotland in beauty, sublimity, and romantic interest; and the Doctor having noticed, with other companions, that he seemed little moved upon one occasion by the sight of such a scene, says—'I doubt if he had much taste for the picturesque.' The personal testimony, however, upon this point is conflicting; but when Dr. Currie refers to certain local poems as decisive proofs that Burns' fellow-traveller was mistaken, the biographer is surely unfortunate. How vague and tame are the poet's expressions in those few local poems, compared with his language when he is describing objects with which his position in life allowed him to be familiar! It appears, both from what his works contain, and from what is not to be found in them, that, sensitive as they abundantly prove his mind to have been in its intercourse with common rural images, and with the general powers of nature exhibited in storm and in stillness, in light or darkness, and in the various aspects of the seasons, he was little affected by the sight of one spot in preference to another, unless where it derived an interest from history, tradition, or local associations. He lived many years in Nithsdale, where he was in daily sight of Skiddaw, yet he never crossed the Solway for a better acquaintance with that mountain;* and I am persuaded that, if he had been induced to ramble among our Lakes, by that time sufficiently celebrated, he would have seldom been more excited than by some ordinary Scottish stream or hill with a tradition attached to it, or which had been the scene of a favourite ballad or love song. If all this be truly said of such a man, and the like cannot be denied of the eminent individuals before named, who to great natural talents added the accomplishments of scholarship or science, then what ground is there for maintaining that the poor are treated with disrespect, or wrong done to them or any class of visitants, if we be reluctant to introduce a railway into this country for the sake of lessening, by eight or nine miles only, the fatigue or expense of their journey to Windermere?—And wherever any one among the labouring classes has made even an approach to the sensibility which drew a lamentation from Burns when he had uprooted a daisy with his plough, and caused him to turn the 'weeder-clips aside' from the thistle, and spare 'the symbol dear' of his country,* then surely such a one, could he afford by any means to travel as far as Kendal, would not grudge a two hours' walk across the skirts of the beautiful country* that he was desirous of visiting.

The wide-spread waters of these regions are in their nature peaceful; so are the steep mountains and the rocky glens; nor can they be profitably enjoyed but by a mind disposed to peace. Go to a pantomime, a farce, or a puppet-show, if you want noisy pleasure*—the crowd of spectators who partake your enjoyment will, by their presence and acclamations, enhance it; but may those who have given proof that they prefer other gratifications continue to be safe from the molestation of cheap trains pouring out their hundreds at a time along the margin of Windermere; nor let any one be liable to the charge of being selfishly disregardful of the poor, and their innocent and salutary enjoyments, if he does not congratulate himself upon the especial benefit which would thus be conferred on such a concourse.

> 'O, Nature, a' thy shows an' forms,
> To feeling pensive hearts hae charms!'*

So exclaimed the Ayrshire ploughman, speaking of ordinary rural nature under the varying influences of the seasons, and the sentiment has found an echo in the bosoms of thousands in as humble a condition as he himself was when he gave vent to it. But then they were feeling, pensive hearts; men who would be among the first to lament the facility with which they had approached this region, by a sacrifice of so much of its quiet and beauty, as, from the intrusion of a railway, would be inseparable. What can, in truth, be more absurd, than that either rich or poor should be spared the trouble of travelling by the high roads over so short a space, according to their respective means, if the unavoidable consequence must be a great disturbance of the retirement, and in many places a destruction of the beauty of the country, which the parties are come in search of? Would not this be pretty much like the child's cutting up his drum to learn where the sound came from?*

Having, I trust, given sufficient reason for the belief that the imperfectly educated classes are not likely to draw much good from rare visits to the Lakes performed in this way, and surely on their own account it is not desirable that the visits should be frequent, let us glance at the mischief which such facilities would certainly produce. The directors of railway companies are always ready to devise or encourage entertainments for tempting the humbler classes to leave their homes. Accordingly, for the profit of the shareholders and that of the lower class of inn-keepers, we should have wrestling matches, horse and boat races without number, and pot-houses and beer-shops would keep pace with these excitements and recreations, most of which might too easily be had elsewhere. The injury which would thus be done to morals, both among this influx of strangers and the lower class of inhabitants, is obvious; and, supposing such extraordinary temptations not to be held out, there cannot be a doubt that the Sabbath day in the towns of Bowness and Ambleside, and other parts of the district, would be subject to much additional desecration.

Whatever comes of the scheme which we have endeavoured to discountenance, the charge against its opponents of being selfishly regardless of the poor, ought to cease. The cry has been raised and kept up by three classes of persons—they who wish to bring into discredit all such as stand in the way of their gains or gambling speculations;* they who are dazzled by the application of physical science to the useful arts, and indiscriminately applaud what they call the spirit of the age as manifested in this way; and, lastly, those persons who are ever ready to step forward in what appears to them to be the cause of the poor, but not always with becoming attention to particulars. I am well aware that upon the first class what has been said will be of no avail, but upon the two latter some impression will, I trust, be made.

To conclude. The railway power, we know well, will not admit of being materially counteracted by sentiment; and who would wish it where large towns are connected, and the interests of trade and agriculture are substantially promoted, by such mode of intercommunication? But be it remembered, that this case is, as has been said before, a peculiar one, and that the staple of the country* is its beauty and its character of retirement. Let then the beauty be undisfigured and the retirement unviolated, unless there be reason for believing that rights and interests of a higher kind and more apparent than those which have been urged in behalf of the projected intrusion will compensate the sacrifice.* Thanking you for the judicious observations that have appeared in your paper upon the subject of railways, I remain, Sir, your obliged,

WM. WORDSWORTH.

Rydal Mount, Dec. 9, 1844.

NOTE.—To the instances named in this letter of the indifference even of men of genius to the sublime forms of nature in mountainous districts, the author of the interesting Essays, in the Morning Post, entitled Table Talk has justly added Goldsmith, and I give the passage in his own words.

'The simple and gentle-hearted Goldsmith, who had an exquisite sense of rural beauty in the familiar forms of hill and dale, and meadows with their hawthorn-scented hedges, does not seem to have dreamt of any such thing as beauty in the Swiss Alps, though he traversed them on foot, and had therefore the best opportunities of observing them. In his poem "The Traveller," he describes the Swiss as loving their mountain homes, not by reason of the romantic beauty of the situation, but in spite of the miserable character of the soil, and the stormy horrors of their mountain steeps—

> Turn we to survey
> Where rougher climes a nobler race display,
> Where the bleak Swiss their stormy mansion tread,
> And force a churlish soil for scanty bread.
> No produce here the barren hills afford,
> But man and steel, the soldier and his sword:
> No vernal blooms their torpid rocks array,
> But winter lingering chills the lap of May;

No Zephyr fondly sues the mountain's breast,
But meteors glare and stormy glooms invest.
Yet still, *even here*, content can spread a charm,
Redress the clime, and all its rage disarm.'*

In the same Essay, (December 18th, 1844,) are many observations judiciously bearing upon the true character of this and similar projects.

NO. II

TO THE EDITOR OF THE MORNING POST

SIR—As you obligingly found space in your journal for observations of mine upon the intended Kendal and Windermere Railway, I venture to send you some further remarks upon the same subject. The scope of the main argument, it will be recollected, was to prove that the perception of what has acquired the name of picturesque and romantic scenery is so far from being intuitive, that it can be produced only by a slow and gradual process of culture; and to show, as a consequence, that the humbler ranks of society are not, and cannot be, in a state to gain material benefit from a more speedy access than they now have to this beautiful region. Some of our opponents dissent from this latter proposition, though the most judicious of them readily admit the former; but then, overlooking not only positive assertions, but reasons carefully given, they say, 'As you allow that a more comprehensive taste is desirable, you ought to side with us'; and they illustrate their position, by reference to the British Museum and National Picture Gallery. 'There,' they add, 'thanks to the easy entrance now granted, numbers are seen, indicating by their dress and appearance their humble condition, who, when admitted for the first time, stare vacantly around them, so that one is inclined to ask what brought them hither?* But an impression is made, something gained which may induce them to repeat the visit until light breaks in upon them, and they take an intelligent interest in what they behold.' Persons who talk thus forget that, to produce such an improvement, frequent access at small cost of time and labour is indispensable. Manchester lies, perhaps, within eight hours' railway distance of London; but surely no one would advise that Manchester operatives should contract a habit of running to and fro between that town and London, for the sake of forming an intimacy with the British Museum and National Gallery? No, no; little would all but a very few gain from the opportunities which, consistently with common sense, could be afforded them for such expeditions. Nor would it fare better with them in respect of trips to the lake district; an assertion, the truth of which no one can doubt, who has learned by experience how many men of the same or higher rank, living from their birth in this very region, are indifferent to those objects around them in which a cultivated taste takes so much pleasure. I should not have detained the reader so long upon this point, had I not heard (glad tidings for the directors and traffickers in shares!) that among the affluent and benevolent manufacturers of Yorkshire and Lancashire are some who already entertain the thought of sending, at their own expense, large bodies of their workmen, by railway, to the banks of Windermere.* Surely those gentlemen will think a little more before they put such a scheme into practice. The rich man cannot benefit the poor, nor the superior the inferior, by anything that degrades him. Packing off men after this fashion, for holiday entertainment, is, in fact, treating them like children. They go at the will of their master, and must return at the same, or they will be dealt with as transgressors.

A poor man, speaking of his son, whose time of service in the army was expired, once said to me, (the reader will be startled at the expression, and I, indeed, was greatly shocked by it), 'I am glad he has done with that *mean* way of life.' But I soon gathered what was at the bottom of the feeling. The father overlooked all the glory that attaches to the character of a British soldier, in the consciousness that his son's will must have been in so great a degree subject to that of others. The poor man felt where the true dignity of his species lay, namely, in a just proportion between actions governed by a man's own inclinations and those of other men; but, according to the father's notion, that proportion did not exist in the course of life from which his son had been released. Had the old man known from experience the degree of liberty allowed to the common soldier, and the moral effect of the obedience required, he would have thought differently, and had he been capable of extending his views, he would have felt how much of the best and noblest part of our civic spirit is owing to our military and naval institutions, and that perhaps our very existence as a free people has by them been maintained. This extreme instance has been adduced to show how deeply seated in the minds of Englishmen is their sense of personal independence. Master-manufacturers ought never to lose sight of this truth. Let them consent to a Ten Hours' Bill, with little or, if possible, no diminution of wages,* and the necessaries of life being more easily procured, the mind would develope itself accordingly, and each individual would be more at liberty to make at his own cost excursions in any direction which might be most inviting to him. There would then be no need for their masters sending them in droves scores of miles from their homes and families to the borders of Windermere, or anywhere else. Consider also the state of the lake district; and look, in the first place, at the little town of Bowness, in the event of such railway inundations. What would become of it in this, not the Retreat, but the Advance, of the Ten Thousand? Leeds, I am told, has sent as many at once to Scarborough. We should have the whole of Lancashire, and no small part of Yorkshire, pouring in upon us to meet the men of Durham, and the borderers from Cumberland and Northumberland. Alas, alas, if the lakes are to pay this penalty for their own attractions!

> '—Vane could tell what ills from beauty spring,
> And Sedley cursed the form that pleased a king.'*

The fear of adding to the length of my last long letter prevented me from entering into details upon private and personal feelings among the residents, who have cause to lament the threatened intrusion. These are not matters to be brought before a Board of Trade, though I trust there will always be of that board members who know well that as we do 'not live by bread alone,' so neither do we live by political economy alone. Of the present board I would gladly believe there is not one who, if his duty allowed it, would not be influenced by considerations of what may be felt by a gallant officer now serving on the coast of South America,* when he shall learn that the nuisance, though not intended actually to enter his property, will send its omnibuses, as fast as they can drive, within a few yards of his modest abode, which he built upon a small domain purchased at a price greatly enhanced by the privacy and beauty of the situation. Professor Wilson (him I take the liberty to name), though a native of Scotland, and familiar with the grandeur of his own country, could not resist the temptation of settling long ago among our mountains. The place which his public duties have compelled him to quit as a residence, and may compel him to part with, is probably dearer to him than any spot upon earth. The reader should be informed with what respect he has been treated. Engineer agents, to his astonishment, came and intruded with their measuring instruments, upon his garden. He saw them; and who will not admire the patience that kept his hands from their shoulders? I must stop.

But with the fear before me of the line being carried, at a day not distant, through the whole breadth of the district,* I could dwell, with much concern for other residents, upon the condition which they would be in if that outrage should be committed; nor ought it to be deemed impertinent were I to recommend this point to the especial regard of Members of Parliament who may have to decide upon the question. The two Houses of Legislature have frequently shown themselves not unmindful of private feeling in these matters. They have, in some cases, been induced to spare parks and pleasure grounds. But along the great railway lines these are of rare occurrence. They are but a part, and a small part; here it is far otherwise. Among the ancient inheritances of the yeomen, surely worthy of high respect, are interspersed through the entire district villas, most of them with such small domains attached that the occupants would be hardly less annoyed by a railway passing through their neighbour's ground than through their own. And it would be unpardonable not to advert to the effect of this measure on the interests of the very poor in this locality. With the town of Bowness I have no *minute* acquaintance; but of Ambleside, Grasmere, and the neighbourhood, I can testify from long experience, that they have been favoured by the residence of a gentry whose love of retirement has been a blessing to these vales; for their families have ministered, and still minister, to the temporal and spiritual necessities of the poor, and have personally superintended the education of the children in a degree which does those benefactors the highest honour, and which is, I trust, gratefully acknowledged in the hearts of all whom they have relieved, employed, and taught. Many of those friends of our poor would quit this country if the apprehended change were realised, and would be succeeded by strangers not linked to the neighbourhood, but flitting to and fro between their fancy-villas and the homes where their wealth was accumulated and accumulating by trade and manufactures. It is obvious that persons, so unsettled, whatever might be their good wishes and readiness to part with money for charitable purposes, would ill supply the loss of the inhabitants who had been driven away.

It will be felt by those who think with me upon this occasion that I have been writing on behalf of a social condition which no one who is competent to judge of it would be willing to subvert, and that I have been endeavouring to support moral sentiments and intellectual pleasures of a high order against an enmity which seems growing more and more formidable every day; I mean 'Utilitarianism,' serving as a mask for cupidity and gambling speculations.* My business with this evil lies in its reckless mode of action by Railways, now its favourite instruments. Upon good authority I have been told that there was lately an intention of driving one of these pests, as they are likely too often to prove, through a part of the magnificent ruins of Furness Abbey—an outrage which was prevented by some one pointing out how easily a deviation might be made;* and the hint produced its due effect upon the engineer.

Sacred as that relic of the devotion of our ancestors deserves to be kept, there are temples of Nature, temples built by the Almighty, which have a still higher claim to be left unviolated. Almost every reach of the winding vales in this district might once have presented itself to a man of imagination and feeling under that aspect, or, as the Vale of Grasmere appeared to the Poet Gray more than seventy years ago. 'No flaring gentleman's-house,' says he, 'nor garden-walls break in upon the repose of this little unsuspected *paradise*, but all is peace,' &c., &c.* Were the Poet now living, how would he have lamented the probable intrusion of a railway with its scarifications, its intersections, its noisy machinery, its smoke, and swarms of pleasure-hunters, most of them thinking that they do not fly fast enough through the country which they have come to see.* Even a broad highway may in some places greatly impair the characteristic beauty of the country, as will be readily acknowledged by those who remember what the Lake of Grasmere was before the new road that runs along its eastern margin had been constructed.*

> Quanto præstantius esset
> Numen aquæ viridi si margine clauderet undas
> Herba—*

As it once was, and fringed with wood, instead of the breastwork of bare wall that now confines it. In the same manner has the beauty, and still more the sublimity of many Passes in the Alps been injuriously affected. Will the reader excuse a quotation from a MS. poem in which I attempted to describe the impression made upon my mind by the descent towards Italy along the Simplon before the new military road* had taken the place of the old muleteer track with its primitive simplicities?

> Brook and road
> Were fellow-travellers in this gloomy pass,
> And with them did we journey several hours
> At a slow step. The immeasurable height
> Of woods decaying, never to be decayed,
> The stationary blasts of waterfalls,
> And in the narrow rent, at every turn,
> Winds thwarting winds bewildered and forlorn,
> The torrents shooting from the clear blue sky,
> The rocks that muttered close upon our ears,
> Black drizzling crags that spake by the way-side
> As if a voice were in them, the sick sight
> And giddy prospect of the raving stream,
> The unfettered clouds and region of the heavens,
> Tumult and peace, the darkness and the light,
> Were all like workings of one mind, the features
> Of the same face, blossoms upon one tree,
> Characters of the great Apocalypse,
> The types and symbols of Eternity,
> Of first, and last, and midst, and without end.
>   1799.*

Thirty years afterwards I crossed the Alps by the same Pass:* and what had become of the forms and powers to which I had been indebted for those emotions? Many of them remained of course undestroyed and indestructible.

But, though the road and torrent continued to run parallel to each other, their fellowship was put an end to. The stream had dwindled into comparative insignificance, so much had Art interfered with and taken the lead of Nature; and although the utility of the new work, as facilitating the intercourse of great nations, was readily acquiesced in, and the workmanship, in some places, could not but excite admiration, it was impossible to suppress regret for what had vanished for ever. The oratories heretofore not unfrequently met with, on a road still somewhat perilous, were gone; the simple and rude bridges swept away; and instead of travellers proceeding, with leisure to observe and feel, were pilgrims of fashion hurried along in their carriages, not a few of them perhaps discussing the merits of 'the last new Novel,' or poring over their Guide-books, or fast asleep.* Similar remarks might be applied to the mountainous country of Wales;* but there too, the plea of utility, especially as expediting the communication between England and Ireland, more than justifies the labours of the Engineer. Not so would it be with the Lake District. A railroad is already planned along the sea coast, and another from Lancaster to Carlisle is in great forwardness: an intermediate one is therefore, to say the least of it, superfluous. Once for all let me declare that it is not against Railways but against the abuse of them that I am contending.

How far I am from undervaluing the benefit to be expected from railways in their legitimate application will appear from the following lines published in 1837, and composed some years earlier.

STEAMBOATS AND RAILWAYS

Motions and Means, on sea & land at war
With old poetic feeling, not for this
Shall ye, by poets even, be judged amiss!
Nor shall your presence, howsoe'er it mar
The loveliness of nature, prove a bar
To the mind's gaining that prophetic sense
Of future good, that point of vision, whence
May be discovered what in soul ye are.
In spite of all that Beauty must disown
In your harsh features, nature doth embrace
Her lawful offspring in man's Art; and Time,
Pleased with your triumphs o'er his brother Space,
Accepts from your bold hands the proffered crown
Of hope, and welcomes you with cheer sublime.*

I have now done with the subject. The time of life at which I have arrived may, I trust, if nothing else will, guard me from the imputation of having written from any selfish interests, or from fear of disturbance which a railway might cause to myself. If gratitude for what repose and quiet in a district hitherto, for the most part, not disfigured but beautified by human hands, have done for me through the course of a long life, and hope that others might hereafter be benefited in the same manner and in the same country, *be* selfishness, then, indeed, but not otherwise, I plead guilty to the charge. Nor have I opposed this undertaking on account of the inhabitants of the district *merely*, but, as hath been intimated, for the sake of every one, however humble his condition, who coming hither shall bring with him an eye to perceive, and a heart to feel and worthily enjoy.* And as for holiday pastimes, if a scene is to be chosen suitable to them for persons thronging from a distance, it may be found elsewhere at less cost of every kind. But, in fact, we have too much hurrying about in these islands; much for idle pleasure, and more from over activity in the pursuit of wealth, without regard to the good or happiness of others.

> Proud were ye, Mountains, when, in times of old,
> Your patriot sons, to stem invasive war,
> Intrenched your brows; ye gloried in each scar:
> Now, for your shame, a Power, the Thirst of Gold,
> That rules o'er Britain like a baneful star,
> Wills that your peace, your beauty, shall be sold,
> And clear way made for her triumphal car
> Through the beloved retreats your arms enfold!
> Heard YE that Whistle? As her long-linked Train
> Swept onwards, did the vision cross your view?
> Yes, ye were startled;—and, in balance true,
> Weighing the mischief with the promised gain,
> Mountains, and Vales, and Floods, I call on you
> To share the passion of a just disdain.
>   WILLIAM WORDSWORTH.

APPENDIX III

A PRODUCTION HISTORY OF WORDSWORTH'S *GUIDE TO THE LAKES*

1810 edition	1820 edition	1822 edition	1823 edition	1835 edition	1842–59 editions
					Introduction
				Directions & Information	*Directions & Information*, incorporating Excursions to Scawfell & Ullswater
INTRODUCTION	TOPOGRAPHICAL DESCRIPTION Adding new paragraphs incorporating	DESCRIPTION OF THE SCENERY SECTION FIRST SECTION SECOND SECTION THIRD	DESCRIPTION OF THE SCENERY SECTION FIRST SECTION SECOND SECTION THIRD	DESCRIPTION OF THE SCENERY SECTION FIRST SECTION SECOND SECTION THIRD	DESCRIPTION OF THE SCENERY SECTION FIRST SECTION SECOND SECTION THIRD
Section I (Best Time for Visiting the Lakes)	Section I of the 1810 edition	Miscellaneous Observations Excursion to Scawfell	Miscellaneous Observations Excursions to Scawfell & Ullswater	Miscellaneous Observations Excursions to Scawfell & Ullswater	Section Fourth
Section II		*Directions & Information*	*Directions & Information*		Sedgwick's geological essays

1807   (Summer) Wordsworth's first mention of preparing a guidebook.

1809   By June, Wordsworth starts to draft the letterpress for Wilkinson's *Select Views* and in Nov. finishes the general introduction, though still working on Sections I and II. He mentions a possibility of publishing a separate guide of his own.

1810   Joseph Wilkinson, *Select Views in Cumberland, Westmoreland, and Lancashire* (London: Ackermann), published in 12 instalments.

1811   (Sept.–Nov. 1812) Wordsworth prepares a new guide of his own (left unfinished in MS; published 1974 in *PrW* ii. as 'An Unpublished Tour').

1820   *The River Duddon, a Series of Sonnets: Vaudracour & Julia: and Other Poems. To which is annexed, A Topographical Description of the Country of the Lakes, in the North of England* (London: Longman).

1821   Joseph Wilkinson, *Select Views in Cumberland, Westmoreland, and Lancashire* (London: Ackermann), 2nd edition.

1822   (June) *A Description of the Scenery of the Lakes in the North of England. Third Edition, (now first published separately) with Additions, and Illustrative Remarks upon the Scenery of the Alps* (London: Longman).

1823   *A Description of the Scenery of the lakes in the North of England. Fourth Edition. With Additions, and Illustrative Remarks upon the Scenery of the Alps* (London: Longman).

1835   (May) Wordsworth writes to the publishers Hudson & Nicholson at Kendal about a new edition of the *Guide*.

1835   (July) *A Guide through the District of the Lakes in the North of England, with a Description of the Scenery, etc. for the Use of Tourists and Residents. Fifth Edition, with considerable additions* (Kendal: Hudson and Nicholson; London: Longman & Co., Moxon, and Whittaker & Co.).

1837   Henry Reed, ed., *The Complete Poetical Works of William Wordsworth: Together with a Description of the Country of the Lakes in the North of England, Now First Published with His Works* (Philadelphia: James Kay, Jun. and Bro.; Boston: James Munroe and Co.; Pittsburgh: John I. Kay & Co.) [includes the text of 1820].

1838   (Sept.) Hudson writes to Wordsworth about a new expanded edition of the *Guide*.

1842   (Mar.) Wordsworth agrees that Hudson will compile a new expanded edition. (May) Wordsworth writes to Adam Sedgwick requesting him to contribute an essay on the geology of the Lake District. (July) *A Complete Guide to the Lakes, Comprising Minute Directions for the Tourist, with Mr Wordsworth's Description of the Scenery of the Country, &c. and Three Letters upon the Geology of the Lake District, by the Rev. Professor Sedgwick.* Edited by the Publishers (Kendal: Hudson and Nicholson. London: Longman and Co., and Whittaker and Co. Liverpool; Webb, Castle St. Manchester; Simms and Co.).

1843   *A Complete Guide to the Lakes,... and Three Letters...* Second Edition. Edited by the Publisher (Kendal: J. Hudson. London: Longman and Co., and Whittaker and Co. Liverpool; Webb, Castle St. Manchester; Simms and Co.).

1844   (June) Wordsworth writes to John Hudson about how to market the *Complete Guide.*

1846   *A Complete Guide to the Lakes,... and Four Letters...* Third Edition. Edited by the Publisher (Kendal: J. Hudson. London: Longman and Co., and Whittaker and Co. Liverpool; Webb, Castle St. Manchester; Simms and Co.).

1853   *A Complete Guide to the Lakes,... and Five Letters...* Fourth Edition. Edited by the Publisher (Kendal: J. Hudson. London: Longman and Co., and Whittaker and Co. Liverpool; Webb, Castle St. Manchester; Simms and Co.).

1859   *A Complete Guide to the Lakes, with Minute Directions for the Tourist, and Mr Wordsworth's Description of the Scenery of the Country, etc; Also Five Letters on the Geology of the Lake District, by the Rev. Professor Sedgwick.* Fifth Edition. Edited by John Hudson (Kendal: Thomas B. Hudson. London: Longman and Co., and Whittaker and Co.). *Hudson's New Hand-Book for Visitors to the English Lakes, with an Introduction by the Late William Wordsworth, Esq. and a New Map of the Lake District; to which is Appended a Copious List of Plants Found in the Adjacent Country. Embellished with Steel Engravings* (Kendal: Thomas B. Hudson. London: Longman and Co., Whittaker and Co., and Hamilton Adams, and Co.).

1860   *Hand-book for Visitors to the English Lakes, with an Introduction by the Late William Wordsworth, Esq. Illustrated with Outlines of Mountains, New Map, and Numerous Full Page Engravings* (Kendal: T. Wilson. London: Longman and Co., and Whittaker and Co. [1860–73]).

1873   *Shaw's Tourist's Picturesque Guide to the English Lakes with an Introduction by the Late Poet Laureate Wordsworth* (Kendal: Titus Wilson. London: The Graphotyping Co., Simpkin Marshall [1873–7]).

1876   Alexander B. Grosart, *The Prose Works of William Wordsworth*, 3 vols (London: Moxon), ii. 215–319.

*c.*1878   *A Description of the Scenery of the District of the Lakes by William Wordsworth* (Windermere: J. Garnett) [comprises 'Description of the Scenery of the Lakes', 'Miscellaneous Observations' and 'Excursions'].

1884   *Ward and Lock's Pictorial and Historical Guide to the English Lakes, their Scenery and Associations, with an Introduction by the Poet Wordsworth* (London: Ward, Lock & Co. [1884–*c*.1894]).

1897   William Knight, ed., *Prose Works of William Wordsworth*, 2 vols (London: Macmillan), ii. 1–121 [Although the volumes are dated 1896, publication was early in 1897 as Mark Reed notes].

1898   *Ward and Lock's Pictorial and Descriptive Guide to the Lakes* (London: Ward, Lock & Co. [1898–*c*.1950, includes extracts from Wordsworth's *Guide*]).

1906   Ernest De Selincourt, ed., *Wordsworth's Guide to the Lakes* (London: Henry Frowde); reissued from Humphrey Milford, 1926; Oxford University Press, 1970, 1977; reprinted with new preface by Stephen Gill (London: Frances Lincoln, 2004).

1921   *Poetry & Prose with Essays by Coleridge, Hazlitt, De Quincey, with an Introduction by David Nichol Smith and Notes* (Oxford: Clarendon Press) [includes two paragraphs from the second section of 'Description of the Scenery of the Lakes'].

1948   J. W. Lucas, introduction, *A Guide through the District of the Lakes in the North of England*, Facsimile of the Definitive Fifth Edition (Malvern: Tantivy Press).

1951   W. M. Merchant, introduction, *A Guide through the District of the Lakes in the North of England*, with Illustrations by John Piper (London: Rupert Hart-Davis).

1974   W. J. B. Owen and Jane Worthington Smyser, eds, *The Prose Works of William Wordsworth*, 3 vols (Oxford: Clarendon Press, 1974), vol. 2.

1984   Peter Bicknell, ed., *The Illustrated Wordsworth's Guide to the Lakes* (Exeter: Webb & Bower).

1991   Jonathan Wordsworth, ed., *A Description of the Lakes, 1822* (Otley, West Yorkshire: Woodstock).

2008   *Select Views in Cumberland, Westmoreland, and Lancashire (1810)*, in Tomoya Oda, ed., *Lake District Tours: A Collection of Travel Writings and Guide Books in the Romantic Era*, vol. 6 (Kyoto: Eurika Press).

2015   Nicholas Mason, Paul Westover, and Shannon Stimpson, eds, *William Wordsworth's Guide to the Lakes: A Romantic Circles Electronic Edition*. Revised, 2020.

2020   Stephen Hebron and Cecilia Powell, eds, *The Country of the Lakes in 1820* (Grasmere: Wordsworth Trust) [reproduces the 1820 edition].

APPENDIX IV

TWO HUNDRED YEARS OF LAKE DISTRICT TOURISM, 1750–1950

The following list offers a chronological sequence of selected key texts and events for the development of Lake District tourism, 1750–1950.

1752   William Bellers, *Six Select Views in the North of England*.

1755   John Dalton, *A Descriptive Poem, addressed to two ladies, at their return from viewing the mines near Whitehaven*...

1762   The road between Kendal and Keswick begins to be turnpiked.

1767   John Brown, *A Description of the Lake at Keswick (and the adjacent country) in Cumberland* [written in 1753, first published in *London Chronicle* in 1766].

1774   William Hutchinson, *An Excursion to the Lakes, in Westmoreland and Cumberland*...

1774   Thomas West, *The Antiquities of Furness*.

1775   Thomas Gray, *The Poems of Mr Gray. To Which are Prefixed Memoirs of his Life and Writings by W. Mason* [includes Gray's journal of his visit to the Lakes in 1769 and Mason's description of the Rydal Lower Fall].

1776   Richard Cumberland, *Odes* [includes John Brown's poem].

1777   Joseph Nicolson and Richard Burn, *The History and Antiquities of the Counties of Westmorland and Cumberland*.

1778   Thomas West, *A Guide to the Lakes* [from the 2nd edition onward (1780–1821), edited and enlarged by William Cockin].

1783   Peter Crosthwaite, *Seven Maps of the Lakes*.

1786   William Gilpin, *Observations, Relative Chiefly to Picturesque Beauty*...*Particularly the Mountains, and Lakes of Cumberland, and Westmoreland*, 2 vols.

1787   James Clarke, *A Survey of the Lakes of Cumberland, Westmorland, and Lancashire*...

1789   Joseph Farington, *Views of the Lakes, &c. in Cumberland and Westmorland* [letterpress by William Cookson].

1792   Peter Holland, *Select Views of the Lakes in Cumberland, Westmoreland & Lancashire*.

1792   Joseph Budworth, *A Fortnight's Ramble to the Lakes in Westmoreland, Lancashire and Cumberland*.

1793   A daily post coach service between Kendal and London begins to operate.

1795   Ann Radcliffe, *A Journey Made in the Summer of 1794, through Holland...to Which are Added Observations during a Tour to the Lakes...*

1795   John 'Warwick' Smith, *Views of the Lakes.*

1798   James Plumptre, *The Lakers: A Comic Opera in Three Acts.*

1800   John Housman, *A Topographical Description of Cumberland, Westmoreland, Lancashire.*

1807   Robert Southey, *Letters from England; by Don Manuel Alvarez Espriella*. Translated from the Spanish, 3 vols.

1809   William Green, *Seventy Eight Studies from Nature.*

1810   William Green, *A Description of Sixty Studies from Nature...Comprising a General Guide to the Beauties of the North of England.*

1810   Joseph Wilkinson, *Select Views in Cumberland, Westmoreland, and Lancashire.*

1812   William Combe and Thomas Rowlandson, *The Tour of Doctor Syntax in Search of the Picturesque. A Poem* [first published in 1809 in a magazine].

1814   W. Wordsworth, *The Excursion.*

1816   Thomas Hartwell Horne, *The Lakes of Lancashire, Westmorland, and Cumberland; Delineated in Forty-Three Engravings, from Drawings by Joseph Farington...*

1819   John Robinson, *A Guide to the Lakes in Cumberland, Westmorland, and Lancashire.*

1819   William Green, *The Tourist's New Guide, Containing a Description of the Lakes, Mountains, and Scenery, in Cumberland, Westmorland, and Lancashire*, 2 vols.

1819   John Wilson, 'Letters from the Lakes, Written during the Summer of 1818', *Blackwood's Edinburgh Magazine.*

1820   William Westall, *Views of the Lake and of the Vale of Keswick* [letterpress by Robert Southey].

1820   W. Wordsworth, *The River Duddon, a Series of Sonnets... A Topographical Description of the Country of the Lakes, in the North of England.*

1820   John Briggs, ed., *The Lonsdale Magazine*, 3 vols, 1820–2 [contains extracts from the Duddon Sonnets (vol. 1, 1820) and 'Excursion to the Top of Scawfell' (vol. 3, 1822)].

1821   T. H. A. Fielding and John Walton, *A Picturesque Tour of the English Lakes...*

1822   W. Wordsworth, *A Description of the Scenery of the Lakes in the North of England. Third Edition.*

1823   W. Wordsworth, *A Description of the Scenery of the Lakes...Fourth Edition.*

1823   Jonathan Otley, *A Concise Description of the English Lakes, and Mountains in their Vicinity*...

1826   The new road between White Moss and Grasmere opened in February.

1827   Charles Cooke, *The Tourist's and Traveller's Companion to the Lakes*...

1830   Edward Baines, *A Companion to the Lakes*, 2nd edn [first edition, 1829].

1832   *Leigh's Guide to the Lakes and Mountains of Cumberland, Westmoreland, and Lancashire*, 2nd edn [first edition, 1830].

1832   Thomas Rose, *Westmorland, Cumberland, Durham, and Northumberland, Illustrated...by Thomas Allom, George Pickering, &c. with Descriptions.*

1832   John Wilson, 'Christopher at the Lakes', *Blackwood's Edinburgh Magazine.*

1833   John Robinson, *Views of the Lakes in the North of England*..., 2 vols.

1834   James Johnson, 'The English Lakes', *Recess, or Autumnal Relaxation in the Highlands and Lowlands*...

1835   Newcastle and Carlisle Railway starts to carry passengers.

1835   'Rydal Lake, and Residence of the Poet Wordsworth, Westmorland', *Mirror of Literature, Amusement, and Instruction*, vol. 26.

1835   W. Wordsworth, *A Guide through the District of the Lakes in the North of England. Fifth Edition.*

1837   'English Lakes', *Penny Magazine*, vol. 6.

1837   'English Lake Scenery, Wordsworth's Residence at Rydal Water', *Saturday Magazine*, vol. 10.

1837   *Allison's Northern Tourist's Guide to the Lakes, of Cumberland, Westmorland, and Lancashire*, 7th edn.

1839   William Ford, *A Description of the Scenery in the Lake District, Intended as a Guide to Strangers* [1839–55].

1840   Lancaster and Preston Junction Railway opened.

1841   *Black's Picturesque Guide to the English Lakes* [1841–1900].

1841   *Onwhyn's Pocket Guide to the Lakes*...

1842   Jonathan Otley, *A Descriptive Guide to the English Lakes, and Adjacent Mountains: with Notices of the Botany, Mineralogy, and Geology of the District. Seventh Edition. To which is Added, an Excursion through Lonsdale to the Caves.*

1842   Hudson and Nicholson (publishers), *A Complete Guide to the Lakes... with Mr Wordsworth's Description of the Scenery of the Country, &c. and Three Letters upon the Geology of the Lake District, by the Rev. Professor Sedgwick.*

1843   J. Hudson (publisher), *A Complete Guide to the Lakes*... 2nd edn.

1844   James Thorne, *Rambles by Rivers: The Duddon*...

1844   W. Wordsworth, 'Kendal and Windermere Railway', *Morning Post*.

1845   Maryport and Carlisle Railway starts through passenger service.

1846   Furness Railway, Lancaster and Carlisle Railway, begin passenger services.

1846   J. Hudson (publisher), *A Complete Guide to the Lakes*... 3rd edn.

1846   Charles Mackay, *The Scenery and Poetry of the English Lakes. A Summer Ramble*.

1847   Kendal and Windermere Railway, Cockermouth and Workington Railway, opened.

1847   T. Atkinson (publisher), *Hand-book to the English Lakes* [1847–57].

1847   John Jackson (publisher), *A Complete and Descriptive Guide to the Lakes*...

1847   'Windermere', Charles Knight et al., eds, *The Land We Live In*, vol. 1.

1847   *Sylvan's Pictorial Handbook to the English Lakes*.

1849   Alexander Craig Gibson, *The Old Man; or Ravings and Ramblings round Conistone*.

1849   George Mogridge, *Loiterings among the Lakes of Cumberland and Westmoreland*.

1851   Christopher Wordsworth, Jr, *Memoirs of William Wordsworth*, 2 vols.

1852   Edward L. Blanchard, *Adams's Pocket Descriptive Guide to the Lake District*...

1852   John Linton, *A Handbook of the Whitehaven and Furness Railway, Being a Guide to the Lake District of West Cumberland and Furness*.

1853   J. Hudson (publisher), *A Complete Guide to the Lakes*... 4th edn.

1853   James Baker Pyne, *The English Lake District*.

1855   Harriet Martineau, *A Complete Guide to the English Lakes* [1855–76].

1857   Harry Hardknot, *Rambles in the Lake District*.

1858   Harriet Martineau, *The English Lakes. Illustrated... by W. J. Linton*.

1858   Thomas Rose, *The British Switzerland; or, Picturesque Rambles in the English Lake District*.

1859   J. M. Wilson, *The English Lakes. Nelson's Hand-books for Tourists*.

1859   James Payn, *Hand-Book to the English Lakes*.

1859   James Baker Pyne, *Lake Scenery of England*.

1859   T. B. Hudson (publisher), *A Complete Guide to the Lakes*... 5th edn.

1859   *Hudson's New Hand-book for Visitors to the English Lakes, with an Introduction by the Late William Wordsworth.*

1860   *Hand-book for Visitors to the English Lakes, with an Introduction by the Late William Wordsworth* [1860–73].

1860   *The Excursion. A Poem. By William Wordsworth. With Topographical Note by Lindsey Aspland.*

1861   Edwin Waugh, *Rambles in the Lake Country and Its Borders.*

1864   Elizabeth Lynn Linton, *The Lake Country, with a Map and One Hundred Illustrations . . .*

1865   Cockermouth, Keswick and Penrith Railway opened for passenger traffic.

1865   Herman Prior, *Ascents and Passes in the Lake District of England.*

1866   *Murray's Handbook for Travellers in Westmoreland and Cumberland.*

1866   G. K. Matthew, *The English Lakes, Peaks, and Passes, from Kendal to Keswick.*

1867   James Payn, *The Lakes in Sunshine: Being Photographic and Other Pictures of the Lake District of Westmorland and North Lancashire.*

1869   W. F. Topham, *The Lakes of England. Illustrated with Eighteen Coloured Etchings.*

1870   James Payn, *The Lakes in Sunshine: Being Photographic and Other Pictures of the Lake District of Cumberland.*

1872   H. I. Jenkinson, *Practical Guide to the English Lake District* [1872–93].

1873   *Shaw's Tourist's Picturesque Guide to the English Lakes with an Introduction by the Late Poet Laureate Wordsworth.*

1875   W. J. Loftie, *English Lake Scenery from Original Drawings by T. L. Rowbotham . . .*

c.1878 *A Description of the Scenery of the District of the Lakes by William Wordsworth.*

1878   William Knight, *The English Lake District as Interpreted in the Poems of Wordsworth.*

1878   Payne Jennings, *The English Lakes* [photographically illustrated].

1880   M. J. B. Baddeley, *The Thorough Guide to the English Lake District* [1880–1921].

1880   Edwin Waugh, *In the Lake Country.*

1880   A. F. Lydon, *English Lake Scenery, Illustrated with a Series of Coloured Plates.*

1884   *Ward and Lock's Pictorial and Historical Guide to the English Lakes, their Scenery and Associations, with an Introduction by the Poet Wordsworth* [1884–c.1894].

1887   Harry Goodwin and William Knight, *Through the Wordsworth Country.*

1891   J. Garnett (publisher), *Guide to the Highways of the Lake District of England*.

1891   (27 July) Dove Cottage opened for visitors.

1894   A. W. Rumney, *Cycling in the English Lake District*.

1896   M. J. B. Baddeley, *Black's Shilling Guide to the English Lakes*. 20th edn.

1898   *Ward and Lock's Pictorial and Descriptive Guide to the English Lakes* [1898–*c*.1950].

1901   A. G. Bradley, *Highways and Byways in the Lake District*.

1902   *Pearson's Gossipy Guide to the English Lakes and Neighbouring Districts*.

1902   W. G. Collingwood, *The Lake Counties*...

1902   F. G. Brabant, *The English Lakes. Illustrated by Edmund H. New*.

1905   W. T. Palmer, *The English Lakes* [with illustrations in colour by Alfred Heaton Cooper].

1906   Ernest De Selincourt, ed., *Guide to the Lakes* [reprint 1926, 1970, 1977].

1912   Ashley P. Abraham, *Beautiful Lakeland*, photograph by G. P. Abraham.

1913   George Dixon Abraham, *Motor Ways in Lakeland*.

1922   *Burrow's Guide to the Lake District* (1922–39).

1929   James Baikie, *Black's Guide to the English Lakes*.

1930   W. T. Palmer, *The English Lakes: Their Topographical, Historical and Literary Landmarks*.

1933   H. H. Symonds, *Walking in the Lake District*.

1937   Maxwell Fraser, *Companion into Lakeland* [1937–73].

1937   Arthur Mee, *Lake Counties*.

1948   J. W. Lucas, introduction. *A Guide through the District of the Lakes*.

1951   W. M. Merchant, introduction. *A Guide through the District of the Lakes*.

1951   The Lake District National Park founded.

EXPLANATORY NOTES

The explanatory notes draw on EdS, *PrW*, and *RCDE*, with further material supplied by the present editor. Additional abbreviations in the following notes:

DW	Dorothy Wordsworth
'Epistle'	'Epistle to Sir George Beaumont' (1842)
Ex	*The Excursion* (1814)
Guide	*Guide through the District of the Lakes* (1835)
HG	*Home at Grasmere*
KWRL	*Kendal and Windermere Railway* (London, 1845), reproduced in Appendix II
MW	Mary (Hutchinson) Wordsworth
PM (1837)	'English Lakes', *Penny Magazine*, vol. 6 (1837)
Pr1805	*The Prelude* (1805)
Pr1850	*The Prelude* (1850)
STC	Samuel Taylor Coleridge
S2SV	Section II of *Select Views in Cumberland, Westmoreland and Lancashire* (1810), reproduced in Appendix I
W	William Wordsworth
Waggoner	*The Waggoner* (1819).

References to guidebooks and travel articles are shown with the author's (or publisher's) names and/or short titles followed by the date of publication in parentheses. Full details of these can be found in Appendix IV.

A GUIDE THROUGH THE DISTRICT OF THE LAKES IN THE NORTH OF ENGLAND (1835)

DIRECTIONS AND INFORMATION FOR THE TOURIST

'Directions and Information for the Tourist' roughly corresponds to Section II of *Select Views* (1810), although much revised and reduced. See Appendix I.

    4 *through Yorkshire*: in the summers of 1788 and 1789, W wandered extensively in Yorkshire, Lancashire, and Dovedale (*CEY* 84, 86, 93). See *Pr1805*, vi. 208–10: 'In summer among distant nooks I roved — | Dovedale, or Yorkshire dales, or through bye-tracts | Of my own native region . . .'.

    4 *great north road*: the main road from London to Edinburgh via York.

4 *this route*: W took this northern route from Greta Bridge over Stainmore to Penrith when he travelled to the Lake District with STC, Oct.–Nov. 1799 (*CEY* 275).

the great fall of the Tees above Middleham: Middleham, a Yorkshire town, is mistaken for Middleton-on-Teesdale, above which is the great fall of High Force (Oda 424–5).

The second road: this follows W's and DW's route, Dec. 1799, from Sockburn in County Durham to their new home at Grasmere. They retraced the route, Oct. 1802, when they took W's newly married wife MW to Dove Cottage. Cf. *HG* (MS B), 218–23: 'Bleak season was it, turbulent and bleak, | When hitherward we journeyed, . . . | Paced the long vales—. . . | Wensley's long Vale and Sedbergh's naked heights'.

5 *the other by Otley . . . the Abbey and grounds*: W and DW took this route, in July 1807, to Bolton Abbey by the River Wharf (*LMY* i. 158).

the banks of the Wharf . . . Burnsall . . . Gordale . . . Malham Cove: after visiting Bolton Abbey in July 1807, W and DW walked along the Wharf to Burnsall, from where they visited Gordale Scar and Malham Cove (*LMY* i. 158). See W's sonnets, 'Malham Cove' and 'Gordale'.

the bridge over the Lune: Devil's Bridge, a medieval three-arched stone bridge at Kirkby Lonsdale.

looking at the Vale of Lune from the Church-yard: Turner painted the view from the churchyard of St Mary's in Kirkby Lonsdale, *c*.1818, and included it in his 'History of Richmondshire' (1822).

The journey . . . through Lancashire: Hudson (1842) here recommends two railway routes for approaching the Lake District: from Preston to Lancaster and from Preston to Fleetwood. Hudson (1846) advised tourists to take the Lancaster and Carlisle Railway (opened 1846) as far as Kendal, and then to board the Kendal and Windermere Railway (opened 20 April 1847) as the route that held 'the least danger and interruption' (p. 3).

crossing the Sands: at low tide it is possible to cross Morecambe Bay on foot. Before the coastal railway was completed this was the shortest route to the Lake District, as evoked in *Pr1850*, x. 562–8: 'all the plain | Lay spotted with a variegated crowd | Of vehicles and travellers, horse and foot, | Wading beneath the conduct of their guide | In loose procession through the shallow stream | Of inland waters; the great sea meanwhile | Heaved at safe distance, far retired'. The passage is quoted in Collingwood (1902). See also note to p. 9 ('The Stranger . . .').

one view mentioned by Gray and Mason: a view of Crook o' Lune, a bend in the River Lune near Caton, visited by Gray, 12 Oct. 1769. The view was painted by Joseph Wilkinson and more famously by Turner: 'Crook of Lune, looking towards Hornby Castle' (*c*.1816–18).

West's Guide: Thomas West's *Guide to the Lakes* was first published in 1778 and after West's death in 1779, William Cockin revised it with additional material, including Gray's journal. West's continued to be updated, reaching the eleventh edition in 1821, and was the most popular guide to the Lake District in the late eighteenth and early nineteenth century.

6 *the viaducts*: the five-arched Wetheral Viaduct over the River Eden and the seven-arched Corby Viaduct over the Corby Beck, built in 1831–4 with local sandstone for the Newcastle and Carlisle Railway. See note to p.143 ('STEAMBOATS . . .').

a fine piece of monumental sculpture by Nollekens: commissioned by Henry Howard, the monument was created by Joseph Nollekens (1737–1823) for Lady Howard, who had died young. See W's sonnet: 'Monument of Mrs Howard (by Nollekens), in Wetheral Church, near Corby, on the Banks of Eden' (*IF* 159).

its eastern side: for W's schoolboy visits to the eastern shore of Windermere, see *Pr1850*, ii. 138–64, inserted in Loftie (1875) and Jennings (1878) at length. The following two lines are quoted in Hudson (1853, 1859), *Shaw's* (1873), *Ward & Lock's* (1884) to introduce Bowness: 'Midway on long Winander's eastern shore, | Within the crescent of a pleasant bay' (138–9).

the Station near the Ferry: Claife viewing station (recommended by West's guide), on the west shore of Windermere, just above the ferry landing. In 1799 the Revd W. Braithwaite, W's model for the hermit in 'Lines left upon a Seat in a Yew-tree', built a two-storeyed octagonal summerhouse here, which was then purchased and remodelled by J. C. Curwen. The upper room offered panoramic views of Windermere through coloured glass panels (*PrW* ii. 429; Matthew Hyde and Nikolaus Pevsner, *The Buildings of England: Cumbria* (New Haven: Yale University Press, 2010), p. 603). Southey in 1807 complained that it was a 'ridiculous edifice' with a banqueting-room 'hung with prints, representing the finest similar landscapes in Great Britain and other countries, none of the representations exceeding in beauty the real prospect before us' (*Letters from England,* Letter XLI). Although it had fallen into disuse by the end of the nineteenth century, the viewing tower is now restored and open to the public. See also *S2SV*, p. 106.

suffered much from Larch plantations: cf. p. 54.

the proprietor, Mr Curwen: Henry Curwen, son of the politician John Christian Curwen.

7 *The Islands may be explored . . . the peaceful Lake*: quoted in Ford (1839). Cf. p. 30 ('There is a beautiful cluster . . . be forgotten'). The river referred to is the Brathay, flowing from Little Langdale. The 'stillness and solemnity' of boating on the lake at evening is evocatively described in *Pr1850*, ii. 164–74, quoted in Loftie (1875).

the lane that leads from Ambleside to Skelgill: on the lane from Ambleside to Troutbeck are situated High Skelghyll and Low Skelghyll, from which pleasant views of Ambleside, Little Langdale, and Lake Windermere can be enjoyed. See Green (1819), i. 178–80.

7 *up the stream under Loughrigg Fell . . . Grasmere Lake*: see note to p. 110 ('turn to a Gate').

Mr Green's Guide to the Lakes: *The Tourist's New Guide* (1819).

8 *'Behold! . . . gladder place'*: *Ex*, ii. 347–68. This passage was quoted first in Baines (1830), with this introduction: 'So completely secluded from the world is this remarkable recess of the mountains, that it might be the chosen abode of a hermit. Wordsworth has made it the residence of his Solitary, and has painted the scene with such perfect fidelity, that I need only copy the passage—observing that he and his friend approached Blea tarn from Great Langdale' (p. 95). Since then, the passage (partly or entirely) was quoted in many guidebooks, including Rose (1832), *Leigh's* (1832), Wordsworth's own *Guide* (1835), Ford (1839), *Black's* (1841), *Onwhyn's* (1841), Mackay (1846), *Sylvan's* (1847), Mogridge (1849), Pyne (1859), Payn (1859, 1867), J. M. Wilson (1859), *Murray's* (1866), Matthew (1866), Topham (1869), Jenkinson (1872), Garnett (1891), *Pearson's* (1902), and Brabant (1902). For a prose description of the place, see *S2SV*, p. 110.

9 *The Stranger, from the moment . . . peacefully led*: this passage was preserved from *Select Views* and retained through Hudson (1842, 1843). Quoted in Martineau (1858). *Black's* (1841) and Waugh (1861, 1880) quote from Felicia Hemans's letter about W's approval of her route across the sands: 'the lake scenery, he says, is never seen to such advantage as after the passage of what he calls its majestic barrier'. *Sylvan's* (1847) recommends the route, while Hudson (1846) advises tourists to take the steamboat from Fleetwood, as crossing the sands is 'somewhat dangerous and objectionable' (p. 3). The 'cluster of mountains' to be seen from the Sands is depicted in *Pr1850*, x. 516–23, and quoted in H. H. Symonds, *Walking in the Lake District* (1933): 'beneath a genial sun, | With distant prospect among gleams of sky | And clouds, and intermingling mountain tops, | In one inseparable glory clad . . .'.

go to the Vale of the Duddon, over Walna Scar: W gave a more detailed explanation in *S2SV* (p. 105). Later, he expanded this description of the Valley and incorporated part of it into the long note to the sonnets XVII and XVIII of *The River Duddon* (1820). In turn, Hudson's editions (1842–59) extracted the following from W's note to the sonnets:

> This recess, towards the close of September, when the after-grass of the meadows is still of a fresh green, with the leaves of many of the trees faded, but perhaps none fallen, is truly enchanting. At a point elevated enough to shew the various objects in the valley, and not so high as to diminish their importance, the stranger will instinctively halt. . . . Russet and craggy hills, of bold and varied outline, surround the level valley which is besprinkled with grey rocks plumed with birch trees. A few home-steads are interspersed in some places, peeping out from among the rocks like hermitages, whose [site] has been chosen for the benefit of sunshine as well as shelter; . . . *Time, in most cases, and nature every where,*

have given a sanctity to the humble works of man, that are scattered over this
peaceful retirement.... (*Poems* iii. 783–4, my italics).

This passage was also quoted at length in *PM (1837)*, *Onwhyn's* (1841),
Blanchard (1852), and *Murray's* (1866). The italicized sentence is quoted in
the 2017 document nominating the Lake District for a World Heritage Site.

10 *a Roman fortress*: Hardknott Fort, founded under Hadrian's rule in the
second century to guard the pass and provide a base for transporting goods
between Ambleside and Ravenglass (Lindop 215). *Murray's* (1866) and
Loftie (1875) quote the following lines from *The River Duddon*: 'into
silence hush the timorous flocks, | That slept so calmly while the nightly
dew | Moisten'd each fleece, beneath the twinkling stars: | These couch'd
'mid that lone Camp on Hardknot's height, | Whose Guardians bent the
knee to Jove and Mars' (XVII, 7–11).

series of Sonnets upon the Duddon . . . Notes: see note to p. 9 ('go to the Vale . . .').

crossing the Lake by the Ferry: returning from Cambridge for his first sum-
mer vacation W got off the coach at Kendal, walked to Bowness, and took
the ferry across Windermere, heading for Hawkshead. See *Pr1805*, iv. 1–9:
'A pleasant sight it was when . . . | . . . as from a rampart's edge, | I over-
looked the bed of Windermere. | I bounced down the hill, shouting amain
| A lusty summons to the farther shore | For the old ferryman; and when
he came | I did not step into the well-known boat | Without a cordial
welcome'.

a passage of the brook: Stock Ghyll, which runs through Ambleside and
joins the river Rothay. See *S2SV*, p. 108.

the Nook also might be visited . . . for the pencil: Scandale Beck, a mountain
stream running parallel with Stock Ghyll, flows into the river Rothay.
Green (1819) and *Leigh's* (1832) remark that the best among numerous
small waterfalls is the one between Nook-end Bridge (Low Sweden
Bridge) and Scandale Bridge (where the present beck crosses the A591).
For more details, see *S2SV* (p. 109).

11 *A foot road passing behind Rydal Mount . . . to Grasmere*: the 'Coffin Path'
between Rydal and Town End, Grasmere, a favourite walk for W's family.
See 'To the Clouds', 64–6: 'An humble walk | Here is my Body doomed to
tread, this Path, | A little hoary line and faintly traced'. On this path, just
behind Rydal Mount, is a spring called Nab Well, used by W's family.

the high road: there are three roads connecting Rydal and Grasmere on the
north side of the lakes: the upper 'foot road' (the 'Coffin Path', see previ-
ous note), the middle 'horse road' (the old high road), and the new 'main
road' along the lake shore, respectively labelled by Thomas Arnold as 'Old
Corruption', 'Bit-by-bit Reform' and 'Radical Reform' (W. Knight 62).
Hudson (1842) explains as follows, drawing on *PM (1837)*: 'Between
Rydal and Grasmere the high road formerly ran winding among, and over
a succession of knolls; and being half hidden in its serpentine course,
afforded a series of exquisite views, without deforming this lovely valley.

But the steepness of the hills was ill suited to the convenience of increasing traffic, and about twelve years ago a new road was made, which runs close along the lower end of Grasmere, and is fenced from it by a long, straight, odious stone wall, which offends the eye, and cuts the sweetest part of the landscape with its rectilinear deformity.' Benjamin the Waggoner toiled up 'Bit-by-bit Reform': 'Now he leaves the lower ground, | And up the craggy hill ascending | Many a stop and stay he makes, | Many a breathing fit he takes;— | Steep the way and wearisome, | Yet all the while his whip is dumb!' (*Waggoner*, i. 34–9). The new road made journeys between Ambleside and Grasmere considerably quicker, although W regretted the change. See note to p. 142 ('before the new road . . .').

On the old high road is the Wishing Gate, of which Hudson (1842) explains: 'a gate, which, time out of mind, has been called the Wishing Gate', drawing on W's head-note to his own poem, 'The Wishing Gate'. When *Black's* (1841) reproduced the poem in full, many other guides followed it, including Atkinson (1847), J. M. Wilson (1859), *Murray's* (1866), Jenkinson (1872), and *Ward & Lock's* (1884). The gate became a popular tourist site in the late nineteenth century.

11 *two small Inns*: The Red Lion (now called The Inn at Grasmere) and The Swan.

the Church: Hudson (1853) quotes here a popular passage, portraying St Oswald's at Grasmere:

> Not framed to nice proportions was the Pile,
> But large and massy; for duration built.
> With pillars crowded, and the roof upheld
> By naked rafters intricately crossed,
> Like leafless underboughs, in some thick grove,
> All withered by the depth of shade above.   (*Ex*, v. 148–53)

After Horne (1816), this verse passage (with slight alterations) was extracted in several guidebooks, including Robinson (1819), Fielding (1821), Rose (1832), Ford (1839), *Black's* (1841), J. M. Wilson (1859), and Waugh (1880), and referenced in *Pearson's* (1902).

The direct road from Grasmere to Keswick: this road is vividly described in *Waggoner*, featuring Dove Cottage, the Swan Inn, Helm Crag, Cherry Tree Inn, and Wythburn Church and quoted in many Victorian guidebooks. The passage depicting Helm Crag's conspicuous crest was popular: 'The Astrologer, sage Sydrophel, | . . . the Ancient Woman: | Cowering beside her rifted cell, . . . | Dread pair, that, spite of wind and weather, | Still sit upon Helm-crag together!' (i. 171–9). See *Black's* (1841), *Sylvan's* (1847), Mogridge (1849), J. M. Wilson (1859), *Murray's* (1866), E. L. Linton (1864), Payn (1859, 1867), Jenkinson (1872), and Garnett (1891). Hudson (1842–59) comments that '[t]he shattered apex of this mountain [Helm Crag] as seen from certain points in the valley, bears a striking resemblance to a lion couchant, with a lamb lying at the end of his nose; and to an old woman cowering', and extracts the following lines from 'To Joanna': 'The rock, like something starting from a sleep, | Took up the Lady's voice, and laugh'd again: | That ancient Woman seated on Helm-crag | Was ready with her cavern; Hammer-Scar, | And the tall Steep of Silver-How sent forth | A noise of laughter . . .' (54–65). These lines were quoted in Robinson (1819), *Leigh's* (1832), Rose (1832), *PM (1837)*, Mackay (1846), and Pyne (1859).

proceed with the Lake on the right: here W recommends taking the western road along Thirlmere. Likewise, Mackay (1846) remarks that Helvellyn should be viewed from the west shore of the lake. When the lake was turned into a reservoir at the end of the nineteenth century, the western road was rebuilt and became popular with cyclists.

if on foot, the Tourist may follow the stream . . . a mile: for a more detailed direction, see *S2SV* (p. 111).

12 *Keswick Lake*: Derwentwater. West's guide offers eight 'stations' for viewing the lake, of which five are named here: Crow Park, Stable Hill, Vicarage at Crosthwaite, Latrigg, and Castle Crag.

following the Watenlath stream downwards to the Cataract of Lodore: for a more detailed direction, see *S2SV* (p. 112).

Solway Frith and the Scotch Mountains: in 'At the Grave of Burns, 1803' W describes a view across Solway Firth. See note to p. 135 ('He lived many . . .')

BORROWDALE: see *S2SV*, pp. 112–13 and note to p. 113.

Bowder-stone: a huge boulder in Borrowdale, about a mile south of Grange Bridge. Gilpin (1786) called it 'Boother-stone', describing it as 'an independent creation', lying 'in a sort of diagonal position; overshadowing a space, sufficient to shelter a troop of horse' (i. 194). It was a popular tourist attraction in the late eighteenth and nineteenth centuries to the extent that a ladder was installed for tourists to climb. For W's interest in huge stones, see p. 28 ('Masses of rock . . . stranded ship'), p. 32 ('huge stones . . . came thither'), and *Ex*, iii. 53–6: 'A Mass of rock, resembling, as it lay | Right at the foot of that moist precipice, | A stranded Ship, with keel upturned,—that rests | Fearless of winds and waves'. When Ford (1839) quoted this passage in reference to the Bowder Stone many guidebooks followed, including *Black's* (1841), Mackay (1846), *Sylvan's* (1847), Atkinson (1847), Mogridge (1849), Blanchard (1852), J. M. Wilson (1859), and Brabant (1902), while Martineau (1855) and E. L. Linton (1864) denied the association. Jenkinson (1872) remarks that the lines 'describing a large stone in Little Langdale Valley, are by many writers erroneously thought to refer to this Bowder Stone' (p. 145). In the draft guide of 1811–12 W has 'the huge mass of Bowder Stone, lying like a stranded Vessel' (*PrW* ii. 345); so he may have had an image of Bowder Stone in mind when he wrote the *Excursion* passage, which is also quoted in Hudson (1853) as a reference to the Bowder Stone.

13 *Mr. Marshall's woods*: Lanthwaite Wood, along the east shore of Crummock, planted by John Marshall, the husband of Jane Pollard, an old friend of DW (*PrW* ii. 385).

13 *a fine view of the Lake of Ennerdale*: cf. *S2SV* (p. 114).

Wastwater: for a more detailed description of Wastwater, arguably by DW, see *S2SV* (p. 115).

14 *The Church-yard Yew-tree still survives at Old Church*: 'Old Church' refers to the house at Old Church Bay on the north-west shore of Ullswater. There had been a thirteenth-century church on this site, with a yew tree that was said to be even more ancient. Marauding Scots destroyed the church in the fifteenth century but the tree still survives.

a New Chapel: All Saints' Church, built in Watermillock in the fifteenth century, was replaced by the present church in 1881.

Bassenthwaite Chapel: St Bega's Church, dating from pre-Norman times, restored 1874.

the Dacre, or Dacor . . . Venerable Bede: Bede (*c.*673–735), often called 'the Father of English History', mentions the Dacre in *Ecclesiastical History of the English People*. At that time, Bede reports, the stream had a monastery beside it (*RCDE*).

15 *a powerful Brook*: the river Airey.

a silent Tarn: Red Tarn. *PM (1837)* quoted from W's 'Fidelity' the following lines: 'It was a Cove, a huge Recess, | That keeps till June December's snow; | A lofty Precipice in front, | A silent Tarn below' (17–20); these lines were in turn quoted in Hudson (1842–59).

16 *the fate of a young man . . . its master*: the accident happened in April 1805. The fate of Charles Gough and his faithful dog is treated in W's 'Fidelity' and Scott's 'Helvellyn'. Several lines of 'Fidelity' were quoted in *Black's* (1841), Mogridge (1849), Hudson (1853, 1859), J. M. Wilson (1859), Jenkinson (1872), *Shaw's* (1873), and *Ward & Lock's* (1884).

the next considerable stream: Deepdale Beck.

Grisdale . . . Helvellyn . . . Deep-dale . . . Fairfield . . . Brotherswater . . . Dove Crag: these place names are mentioned in *Pr1805*, viii. 228–44, which tells of a shepherd and his son searching for a sheep lost in this neighbourhood (*PrW* ii. 387). 'Written in March' was composed on Cow Bridge over Goldrill Beck, at the foot of Brothers Water (*CMY* 160–1; Lindop 256).

passed Hartsop Hall, a Stream soon after issues . . . the wildness of the scenery: quoted in *PM (1837)* and Mackay (1846). The 'Stream' refers to Hartsop (Dovedale) Beck. It was above Hartsop Hall that in Sept. 1807 W and MW saw the magnificent vision of mists, vapours, and light that inspired the scene in *Ex*, ii. 859–95 (*IF* 82, *CMY* 362). See note to p. 71.

one of which: Goldrill Beck.

The other: Howegrain Beck.

17 *About 200 yards . . . the public road*: Thrang Crag, also known as 'Wordsworth's Seat', is a boulder with steps cut in it, situated on the north-east shore of Rydal Water. In 1855 Nathaniel Hawthorne sat here, fancying that 'Wordsworth has doubtless sat there hundreds of times'

('A Passage from Hawthorne's English Note-Books' (1867), p. 16). By the 1860s the rock was believed to be where W had composed many poems. *Shaw's* (1873) slightly changed W's text as follows: 'the road is cut through a low wooded rock, called Thrang Crag. The Top of it is reached by a few steps cut in the rock' (p. 29); *Ward & Lock's* (1884) made a clearer statement: 'the road is cut through a low wooded rock, called *Wordsworth's Seat*. The top of it is reached . . .' (p. 131). Wordsworth's Seat was a popular tourist site until the Second World War.

DESCRIPTION OF THE SCENERY OF THE LAKES

SECTION FIRST: VIEW OF THE COUNTRY AS FORMED BY NATURE

19 *spokes from the nave of a wheel*: the 'wheel' analogy was mentioned in *Sylvan's* (1847), Mogridge (1849), J. M. Wilson (1859), Rose (1858), and *Ward & Lock's* (1884). E. L. Linton (1864) remarks that it is 'a simile often used, but it is too good to be discarded' (p. 52).

a short and narrow æstuary . . . Ravenglass: the rivers Irt, Mite, and Esk meet here, forming what STC termed a 'Trident' in a narrow channel cut off from the sea by dunes (*CL* ii. 858). In Roman times Ravenglass was an important port.

20 *the ruins of the castle*: the medieval castle on a mound above the River Ehen, the setting of W's 'The Horn of Egremont Castle'.

four or five miles: *PM (1837)* notes that 'Mr Wordsworth has underestimated the distance—read eight or nine' (p. 242).

from elegance and richness . . . grandeur and sublimity: cf. 'it will appear to most advantage . . . humbler excitement' (pp. 71–2).

21 *in the vale of Winandermere, if the spectator looks for . . . splendour*: quoted in *PM (1837)*, *Land We Live In* (1847), Blanchard (1852), Rose (1858), and Lydon (1880). W's description of light diffused from the sun setting behind mountains was often referenced by guidebooks. For instance, Rose (1832) quoted from *Ex*, ix. 592–608: 'rays of light— | Now suddenly diverging from the orb | Retired behind the mountain tops or veiled | By the dense air—shot upwards to the crown | Of the blue firmament . . .'. Jennings (1878) extracted from *Pr1850*, viii. 463–75: 'I watched the golden beams of light | Flung from the setting sun, . . . | "Dear native Region, wheresoe'er shall close | My mortal course, there will I think on you; . . . | Even as this setting sun (albeit the Vale | Is no where touched by one memorial gleam) | Doth with the fond remains of his last power | Still linger, and a farewell lustre sheds | On the dear mountain-tops where first he rose"'.

22 *the MOUNTAINS*: W's geological description of Lakeland mountains in the ensuing three paragraphs was excerpted in guidebooks and travel articles, including *The Mirror* (1835), *Saturday Magazine* (1837), and Mogridge (1849).

23 *In the ridge that divides Eskdale from Wasdale ... a dove's neck*: W was inter-
ested in geology and mineralogy and asked Adam Sedgwick, geologist
of Dent, to contribute geological essays to Hudson's enlarged edition of
the *Guide*. For the image of 'a dove's neck', see note to p. 115 ('This
Water ...'). W also describes the colours of the rock at Hardraw Scar as
'dove colour'd' in his letter to STC, Dec. 1799 (*LEY* 280).

The brilliant and various colours ... decay: for W's admiration for autumnal
colours, see pp. 69–70 ('the six weeks following ... cottages') and note.

the mountains are of height sufficient ... aërial hues: for the effect of distance
on the appearance of mountains, see *Ex*, ii. 96–100: 'mountains stern and
desolate; | But in the majesty of distance now | Set off, and to our ken
appearing fair | Of aspect, with aerial softness clad, | And beautified with
morning's purple beams'. These lines are cited in Baines (1830) and Ford
(1839) in reference to Langdale.

the effect indeed of mist or haze ... magic: for the magical effects of vapours,
see also p. 35 ('Vapours exhaling ... departed ancestors'). For a visionary
landscape created by mists, see *Ex*, ii. 859–904, partly quoted in note to
p. 71. See also *Ex*, iv. 521–5: 'the Mists | Flying, and rainy Vapours, call
out Shapes | And Phantoms from the crags and solid earth | As fast as
a Musician scatters sounds | Out of an instrument'.

24 *the memorandum-book of a friend*: the friend is STC and the ensuing quota-
tion draws on his notebook entry for Friday, 5 Jan. 1804. Quoted in
Mogridge (1849).

25 *a single cottage, or cluster of cottages ... upon their sides*: cf. the MS poem
inserted at p. 46. See also *Ex*, v. 87–9: 'Fair Dwellings, single or in social
knots; | Some scattered o'er the level, others perched | On the hill sides,
a cheerful quiet scene'. This passage was a popular quote; see Fielding
(1821), Ford (1839), *Black's* (1841), Mackay (1846), Jackson (1847), and
J. M. Wilson (1859).

26 *contemplated with that placid and quiet ... no current*: W's fascination with
still water can be seen at p. 36 ('while looking on the unruffled waters ...
purer element') and in *Pr1805*, ii. 176–80: 'the calm | And dead still
water lay upon my mind | Even with a weight of pleasure, and the sky, |
Never before so beautiful, sank down | Into my heart and held me like
a dream'. See also the simile in *Pr1805*, iv. 247–61: 'As one who hangs
down-bending from the side | Of a slow-moving boat upon the breast |
Of a still water ...'.

expressing also and making visible ... the atmosphere: cf. p. 79 ('the fine daz-
zling trembling ... endless variety'). *Ex*, vii. 426–8 captures the lake sur-
face responding to the winds: 'When stormy winds | Were working the
broad bosom of the lake | Into a thousand thousand sparkling waves ...'.
These lines are quoted in Horne (1816), Robinson (1819), and Rose
(1832). See also *An Evening Walk* (1836): 'Gleams that upon the lake's still
bosom fall; | Soft o'er the surface creep those lustres pale | Tracking the
motions of the fitful gale' (303–5).

The visible scene ... lake!: 'There was a Boy', 21–5 (later incorporated in *Pr1805*, v. 409–13). This verse quotation, with its preceding prose explanation, was largely preserved from *S2SV*. Extracting the passage from the second edition (1820) of the *Guide*, *The Mirror* (1835) describes Rydal Water and Rydal Mount. Mogridge (1849) quotes the prose part and *Land We Live In* (1847) quotes the poem.

several of the largest, such as Winandermere ... a magnificent river: cf. *Pr1850*, iv. 5–6: 'I overlooked the bed of Windermere, | Like a vast river, stretching in the sun'. These lines were quoted in Hudson (1853–9), J. M. Wilson (1859), *Shaw's* (1873), Loftie (1875), Jennings (1878), and *Ward & Lock's* (1884).

28 *Masses of rock ... like stranded ships*: see p. 32 ('huge stones and masses of rock ... came thither') and note to p. 12 ('Bowder-stone').

water-lilies ... heaving upon the wave: cf. 'Elegiac Stanzas. 1824': 'Or lily heaving with the wave | That feeds it and defends' (44–5).

the birds that enliven the waters: for W's fondness for water birds, see 'Farewell Lines', 13–16, describing 'a pair of herons' upon 'a rocky islet ... [d]rying their feathers in the sun'; and *An Evening Walk* (1793), 301–8 capturing a 'dabbl[ing]' duck, a swan 'stirr[ing] the reeds', and a heron 'darting his long neck'. See also 'The Wild Duck's Nest', 'Lines Left on a Seat in a Yew-tree', and the verse inserted at p. 29.

29 *wild swans*: cf. *HG* (MS B), which features swans in the verse paragraph (lines 322–57) beginning: 'But two are missing—two, a lonely pair | Of milk-white Swans'. See also *An Evening Walk* (1793), 199–240.

goldings: W seems to be referring to goldeneyes, a species of migratory northern duck.

Mark how the feather'd tenants ... and rest!: first published in the 1823 fourth edition of the *Guide*, these lines generally correspond to *HG* (MS D), 203–29. Although the poem remained unpublished in W's lifetime, these lines were published under the title of 'Water-fowl' in *Poetical Works* (1827). Quoted in Mogridge (1849).

30 *a beautiful cluster on Winandermere*: three islands are featured in *Pr1850*, ii. 55–65, describing boys enjoying boat racing on summer afternoons. Quoted in *Ward & Lock's* (1884). See also *An Evening Walk* (1836), 9–10: 'Winander sleeps | 'Mid clustering islets ....'.

the solitary green island of Grasmere: this island appears in several of W's poems: 'Where peace to Grasmere's lonely island leads' (*An Evening Walk*, 1793, 9); 'Its one green Island and its winding shores' (*HG*, MS B, 138); 'Grasmere's silent Lake | And one green Island gleam between the stems | Of the close firs' ('When first I journey'd hither, to a home', 98–100). See also 'Inscription for the House (an Outhouse) on the Island at Grasmere'.

'The haunt of cormorants ... clang': misquoted from Milton, *Paradise Lost*, xi. 835: 'The haunt of Seals and orcs, and sea-mew's clang'.

the Floating . . . the Buoyant, Island: an island seemingly appearing and dis-
appearing at irregular intervals attracted the attention of early writers on the
Lake District, including Hutchinson (1774), Clarke (1787), Green (1819),
and Otley (1823) (*PrW* ii. 395). DW wrote a poem, 'Floating Island', included
in W's volume of 1842. W himself wrote about it in *Pr1805*, iii. 340–3: 'A
floating island, an amphibious thing, | Unsound, of spungy texture, yet
withal | Not wanting a fair face of water-weeds | And pleasant flowers'.

30 *'fas habeas . . . natantes'*: from Walter Savage Landor's 'Catillus and Saila'
(1820), 133–4, meaning 'You really ought to visit the fields of Tivoli, and
the lake of Albunea, with its leafy floating islands' (*RCDE*).

'vivi lacus': Virgil, *Georgics*, ii. 469. The phrase is used in Gilpin (1786) in
a similar context (i. 95).

31 *Carver . . . Erie or Ontario*: Jonathan Carver (1732–80), a popular American
travel writer, actually described Lake Superior, not Lake Erie or Ontario
(EdS 176–7). For the image of a boat floating on pure water, see
'To H. C. Six Years Old': 'Thou Faery Voyager! that dost float | In such
clear water, that thy Boat | May rather seem | To brood on air than on an
earthly stream; | Suspended in a stream as clear as sky, | Where earth and
heaven do make one imagery' (5–10).

TARNS: the ensuing explanation about the role of tarns in the economy of
nature is referenced by Ford (1839), Mogridge (1849), and *Murray's* (1866).

32 *the water where the sun is not shining upon it*: Scale (or Threlkeld) Tarn,
situated deeply among crags high up on Blencathra, is rumoured to be
a place where the sun never shines and stars are visible at noon-day.
Many guidebooks referred to this saying. See also Scott's 'The Bridal of
Triermain'.

huge stones and masses of rock . . . thither: cf. 'Resolution and Independence':
'As a huge Stone is sometimes seen to lie | Couch'd on the bald top of an
eminence; | Wonder to all who do the same espy | By what means it could
thither come, and whence' (64–7). See also p. 28 ('Masses of rock . . . like
stranded ships'), the Bowder-stone at p. 12 and note.

'There, sometimes does a leaping fish . . . sounding blast': from 'Fidelity',
25–31. These lines are quoted in *PM (1837)*, Ford (1839), *Murray's*
(1866), and Jenkinson (1872).

33 *The water is perfectly pellucid . . . blue gravel . . . cerulean . . . Derwent and
Duddon*: see p. 73. Cf. *The River Duddon*: 'In this pellucid Current slaked
his thirst' (VIII, 3); 'Thou, of placid mien, | Innocuous as a firstling of
a flock, | And countenanced like a soft cerulean sky' (XX, 8–10); 'A sky-
blue stone, within this sunless cleft, | Is of the very foot-marks unbereft |
Which tiny Elves impress'd' (XI, 2–4). See also *Ecclesiastical Sketches*,
Part I: 'I, who descended with glad step to chase | Cerulean Duddon from
his cloud-fed spring' (I, 1–2). For W's love for the River Derwent, see
Pr1805, i. 271–89: 'Was it for this | That one, the fairest of all rivers, loved
| To blend his murmurs with my nurse's song . . .'. See also 'To the River
Derwent': 'Among the mountains were we nursed, loved stream! | Thou

near the Eagle's nest—within brief sail, | I, of his bold wing floating on the gale, | Where thy deep voice could lull me!' (1–4).

34 *the sycamore . . . with the fir . . . screen their dwellings*: the image of a shelter- ing sycamore and fir is celebrated in *Ex*, vii. 631–9: 'Yon household Fir, | A guardian planted to fence off the blast, | But towering high the roof above, as if | Its humble destination were forgot; | That Sycamore, which annually holds | Within its shade, as in a stately tent | On all sides open to the fanning breeze, | A grave assemblage, seated while they shear | The fleece-incumbered flock'. See also pp. 62–3 ('The Scotch fir . . . the lighter trees').

The neighbourhood of Rydal . . . distinguished: cf. the ancient trees in the upper Rydal Park mentioned in 'To M. H.', 1: 'Our walk was far among the ancient trees' (*IF* 19). For the 'havoc' made in Rydal forest, see p. 109.

the broom that spreads . . . golden blossoms: cf. 'To Joanna', 38–50: '"Twas that delightful season, when the broom, | Full flower'd, and visible on every steep, | Along the copses runs in veins of gold . . .'. These lines are quoted in J. M. Wilson (1859) to describe the River Rothay.

35 *'skiey influences'*: *Measure for Measure*, III. i. 9.

The rain here comes down heartily . . . bright weather: W's positive account of Lakeland weather was welcomed by guidebooks, including James Johnson (1834), Ford (1839), and *Murray's* (1866). Ford (1839) repeats this passage almost verbatim, quoting lines from *Ex* describing mountain streams after rain: 'Descending from the region of the clouds | And starting from the hollows of the earth | More multitudinous every moment—rend | Their way before them' (iv. 528–31). These lines are also quoted in Rose (1832). To demonstrate positive aspects of Lakeland rain, Payn (1867) quotes the opening lines of 'Resolution and Independence' (1–14).

Days of unsettled weather . . . to the ear: in her review of De Selincourt's edition of the *Guide* (1906) Virginia Woolf quotes this passage as an example of W's combination of 'obstinate truth and fervent imagination'. In asso- ciation with the passage, Ford (1839) extracts the following lines from *Ex*: 'the clouds, | The mist, the shadows, light of golden suns, | Motions of moonlight, all come thither—touch, | And have an answer—thither come, and shape | A language not unwelcome to sick hearts | And idle spirits' (ii. 739–44).

the feelings of those simple nations . . . departed ancestors: in his note to 'Winter', 875, James Thomson remarks that vapours rising from a lake are deemed by the people of Niemi in Lapland to be 'guardian spirits of the mountains' (*PrW* ii. 398). This episode is also referenced by Hutchinson (1774) when he describes mists on moonlit Derwentwater, 'whirled round, and carried upwards like a column', resembling 'a pillar of light' (pp. 153–4).

36 *congratulate himself . . . a sad spectacle*: referring to this passage, Edward Thomas comments that 'in his soberest and his wildest moments this country delighted [Wordsworth]' (*Literary Pilgrims in England* (1917; Oxford University Press, 1980), p. 265).

36 *while looking on the unruffled waters . . . a purer element*: Woolf quotes the passage as most characteristic of W. Cf. 'contemplated with that placid and quiet . . . *steady* lake' (p. 26) and *HG* (MS D), 571–9: 'Behold the universal imagery | Inverted, all its sun-bright features touched | As with the varnish and the gloss of dreams; | Dreamlike the blending also of the whole | Harmonious Landscape, all along the shore | The boundary lost—the line invisible | That parts the image from reality; | And the clear hills, as high as they ascend | Heavenward, so deep piercing the lake below'. See also *Ex*, ix. 442–51 (quoted in note to p. 79: 'The water of the English lakes . . .').

37 *all else speaks of tranquillity; . . . quiet of a time*: for W's sensitivity to breeze-less tranquillity, see 'Airey-force Valley', 1–7: 'Not a breath of air | Ruffles the bosom of this leafy glen. | . . . the brook itself, | Old as the hills that feed it from afar, | Doth rather deepen than disturb the calm | Where all things else are still and motionless'.

the voice of the real bird . . . awakens: for W's keen ear for the call of a bird while flying, see *Ex*, iv. 1171–81: 'Within the circuit of this Fabric huge, | One Voice—the solitary Raven, flying | Athwart the concave of the dark-blue dome, | Unseen, perchance above the power of sight— | An iron knell! with echoes from afar, | Faint—and still fainter—as the cry, with which | The wanderer accompanies her flight | Through the calm region, fades upon the ear, | Diminishing by distance till it seemed | To expire . . .'. This passage is quoted in Rose (1832) and *Murray's* (1866). See also *HG* (MS D), 580–7.

Milton . . . to Paradise: *Paradise Lost*, iv. 606–7: 'the moon | Rising in clouded majesty'.

The stars, taking their stations above the hill-tops: for an image of the starry sky above Langdale Pikes, see *Ex*, ii. 746–9: 'between those heights | And on the top of either pinnacle, | More keenly than elsewhere in night's blue vault, | Sparkle the Stars as of their station proud'.

the Abyssinian recess of Rasselas: cf. Samuel Johnson's *The History of Rasselas, Prince of Abyssinia* (1759). De Selincourt points out that the Abyssinian Happy Valley in *Rasselas* resembles valleys in the Lake District (EdS 182). See *Pr1850*, vi. 661–2: 'confined as in a depth | Of Abyssinian privacy'.

SECTION SECOND: ASPECT OF THE COUNTRY,
AS AFFECTED BY ITS INHABITANTS

39 *the primeval woods . . . the change*: Woolf quotes the passage to illustrate W's sensitivity towards 'the loneliness of nature'.

'When the first settlers . . . beasts': with slight alteration, extracted from West, *Antiquities* (1774), p. xlvii.

40 *the leigh . . . extinct*: cf. West, *Antiquities* (1774), p. xlvi.

Roman forts . . . at Ambleside, and upon Dunmallet: Galava Roman Fort at Ambleside and Dunmallard, a hillfort near Pooley Bridge on Ullswater. Also mentioned on p. 55.

a few circles of rude stones attributed to the Druids: during the nineteenth century the stone circles of the north were associated with Druids. For further mentions of the Druids, see also pp. 53, 92.

41 *It is not improbable . . . the proud*: footnote added in 1822. The 'friend of the author' is Thomas Wilkinson. 'Karl Lofts' was a stone monument found to the south of Shap, 'composed of two lines of huge unhewn masses of granite, enclosing an area of half a mile in length, and from twenty to thirty yards in breadth' (Ford 131). It is all destroyed now. 'Long Meg and her Daughters', consisting of a monolith and a stone circle, is the third largest prehistoric stone circle in Britain, situated six miles north-east of Penrith. W came across the stones by chance, in early 1821, while visiting the Eden valley (*LLY* i. 4–5). The sonnet addressed to 'Giant-mother', first published in the third edition of the *Guide* (1822), was later revised and included in *The Sonnets of William Wordsworth* (1838) and became a favourite quote in Victorian guidebooks. Ford (1839), Mogridge (1849), *Murray's* (1866), and Jenkinson (1872) opt for the *Guide* version of the sonnet, while *Black's* (1841) quotes the poem and footnote from *Sonnets of Wordsworth*. Blanchard (1852), J. M. Wilson (1859), Matthew (1866), and *Ward & Lock's* (1884) also use the 1838 version.

a hostile kingdom: Scotland.

Hence these lakes and inner vallies . . . the Dacres: on the southern periphery, near Dalton-in-Furness stands Furness Abbey and about three miles to its east lie the ruins of medieval Gleaston Castle, once a residence of the Fleming family of Rydal (*Sylvan's* 119–20). On the western periphery, about four miles south of Egremont, is Calder Abbey. On the northern periphery, about twelve miles north-east of Carlisle, stands Lanercost Priory, depicted in Wilkinson's plate No. 48. The Cliffords had castles at Brougham, Appleby, Pendragon near Kirkby Stephen, and Skipton in North Yorkshire; the De Lucys had castles at Cockermouth and Egremont; the Dacres had Dacre Castle and Naworth Castle near Lanercost (*PrW* ii. 404–5).

43 *West's Antiquities of Furness*: in citing *Antiquities*, W quotes from pp. xxiii– xxiv and p. xlv, omitting and adding a few sentences so as to fit his own historical view of the Lake District (*PrW* ii. 405–6).

Danish or Norse origin, as the dialect indicates: Hudson (1843–59) offers a glossary of terms of Danish or Norse origin: e.g. pike (a peak), beck (a stream), ghyll (a fissure in a mountain), nab (a nose) as in Nabscar, thwaite (clearing) as in Esthwaite.

44 *'Sir Launcelot Threlkeld . . . to the wars'*: the reference is to Nicolson and Burn, i. 498. Crosby-Ravensworth is situated five miles south-west of Appleby-in-Westmorland. Yanwath Hall is located to the south of Penrith, on the banks of the River Eamont; its fourteenth-century pele tower and fifteenth-century hall are still well preserved. Threlkeld Hall is described in *Waggoner*, iv. 626– 31: 'The ruined towers of Threlkeld-hall | Lurking in a double shade, | By trees and lingering twilight made! | There, at Blencathara's rugged feet, |

Sir Lancelot gave a safe retreat | To noble Clifford'. These lines are quoted in *Black's* (1841), *Sylvan's* (1847), and J. M. Wilson (1859). During the War of the Roses (1455–85), the young Henry, Lord Clifford, a Lancastrian, was sheltered here for twenty-four years, disguised as a shepherd (*Black's*). The restoration of Lord Clifford is celebrated in W's 'Song, at the Feast of Brougham Castle', often referenced in guidebooks.

45 *kraels*: kraal, a poor hut or hovel (*OED* 1b).

  a community of shepherds and agriculturists: see notes to pp. 50 ('a perfect Republic . . .') and 67 ('estatesman').

46 *'that the Blomaries . . . the cattle'*: West's *Antiquities* (1774) summarizes the history of the bloomeries in Furness (p. xxxvii).

  merely habitations of man and coverts for beasts: cf. 'Inscription for the House (an Outhouse) on the Island at Grasmere', 13–15: 'It is a homely pile, yet to these walls | The heifer comes in the snow-storm, and here | The new-dropp'd lamb finds shelter from the wind'. These lines are quoted in Horne (1816), Robinson (1819), and Rose (1832).

  the COTTAGES: *Penny Magazine*, 5.252 (5 Mar. 1836) reproduces the ensuing paragraph (pp. 46–8) under the title of 'Mountain Cottages'. Ford (1839) refers to the passage in describing Lakeland cottages. An exemplary cottage garden in the Lake District is featured in *Ex*, vi. 1183–210, of which the following lines are quoted in Jennings (1878): 'Brought from the woods the honeysuckle twines | Around the porch, and seems, in that trim place, | A Plant no longer wild; the cultured rose | There blossoms, strong in health, and will be soon | Roof-high; the wild pink crowns the garden wall, | And with the flowers are intermingled stones | Sparry and bright, the scatterings of the hills' (vi. 1189–95).

  Cluster'd like stars . . . clouds between: *HG* (MS B), 141–4. Cf. p. 25 ('where these rocks and hills . . . upon their sides').

47 *rough-cast and white wash . . . sober and variegated*: cf. p. 59 ('the glare of white-wash . . . weather-stains') and note.

  these humble dwellings . . . the native rock: cf. *Ex*, vi. 1179–86: 'The Abode, | . . . to our sight | Would seem in no distinction to surpass | The rudest habitations. Ye might think | That it had sprung self-raised from earth, or grown | Out of the living rock, to be adorned | By Nature only'. In the early twentieth century, G. D. Abraham's *Motor Ways in Lakeland* (1913) likewise comments that old Lake District houses 'seem scarcely of man's handiwork', with 'more the appearance of growth than of ordinary construction' (p. 10).

  Nor will the singular beauty of the chimneys . . . the still air: according to Rawnsley, almost all the chimneys in the Rydal area were built following W's advice, including Thomas Arnold's Fox How ('Reminiscences', p. 93). The passage is referenced and quoted in Ford (1839) and *Pearson's* (1902).

  rough and uneven in their surface . . . the living principle of things: in his *Morning Post* letters of 1844, W laments the lack of public appreciation for this kind of 'romantic' natural beauty (p. 134).

48 *the walls themselves, if old . . . the geranium, and lichens*: see W's poem 'Poor
Robin' on a wild geranium growing from a gap in the stone wall. In his
note to the poem, W says that '[t]his little wild flower "Poor Robin" is here
constantly courting my attention & exciting what may be called a domestic
interest with the varying aspects of its stalks & leaves & flowers' (*IF* 75).
Cf. *KWRL*, p. 134.

49 *Written some time ago . . . liberty*: footnote added in 1823. The quotation
within is from Horace, *Epistles*, II. ii. 55, meaning 'The years as they pass
plunder us of one thing after another' (*RCDE*).

In some places . . . precious: footnote added in 1822. In his note to *The River
Duddon*, W recounts how the Revd Robert Walker taught a school in
Seathwaite Chapel.

50 *the chapel of Buttermere . . . scattered near it*: situated on a rocky outcrop,
St James's chapel at Buttermere was consecrated in 1507. The present
chapel dates from 1840, and is not the building W and STC visited during
their walking tour, Nov. 1799 (*CEY* 279). W describes the original chapel
in *Pr1850*, vii. 324–8: 'Beside the mountain chapel, sleeps in earth | Her
new-born infant, fearless as a lamb | That, thither driven from some
unsheltered place, | Rests underneath the little rock-like pile | When
storms are raging'. These lines, with the account of the Maid of Buttermere
(vii. 296–333), are inserted in Loftie (1875).

To these houses . . . majestic timber: Rydal Park and Lowther Castle were
among the few places where magnificent timber trees were preserved (see
pp. 17, 34). For Wordsworth's comment on ancient woods, see also the
verse quotation at p. 66.

specimens of those fantastic and quaint figures . . . petty art: W refers to topi-
ary. Cf. *KWRL*, p. 132 ('Elaborate gardens, with topiary works') and note.
He may well have in mind the famous topiaries in the gardens of Levens
Hall in Kendal. *Black's* (1841) describes them with reference to *White Doe
of Rylstone*: 'this spacious plot | For pleasure made, a goodly spot, | With
lawns, and beds of flowers, and shades | Of trellis-work, in long arcades,
| And cirque and crescent framed by wall | Of close-clipt foliage green
and tall, | Converging walks' (iv. 981–7).

a perfect Republic of Shepherds and Agriculturists: W's ideal community is
epitomized here. See *Pr1805*, ix. 218–32: 'a poor district, and which yet |
Retaineth more of ancient homeliness, | Manners erect, and frank sim-
plicity, | Than any other nook of English land, | . . . a republic, where all
stood thus far | Upon equal ground, that they were brothers all | In honour,
as of one community'. See p. 45 ('a community of shepherds and agricul-
turalists'), and the note to p. 67 ('estatesman').

51 *the land, which they walked . . . their name and blood*: cf. 'The Brothers',
202–5: 'For five long generations had the heart | Of Walter's forefathers
o'erflow'd the bounds | Of their inheritance, that single cottage, | . . . and
those few green fields'.

SECTION THIRD: CHANGES, AND RULES OF TASTE
FOR PREVENTING THEIR BAD EFFECTS

52 *within the last sixty years*: in this paragraph W refers to the changes made
between the 1770s and 1830s. West's guide (1778) comments on the new
trend of searching for 'select parts of natural scenery': 'The taste for land-
scape . . . induce[s] many to visit the lakes of Cumberland, Westmorland,
and Lancashire, there to contemplate, in Alpine scenery, finished in
nature's highest tints, what refined art labours to imitate; the pastoral and
rural landscape, varied in all the stiles, the soft, the rude, the romantic, and
sublime' (pp. 1–2). Cf. *KWRL*, pp. 132–3.

A practice . . . natural scenery: 'Ornamental Gardening' or landscape gar-
dening, proposed by William Kent and promoted by Lancelot 'Capability'
Brown, prevailed in England in the latter half of the eighteenth century,
replacing formally laid out gardens with landscaped effects. The extremes
of Brown's landscaping were objected to by Gilpin, Uvedale Price, and
Richard Payne Knight (*PrW* ii. 408).

'Not a single red tile . . . attire': quoted from Gray's journal, 8 Oct. 1769,
with slight alteration. The passage is also referenced in *KWRL*, p. 141.
Reproduced in West's guide, Gray's paradisal view of Grasmere became
a popular quote in guidebooks throughout the nineteenth century, includ-
ing *Black's* (1841), Mackay (1846), *Sylvan's* (1847), and *Murray's* (1866).

53 *its native proprietor*: Sir Wilfred Lawson, who *c*.1761 cut down the trees on
St Herbert's Island and replanted it with conifers (*PrW* ii. 409). The
island is now covered with deciduous trees.

Scotch firs . . . melancholy phalanx . . . the winds: W thought that firs need
space and should not be stifled in thick plantations (*PrW* ii. 416). See p. 62
('The Scotch fir . . . becomes a noble tree'). See also p. 48 ('a tall fir, through
which the winds sing').

Œolus: the god of the winds in Greek mythology.

At the bidding of an alien improver . . . approaching invader: Vicar's Island
(now called Derwent Isle) formerly belonged to Fountains Abbey in
Yorkshire; after the Dissolution of the Monasteries it changed owners sev-
eral times until 1778 when it was purchased by Joseph Pocklington, who
added 'improvements', including a house, gravelled walks, a ruined
chapel, a small Druidic circle, and several model forts with cannons (*PrW*
ii. 409).

The taste of a succeeding proprietor . . . its puerilities: in the early nineteenth
century the island's new owner General William Peachy removed
Pocklington's various 'improvements' (*PrW* ii. 410).

the circle upon the opposite hill: Castlerigg Stone Circle. See *Ex*, ix. 707–8:
'A few rude Monuments of mountain-stone | Survive; all else is swept
away', quoted in Ford (1839). Keats visited here in July 1818 and describes
the stone circle in *Hyperion*, ii. 34–6: 'a dismal cirque | Of Druid stones,
upon a forlorn moor, | When the chill rain begins at shut of eve . . .'.

54 *the changes . . . Winandermere, and in its neighbourhood*: in 1774 Thomas
English built a round house and a formal garden on Belle Isle, the struc-
ture forming 'a perfect circle, fifty-four feet in diameter, surmounted by
a dome-shaped roof', according to *Black's* (1846). The building was
deplored by West, Gilpin, Hutchinson, and Green. The island was
acquired in 1781 by Isabella Curwen, who, with her husband John
Christian Curwen, re-landscaped the grounds, but not for the better, in
DW's view (*Grasmere and Alfoxden Journals*, pp. 106–7; Nicholas Mason,
'Larches, Llandaff, and Forestry Politics in Wordsworth's *Guide to the Lakes*').

What could be more unfortunate . . . destroyed: for W's regret at changes on
the islands of Derwentwater and Windermere, see also pp. 30, 107, 133.

Winds and waves work with a careless and graceful hand . . . left behind: for
water's land-shaping power, see p. 28.

plantations in general: for W's discussion of plantations, see pp. 61–6.

These are disappearing fast . . . place: 'the present Proprietor': Henry
Curwen, son of John Christian Curwen, who died in 1828 (Mason,
'Larches'). This footnote was added in the 1835 fifth edition. Cf. p. 6.

55 *the perception of the fine gradations . . . into another*: Wordsworth uses such
terms as 'gradations', 'gently incorporated into nature', 'harmonise',
'delicate blending', 'a transition . . . without abruptness', and 'intermedi-
ate' several times in the *Guide* to describe harmonious variety in nature.
Cf. 'Essays supplementary to Preface' (1815): 'In nature everything is dis-
tinct, yet nothing defined into absolute independent singleness'.

The hill of Dunmallet . . . each avenue: the symmetrical ranks of conifers
planted on the hill in the eighteenth century were often blamed for spoil-
ing the view (Lindop 269).

56 *'Into that forest . . . well delight'*: *Faerie Queen*, III. v. 39–40.

"not obvious, not obtrusive, but retired": *Paradise Lost*, viii. 504.

57 *its titles are from antiquity . . . vicegerent of Nature*: cf. 'Address to Kilchurn
Castle, upon Loch Awe', 18–23: 'submitting | All that the God of Nature
hath conferred, | All that he has in common with the Stars, | To the
memorial majesty of Time | Impersonated in thy calm decay! | Take,
then, thy seat, Vicegerent unreproved!'

'Child of . . . thy age!': 'Address to Kilchurn Castle', 1–3.

58 *an over-prevalence of a bluish tint*: in the introduction to *Select Views* W
gave further explanation: 'This blue tint proceeds from the diffused water,
and still more from the rocks which the reader will remember are generally
of this colour' (p. xxvi).

59 *the glare of white-wash has been subdued . . . by weather-stains*: cf. De
Quincey's description of Dove Cottage: when he came to live here in 1809,
the front of the cottage was covered with roses that 'with as much jessa-
mine and honeysuckle as could find room to flourish . . . performed the
acceptable service of breaking the unpleasant glare that would else have
wounded the eye from the white-wash; a glare which, having been

renewed . . . could not be sufficiently subdued in tone for the artist's eye until the storm of several winters had weather-stained and tamed down its brilliancy' ('Sketches of Life and Manners, from the Autobiography of an English Opium-Eater', *Tait's Edinburgh Magazine*, 7 (1840), p. 32).

59 *The supposed necessity . . . whitening buildings*: W's negative view of white-wash in the mountainous country, demonstrated in the subsequent two paragraphs, can be seen also in 'Lines Written with a Slate pencil upon a Stone, . . . upon one of the Islands at Rydale', where a mansion 'blaze[s] | In snow-white splendour' (30–1). The poem is quoted in Fielding (1821) and Loftie (1875). By contrast, W depicts the 'snow-white church' at Hawkshead sitting 'like a thronèd lady' favourably in *Pr1805*, iv. 13–15. Opposing W's 'anti-whitewashing theory', Gibson (1849) praises 'a liberal sprinkling over the landscape of pure white cottages, embosomed, . . . each in its own nest of sheltering trees' and 'the cleanly, pleasant appearance derivable from a plentiful periodical application of white-wash' (pp. 31–2).

60 *white destroys the gradations of distance*: W draws on Gilpin's *Observations on the River Wye, and Several Parts of South Wales* (2nd edn, 1789), pp. 94–8, for his criticism of white in landscape (*PrW* ii. 414).

it is after sunset, . . . white objects are most to be complained of: in *An Evening Walk* (1836), W says that evening light softens the glare of white: 'How pleasant, as the sun declines, to view | The spacious landscape change in form and hue! | . . . | Even the white stems of birch, the cottage white, | Soften their glare before the mellow light' (97–104).

61 *Larch and fir plantations*: W's discussion of plantations in the ensuing six paragraphs (pp. 61–6), largely unchanged from *Select Views*, was repro-duced in full or referenced in the *Westmorland Advertiser and Kendal Chronicle* (19 and 26 Sept. 1812), Elizabeth Kent's *Sylvan Sketches; or, A Companion to the Park and the Shrubbery* (1825), and William Howitt's *Rural Life of England* (1838). (Mason, 'Larches'.)

I would utter first a regret . . . the neighbouring moors: used as the epigraph for Chapter 1, 'A Thing of Beauty', in H. H. Symonds, *Afforestation in the Lake District* (1936). W's objections to commercial plantation in the Lake District informed the Friends of the Lake District's anti-afforestation campaigns in the mid-twentieth century. Mason argues that the rapid growth of commer-cial forestry in the Central Lake District in the early nineteenth century inspired Wordsworth's vehement response (Mason, 'Larches').

62 *a charge of inconsistency . . . acknowledged*: for the inconsistency of those who admire the beauties of the Lake District but use the railways that arguably threatened them, see *KWRL*, p. 136 ('What can, in truth, . . . came from?').

The Scotch fir . . . the house: see p. 34 ('the sycamore . . . their dwellings') and note.

65 *the native deciduous trees . . . barren tracts*: cf. 'good soil and sheltered situ-ations . . . barren and exposed ground' (p. 61).

66 *'Many hearts . . . yet remain'*: 'Composed at — Castle', 8–14; quoted in Fielding (1821). In *Ex*, vii. 610–20, the Pastor regrets the 'works of havoc'

performed by the woodman: 'Full oft his doings leave me to deplore | Tall ash-tree sown by winds, by vapours nursed, ... | Light birch, aloft upon the horizon's edge, ... | And oak whose roots by noontide dew were damped ...'.

let the images of nature ... in a few words: cf. 'work, where you can, in the spirit of nature' (p. 55).

67 *an unfortunate alteration ... native peasantry*: in the ensuing paragraph W describes the social and economic changes that befell small independent proprietors of land around the turn of the century; 'Michael' and 'The Brothers' illustrate the effects of these changes.

estatesman: in his letter to Charles James Fox, 14 Jan. 1801, W explains 'estatesmen' or 'statesmen' as 'small independent *proprietors* of land, ... men of respectable education who daily labour on their own little properties' (*LEY* 314). See also W's comment on the community of 'shepherds and agriculturists' (pp. 45, 50). Sharing W's concerns, *Murray's* (1866) further points out that owing to the social revolution brought by railways the 'statesmen' in Cumberland and Westmorland have been more often 'obliged to sell the land which had belonged to their ancestors for generations' (p. xxii).

68 *a sort of national property ... a heart to enjoy*: this famous declaration was retained unchanged from *Select Views* (1810) and repeated again with a slight change towards the end of his pamphlet *Kendal and Windermere Railway* (p. 144). Cf. *Ex*, ix. 513–18: '—Ah! that such beauty, varying in the light | Of living nature, cannot be pourtrayed | By words, nor by the pencil's silent skill; | But is the property of him alone | Who hath beheld it, noted it with care, | And in his mind recorded it with love!'. These lines are quoted in Horne (1816), Robinson (1819), and Ford (1839).

Select Views had another paragraph here, to conclude the essay on man's relationship with nature: 'The Writer may now express a hope that the end, which was proposed in the commencement of this Introduction, has not been wholly unattained; and that there is no impropriety in connecting these latter remarks with the Etchings now offered to the public. For it is certain that, if the evil complained of should continue to spread, these Vales, notwithstanding their lakes, rivers, torrents, and surrounding rocks and mountains, will lose their chief recommendation for the eye of the painter and the man of imagination and feeling. And, upon the present occasion, the Artist is bound to acknowledge that, if the fruit of his labours have any value, it is owing entirely to the models which he has had before him, in a country which retained till lately an appearance unimpaired of Man and Nature animated, as it were, by one spirit for the production of beauty, grace, and grandeur.'

MISCELLANEOUS OBSERVATIONS

'Miscellaneous Observations' originated from Section I of *Select Views* (1810). Hudson's enlarged editions (1842–59) adapted the first half of 'Miscellaneous

Observations' for the new introduction and the latter half as a new Fourth Section of 'Description of the Scenery of the Lakes', titled 'Alpine Scenes, Compared with Cumbrian'.

69 *the best season for visiting this country*: this paragraph discussing when to visit the Lake District was reproduced entirely or partly in *PM (1837)*, Ford (1839), *Onwhyn's* (1841), Mogridge (1849), J. B. Pyne (1859), and Waugh (1880).

  the colouring of the mountains and woods: for seasonal colours, see also pp. 23–5, 34–5.

  rainy weather: for the characteristics of rain in the Lake District, see p. 35.

  those deluges of rain . . . the Nile: see *Pr1850*, vi. 614–16: 'like the mighty flood of Nile | Poured from his fount of Abyssinian clouds | To fertilise the whole Egyptian plain'. See also note to p. 37 ('the Abyssinian recess of Rasselas').

70 *the six weeks following the 1st of September . . . the cottages*: quoted in Pyne (1859). Compare this passage with W's description of the beauty of the Duddon Valley in early September, quoted in note to p. 9 ('go to the Vale . . .'). For autumnal colours in the Lake District, see p. 23 and *Pr1850*, vi. 10–13: 'the coves and heights | Clothed in the sunshine of the withering fern; | . . . the mild magnificence | Of calmer lakes and louder streams'.

  the golden flowers of the broom . . . interveined: see note to p. 34 ('the broom . . .').

  English warblers . . . broad still waters: cf. 'By the Side of Rydal Mere' (*Evening Voluntaries*): 'The Linnet's warble, sinking towards a close, | Hints to the Thrush 'tis time for their repose; | The shrill-voiced Thrush is heedless, and again | The Monitor revives his own sweet strain; | . . . | O Nightingale! Who ever heard thy song | Might here be moved, till Fancy grows so strong | That listening sense is pardonably cheated | Where wood or stream by thee was never greeted' (1–16). These lines are quoted in Loftie (1875).

  an imaginative influence . . . a flat country: quoted by Woolf as one of the most impressive passages in W's *Guide*. The effect of the cuckoo's voice in a mountain valley inspired W to produce several verses, including 'To the Cuckoo', 'O Blithe New-comer', 'Yes! full surely 'twas the Echo' and 'The Cuckoo at Laverna'.

71 *no traveller, provided he be in good health . . . accompanied*: with this passage in mind, *PM (1837)* remarks that for those with 'good health and a good temper' even the 'stormiest' weather would be enjoyable as presenting 'those occasional revelations of grandeur' as captured in *Ex*, ii. 859–86: 'when a step, | A single step, that freed me from the skirts | Of the blind vapour, opened to my view | Glory beyond all glory ever seen | By waking sense or by the dreaming soul! | . . . | By earthly nature had the effect been wrought | Upon the dark materials of the storm | Now pacified; on them,

and on the coves | And mountain-steeps and summits, whereunto | The vapours had receded, taking there | Their station under a cerulean sky'. In addition to these lines, Rose (1832) further quotes *Ex*, ii. 887–904: 'O 'twas an unimaginable sight! | Clouds, mists, streams, watery rocks and emerald turf, | Clouds of all tincture, rocks and sapphire sky, | Confused, commingled, mutually inflamed, | Molten together, and composing thus, | Each lost in each, that marvellous array | Of temple, palace, citadel, and huge | Fantastic pomp of structure without name . . .'.

72 *it will appear to most advantage . . . humbler excitement*: West's guide (1778) makes a similar point: 'The Windermere, like Coniston Lake, is viewed to greatest advantage by facing the mountains, which rise in grandeur on the eye, and swell upon the imagination as they are approached' (p. 59). Cf. 'from elegance and richness, to their highest point of grandeur and sublimity' (*Guide*, p. 20).

It is not likely that a mountain . . . from centre to circumference: quoted in Robinson (1833), from the 1823 edition. Compare the Snowdon episode (*Pr1805*, xiii. 36–51); see also *Ex*, ii. 859–904 (quoted in note to p. 71).

A stranger to a mountainous country . . . should be taken: quoted in Ford (1839). For the effects of light and shadow on a mountainous landscape and the tourist's experiences of landscape at different times of the day, see p. 21 and note ('in the vale of Winandermere . . .').

it is upon the mind . . . principally depend: quoted as the epigraph on the title page of Ford (1839). W also says that he wishes 'to teach the *Touring World*, which is become very numerous, to look thro' the clear eye of the Understanding as well as thro' the hazy one of vague Sensibility' (*LLY* i. 303). Cf. the opening remark of the *Guide* (p. 4).

Nothing is more injurious . . . that of another: the ensuing three paragraphs are reproduced at length in the conclusion of Blanchard (1852). For W's criticism of an analytical attitude towards nature, see *Pr1805*, xi. 153–63: 'disliking here, and there | Liking, by rules of mimic art transferred | To things above all art. . . . | . . . giving way | To a comparison of scene with scene, | Bent overmuch on superficial things, . . .'.

Qui bene distinguit bene docet: 'He who distinguishes well, teaches well' (*RCDE*).

73 *the unrivalled brilliancy of the water . . . character*: for the brilliancy and animated motion of mountain streams, see note to p. 33; *Pr1805*, iv. 39–40: 'that unruly child of mountain birth, | The froward brook'; and *The River Duddon*, IV, 3–10: 'A Protean change seems wrought while I pursue | The curves, a loosely-scattered chain doth make; | Or rather thou appear'st a glistering snake, | Silent, and to the gazer's eye untrue, | Thridding with sinuous lapse the rushes, through | Dwarf willows gliding, and by ferny brake. | Starts from a dizzy steep the undaunted Rill | Rob'd instantly in garb of snow-white foam'.

'While the coarse rushes . . . melodies': 'The Pass of Kirkstone', 39–40.

73 *tranquil sublimity*: after inserting the preceding three paragraphs, Blanchard (1852) remarks that 'this is the spirit in which the scenery of the Lake region should be viewed, for its leading attraction is that tranquil sublimity alluded to by the poet' (p. 122).

Havoc, and ruin . . . such changes: for the Alpine scenery that suggests 'Havoc, ruin, and desolation', see the Simplon Pass episode in *Pr1850*, vi. 621–40. See also the verse inserted at p. 142 and note.

74 *It is generally supposed that waterfalls . . . some drawbacks*: for a general view of waterfalls, see West's guide (1778): 'In mountainous countries, cascades, water-falls, and cataracts are frequent, but are only seen in high beauty when in full torrent, and that is in wet weather, or soon after it' (p. 78).

the breath of the precipitous water?: W was fascinated with how a waterfall could stir a breeze; see his note to 'Lines written in Early Spring': 'The brook fell down a sloping rock so as to make a waterfall . . . and, across the pool below, had fallen a tree . . . and, from the underside of this natural sylvan bridge depended long & beautiful tresses of ivy which waved gently in the breeze that might poetically speaking be called the breath of the water-fall' (*IF* 36–7).

the principal charm of the smaller waterfalls . . . surrounding images: the charms of Lakeland waterfalls are captured in several of W's poems, including 'Epistle': 'quieted and soothed, a torrent small, | A little daring would-be waterfall' (177–8); and *Ex*, i. 317–22: 'he scanned the laws of light | Amid the roar of torrents, where they send | From hollow clefts up to the clearer air | A cloud of mist, which in the sunshine frames | A lasting tablet—for the observer's eye | Varying it's rainbow hues'. These lines are quoted in Rose (1832) and Ford (1839). See also 'Rydal Waterfalls' in the Glossary.

As a resident among the Lakes: in the remaining paragraphs of 'Miscellaneous Observations' (incorporated as Section Fourth in Hudson's editions, 1842–59), W compares the Lake District and Alpine scenes in favour of the former; this part was reprinted as an independent article, 'Alpine Scenes Compared with Cumbrian', in *The Visitor* (1846), pp. 467–71.

76 *Monks-hood*: aconite with blue flowers. DW describes the flower in her *Journal of a Tour on the Continent*: 'the monkshood of our gardens, growing at a great height on the Alps has a brighter hue than elsewhere. It is seen in tufts, that to my fancy presented fairy groves upon the green grass, and in rocky places, or under trees' (*Journals* ii. 127).

Titian passed his life . . . the Italian Alps: Titian (1489–1576) was born in a district in the Venetian Alps; Nicolas Poussin (1594–1665), Gaspard Poussin (1615–75), and Claude de Lorrain (1600–82) were landscape painters, influential in the cult of the Picturesque. Pellegrino Tibaldi (1527–96) was born in Puria in Valsolda and Bernardino Luini (*c*.1475–1532) was born in Luino on Lago Maggiore (*PrW* ii. 421).

A few experiments . . . attempt: W seems to allude to the painter J. M. W. Turner (*PrW* ii. 421–2).

77 *Lucretius . . . circúm*: the quotation is from Lucretius's *De Rerum Natura* (*The Nature of Things*), v. 1369–77. The English translation by William Ellery Leonard runs: 'And day by day they'd force the woods to move | Still higher up the mountain, and to yield | The place below for tilth, that there they might, | On plains and uplands, have their meadow-plats, | Cisterns and runnels, crops of standing grain, | And happy vineyards, and that all along | O'er hillocks, intervales, and plains might run | The silvery-green belt of olive-trees, | Marking the plotted landscape; even as now | Thou seest so marked with varied loveliness | All the terrain which men adorn and plant | With rows of goodly fruit-trees and hedge round | With thriving shrubberies sown' (*RCDE*).

78 *such wild graces . . . the Ratcliffes*: for aiding the Jacobite insurrection of 1715, James Radcliffe, Earl of Derwentwater, was executed and his island estate on Derwentwater was confiscated; despite local opposition, the island's woods were felled (Lindop 147). The trees have since been replanted.

LANDOR: Walter Savage Landor (1775–1864). The poem cited is 'Ad Larium' ('To Lake Como') from his 1820 collection. English translation by John Talbot: 'O Como! Along your ragged shores | You deny none of the pious the shelter | Of a painted wall and stone roof; | From where you are, you hear the sailors' many reports | Of astonishing storms, nor do you repel them from your peaceful shore; | But you soon prepare new wonders, either in the form of the south and east winds | Battering the caves even in summer, | Or a blinding hailstorm drawn up | From the bed of the surging River Adda' (*RCDE*).

79 *The water of the English lakes . . . duplicate begins*: reflections in clear water captured W's imagination (see pp. 26, 30–1, 36–7). See also *Ex*, ix. 442–51: 'In a deep pool, by happy chance we saw | A two-fold Image; on a grassy bank | A snow-white Ram, and in the crystal flood | Another and the same! . . . | Each had his glowing mountains, each his sky, | And each seemed centre of his own fair world'. The passage is quoted in Horne (1816) and Robinson (1819).

two comprehensive tours among the Alps: W visited the Alps in 1790 with his friend Robert Jones and again in 1820 with MW, DW, and several friends (*CEY* 97–114, *Journals* ii. 85–306).

the fine dazzling trembling . . . endless variety: see note to p. 26 ('expressing also . . .').

The subject of torrents and water-falls . . . touched upon: see p. 74.

a calm September morning: this phenomenon actually occurred on 17 Nov. 1799, when W was accompanying STC on his first trip to the Lake District (*PrW* ii. 423). Referring to this episode Mackay (1846) comments: 'I have myself witnessed similar optical illusions among the wilder and more magnificent scenery of the Highland lochs. . . . The mist is in this respect a clever wizard' (p. 70).

EXCURSIONS TO THE TOP OF SCAWFELL
AND ON THE BANKS OF ULSWATER

83 *It was my intention . . . abandoned*: after publication of the letterpress for *Select Views*, W planned to expand his text into a more detailed guidebook but abandoned this project unfinished in early 1812. See Introduction, pp. xvi–xvii.

if well executed . . . by anticipation: in the 1811–12 draft guide, W expresses hesitation about writing a guidebook: 'I much wish that my companion could have been brought to it without directions or previous knowledge of what he was about to see' (*PrW* ii. 320).

the following extract from a letter to a Friend: the extract is an extensively altered version of DW's letter to William Johnson, 21 Oct. 1818 (for DW's original script, see *PrW* ii. 364–8). Included in the third edition (1822) for the first time, the account was reproduced in full in *Lonsdale Magazine*, vol. 3 (1822), *New European Magazine*, vol. 1 (1822), and in John Wilson's 'Christopher at the Lakes' (1832); it was also extensively reproduced in J. M. Wilson (1859), *Shaw's* (1873), and *Ward & Lock's* (1884). In the latter three cases, the account is dealt with as if written by W himself.

Ash-course: Esk Hause. DW supposes that Ash-course is a corruption of Esk Hawes (*PrW* ii. 364). Hudson (1843–59) notes that Esk Hause is pronounced 'Ash-course' by the dalesmen.

84 *the Stone Man*: a cairn, or pile of stones, often built on conspicuous points of mountains. In 'Rural Architecture' W describes how local boys 'built up without mortar or lime | A Man on the peak of the crag | . . . of stones gather'd up as they lay' (5–7), and how, when strong wind 'blew the Giant away . . . they built up another' (16–18).

On the summit of the Pike: the ensuing three paragraphs (up to p. 85) were cited in Martineau (1855, 1858) as 'the best account we have of the greatest mountain-excursion in England'. Extracted also in *PM (1837)* and partly in *Onwhyn's* (1841). For the changeable weather on the mountain, see 'Michael' and *Ex*, ii. 859–86 (quoted in note to 'no traveller . . .', p. 71). Hutchinson (1774) offers a lively description of stormy weather on the top of Skiddaw.

on its highest point . . . spotless snow: W's addition, echoing a passage in *S2SV* (p. 116).

85 *round the top of Scawfell-PIKE . . . this happen!*: extracted in *PM (1837)*, *Onwhyn's* (1841), *Land We Live In* (1847), various editions of Black's guides (1841–1900), *Murray's* (1866), *Shaw's* (1873), and *Ward & Lock's* (1884); the last sentence ('Flowers . . . happen') is quoted by Woolf as an example of the poet's peculiar sensitivity towards the 'loneliness of nature', although the passage was actually written by DW.

87 *TO——, ON HER FIRST ASCENT . . . their majesty*: the addressee is Miss Blackett, then residing with Mr Montague Burgoyne at Fox Ghyll (*IF* 16). The fourth stanza is quoted in *Murray's* (1866).

A.D. 1805: the ensuing paragraphs (pp. 87–94) are based on DW's journal account of an excursion through the tributary vales of Ullswater by DW and W, Nov. 1805, with extensive revision by the latter (for DW's original script, see *PrW* ii. 368–78). Added in the fourth, 1823 edition. For W's own descriptions of the same region, see pp. 14–17.

88 *Ammonian horns*: curling horns, like those of the Egyptian god Ammon.

the lake, clouds, and mists . . . shifting vapours: cf. 'Days of unsettled . . . to the ear' (p. 35) and note.

89 *we fixed . . . began to build*: here, W and DW are attracted to a piece of ground called Broad How for building their own house. W owned the land until 1834 but did not build there after all (Moorman, ii. 59–62).

white dog, lying in the moonshine: De Selincourt discerns in this image an inspiration for the description of the white doe in lines 940–1011 of *White Doe of Rylstone* (EdS 203).

The torrents murmured softly . . . there: W's addition. The concluding quotation is from *Ex*, ii. 907: 'I saw not, but I felt that it was there'. In his letter to Walter Scott, 7 Nov. 1805, W points out the Ossianic quality of Patterdale, transcribing 'Glen Almain': 'In this still place, remote from men, | Sleeps Ossian, in the Narrow Glen' (*LEY* 643).

90 *A raven was seen aloft . . . destroyer*: W expands DW's brief comment on a raven. For 'the iron tone of the raven's voice', see *Ex*, iv. 1172–5 (quoted in note to p. 37: 'the voice of the real bird . . .'). For the image of 'the adventurous destroyer' in Hawkshead, see the Raven's nest episode in *Pr1805*, i. 333–50.

'retiredness is a piece of majesty': line 35 of the poem 'Loyalty Confined' (1671), attributed to Sir Roger L'Estrange in Percy's *Reliques of Ancient English Poetry* (*RCDE*).

'bare ring of mossy wall': the same phrase appears on p. 119. Cf. the chapel at Ennerdale described in 'The Brothers', 26–7: 'the parish chapel stood alone, | Girt round with a bare ring of mossy wall'.

91 *On leaving the fields of Sandwyke . . . in sycamore*: W's addition. Cf. *S2SV*, p. 119.

like Stybarrow . . . a green-house: W's addition. Cf. *S2SV*, p. 119.

92 *a small ruin, called at this day the chapel*: better known as the 'Chapel in the Hause', according to local tradition this ruined chapel in Boredale Hause was built by St Patrick in the fifth century (*RCDE*). W heard about an old man who took refuge here during a storm in summer 1805, an episode that is recounted in *Ex*, ii. 758–929 (McCracken 132–3, 250). The 'chapel' is described as follows: 'A heap of ruin, almost without walls | And wholly without roof (in ancient time | It was a Chapel, a small Edifice | In which the Peasants of these lonely Dells| For worship met upon that central height)' (ii. 838–42)—these lines are extracted in Fielding (1821).

what happened . . . drowned there: in Dec. 1785 two young brothers were drowned when the ice broke beneath them. Since then, Broadwater has been known as Brothers Water (Lindop 254–5).

92 *the victory at Trafalgar*: 21 Oct. 1805.

93 *In the rebellion of the year 1745 . . . curiosity alone*: W's addition. During the Jacobite Rising of 1745, the poet's grandfather Richard Wordsworth, agent for James Lowther and receiver general of Westmorland, protected the county's money from the Jacobite invaders.

The morning was clear . . . melted hoar-frost: W considerably revised DW's description of the earth steaming with melted frost.

the lemon-coloured leaves . . . crystal: praised by Woolf, this is actually DW's description.

97 ODE. THE PASS OF KIRKSTONE . . . *portion fair!*: quoted in *PM (1837)*, *Black's* (1841), Mackay (1846), *Sylvan's* (1847), and *Murray's* (1866). Wilkinson's plates include a view of Kirkstone (No. 46).

SECTION II OF *SELECT VIEWS IN CUMBERLAND, WESTMORELAND, AND LANCASHIRE* (1810)

104 *The beautiful Lake of Coniston . . . outlet*: like West, W recommends crossing the Lancaster Sands and going up along the River Crake to approach Coniston Lake. Wilkinson's plate No. 3 shows the river Crake with its bridge, looking towards Coniston (see Figure 1).

given in the Introduction: that is, the Introduction to *Select Views*, corresponding to 'Description of the Scenery of the Lakes' of the 1835 *Guide*. See particularly the second paragraph of p. 20.

105 *a road*: Walna Scar Road.

Chapel of Seathwaite: famous for its priest, Robert 'Wonderful' Walker.

a Farm-house: the present Newfield Inn at Seathwaite, where W stayed with MW when they made a Duddon tour in Sept. 1811 (*LMY* i. 509–10).

The whole scene . . . the Church stands: in June 1850 Sarah Hutchinson (niece of MW) visited Ulpha Kirk with her sister and mother, and recorded in her journal: 'we then wandered out to the Churchyard, which commanded a magnificent view on all sides, the lovely Duddon was flowing at our feet, & we tracked its winding course for some time, and at last sat down under a rock, and read dear Uncles sonnets in praise of this enchanting stream' (Sarah Hutchinson's Journals. June to August 1850. The Wordsworth Trust, Grasmere [WLMSH|2|6|journals|6])

I have recommended . . . its outlet: cf. the Duddon Sonnets, which trace the river from source to estuary. When the railway came to Broughton in 1846, tracing the river upstream to Seathwaite became popular with tourists and the 31st sonnet, depicting the estuary, was often inserted in guidebooks; see Mackay (1846), *Sylvan's* (1847) and J. M. Wilson (1859).

106 *a fine view . . . of the Lake of Estwaite*: see Figure 2.

these Etchings: Wilkinson offers two views of Lake Windermere (Nos. 9, 10).

a Pleasure-house belonging to J.C. Curwen, Esq.: see note to p. 6 ('the Station near the Ferry').

through Stavely . . . Windermere: W and DW took this route when they walked to their new home at Grasmere in Dec. 1799, and again in Oct. 1802, when they brought MW to their home (*Journals* i. 182). Later the Kendal and Windermere Railway would follow the route; hence these lines in W's sonnet 'Is then no nook of English ground secure': 'Baffle the threat, bright Scene, from Orrest-head | Given to the pausing traveller's rapturous glance' (9–10).

107   *Inn of Bowness*: cf. *Pr1805*, ii. 145–62: 'Upon the eastern shore of Windermere, | Above the crescent of a pleasant bay | There was an inn, no homely-featured shed, . . . | But 'twas a splendid place, the door beset | With chaises, grooms, and liveries, and within | Decanters, glasses, and the blood-red wine . . .'.

     discussed at large in the Introduction: for corresponding discussion in the *Guide*, see pp. 61–6.

108   *Upon the largest are a few old trees . . . left behind*: corresponding to *Guide*, p. 54. See also pp. 30 and 133.

     round chimneys: see *Guide*, p. 47 ('Nor will the singular beauty . . . still air') and note.

     The Brook: Stock Ghyll.

109   *From this Bridge . . . a trespass*: in 1799, when walking from Ambleside to Rydal, W and STC made this trespass and were reproved by a servant of Sir Michael le Fleming (see STC's notebook entry for 5 Nov. 1799).

     'Whose boughs . . . dry antiquity': *As You Like It*, IV. iii. 104–5.

     the Water-fall: the Rydal Lower Fall. See 'Rydal Waterfalls' in the Glossary.

110   *'Into the chasm . . . Waterfall'*: 'The Idle Shepherd-Boys', 51–5; while omitted from later editions of W's *Guide*, these lines were repeatedly quoted in other Lake District guidebooks, including Fielding (1821), *Leigh's* (1832), *Black's* (1841), *Sylvan's* (1847), Atkinson (1847), Mogridge (1849), Hudson (1853, 1859), J. M. Wilson (1859), Payn (1859, 1867), Topham (1869), Loftie (1875), Jennings (1878), *Ward & Lock's* (1884), and Garnett (1891).

     Blea Tarn is not an object . . . fields: cf. *Ex*, ii. 347–68, extracted in p. 8.

     a grand view of the River Brathay . . . Langdale, &c.: see Figure 3.

     the Bridge over the Rothay . . . Clappersgate: there is no plate corresponding to this explanation. W may have taken plate No. 14, 'Brathay Bridge, near Ambleside' (see Figure 4), as depicting Rothay Bridge. The former, over the Brathay, is double-arched, while the latter, over the Rothay, is a single-arched bridge. Joseph Farington's *Views of the Lakes* (1789) includes a plate of Brathay Bridge seen from the same angle as Wilkinson's.

     turn to a Gate on the right hand . . . Rydale: this is a path under Loughrigg, dotted with houses occupied at various times by W's relatives and friends, including Fox How (Arnold), Fox Ghyll (De Quincey), Loughrigg Holme (Quillinan), and Stepping Stones (William Wordsworth, Jr, and his son Gordon Wordsworth).

111 *frequently*: following this sentence, MS Prose 25 offers a long passage
    describing Grasmere, Dunmail Raise, Wythburn, and Thirlmere, corres-
    ponding to Wilkinson's plates Nos. 16 and 17; W's text was left unfinished
    and not included in any version of his *Guide*. The passage is reproduced in
    a footnote at *PrW* ii. 271–3.

    descend into the Vale of Keswick while the sun-beams are upon it: see p. 21 for
    evening glory in the Vale of Keswick.

    We have now reached Keswick: the ensuing four paragraphs (pp. 111–16)
    correspond to *Guide*, pp. 12–13. *Select Views* devotes more paragraphs to
    the northern and western regions of the Lake District than the *Guide*.

    This concealed spot . . . mass of Skiddaw: see Figure 5.

112 *the whole splendour . . . Lakes and Mountains spread before your eyes*: from
    Applethwaite there are fine views of Derwentwater to the south
    (cf. Wilkinson's plate No. 22) and Bassenthwaite Lake to the west.

    From both these spots I have given Views: as can be seen in this example, the
    text for *Select Views* sometimes sounds as if the artist himself were writing
    his own commentary. These alterations were probably added by Wilkinson
    (*PrW* ii. 127).

    the single Cottages and clusters of Houses . . . like them: for simple, unobtru-
    sive cottages, see pp. 46–8.

113 *the noblest Yew-trees . . . a fourth a little detached*: see 'Yew-Trees', 13–18:
    'But worthier still of note | Are those fraternal Four of Borrowdale, |
    Joined in one solemn and capacious grove; | Huge trunks! —and each
    particular trunk a growth | Of intertwisted fibres serpentine | Up-coiling,
    and inveterately convolved . . .'. Although W did not include the poem in
    any edition of his *Guide* (1810–35), the poem was incorporated in Hudson's
    enlarged editions (1842–59) and became a stock quotation in guidebooks;
    see *PM (1837)*, *Black's* (1841), *Onwhyn's* (1841), Mackay (1846), *Sylvan's*
    (1847), Atkinson (1847), Jackson (1847), Mogridge (1849), J. M. Wilson
    (1859), *Murray's* (1866), Matthew (1866), Topham (1869), Payn (1870),
    Jenkinson (1872), Loftie (1875), and *Ward & Lock's* (1884). *Pearson's*
    (1902) remarks that the famous 'fraternal four' were severely damaged by
    a storm in December 1883. Three of them are still thriving.

115 *The Views which . . . on the right*: see Figure 6. Lingmoor should be
    Lingmell.

    This Valley has been described in the Introduction: for the corresponding
    passage in the *Guide*, see p. 19 ('Next, almost due west . . . the river Esk').

    This Water for the Lakes . . . many generations: Owen and Smyser surmise
    that this section might have been written by DW. She had used the image
    of a dove's neck in *Recollections of a Tour in Scotland* (1805), in describing
    the screes in the Pass of Branda (Moorman ii. 160).

116 *I cannot deny myself . . . spotless snow*: this passage was later incorporated in
    'Excursion to the top of Scawfell' in the 1835 *Guide* (p. 84).

    Stye-Head Tarn (for which see No. 43): see Figure 7.

It remains that we should speak of Ullswater: the ensuing five paragraphs describing the east part of the Lake District (pp. 116–20) are generally preserved in the *Guide* (pp. 14–17), with some insertions and omissions.

118 *the mind is overcome with a sensation . . . so fortunate*: omitted from the *Guide*.

119 *Lyulph's Tower and Gowbarrow Park*: see Figure 8.

This stream flows down Martindale . . . aboriginal herds: incorporated in the 1822 edition but deleted later; interspersed in 'Excursion on the Banks of Ulswater' in the *Guide* (pp. 90, 91).

120 *Hawes-water, which has furnished . . . an Etching*: cf. Wilkinson's plate No. 47.

I must now express my hope: the last paragraph was omitted from the later versions.

KENDAL AND WINDERMERE RAILWAY.

TWO LETTERS REPRINTED FROM THE *MORNING POST*

When the bill to approve the Lancaster and Carlisle Railway was passed in June 1844, it became evident that a branch line connecting Oxenholme, Kendal, and Windermere would be necessary. The new line was proposed in late August. On hearing about the project, Wordsworth immediately expressed his opposition in a sonnet, published in the *Morning Post* on 16 October 1844. Within six weeks the sonnet was reprinted nationwide in more than sixty newspapers, provoking vigorous controversy that included poetic ripostes. To defend himself, Wordsworth published two open letters and another sonnet in the *Morning Post* on 11 and 20 December 1844, all of which provoked further controversy. Wordsworth's campaign against the Kendal and Windermere Railway proved ineffectual, but he saw the matter in a longer perspective: in order to prepare for effective opposition to further railway projects, he decided to revise the two letters with some additional matter and publish them with the two sonnets as a pamphlet, which was issued in January/February 1845 in Kendal and then in London. Reproduced here is the final London version.

131 *so offensive . . . proprietors*: according to the *Kendal Mercury* (16 Nov. 1844), out of forty-four landowners, forty signed their names against the construction of the railway.

the terminus is . . . Bowness: the original plan was to bring the railway to the head of Windermere, near Ambleside, but engineering difficulties pushed back the terminus to the present Windermere station.

But as no guarantee . . . Grasmere: an extension of the railway to Ambleside, and onwards through Grasmere to Keswick, was repeatedly projected throughout the late nineteenth and early twentieth centuries. For more details, see Yoshikawa, *Wordsworth and Modern Travel*, ch. 2.

Summer TOURISTS . . . notion of a railway: Ian Ousby suggests that W 'meant that the railway excursionist went from A to B and back again on his return ticket, whereas the tourist made a tour or circuit' (*The Englishman's England*, p. 14).

131 *The staple of the district ... retirement*: see note to p. 137.

132 *easy access for all persons*: by the time W wrote this letter, Dec. 1844, the Lake District was almost surrounded by railways: in addition to the Lancaster and Carlisle Railway (with stations at Oxenholme and Penrith), the Maryport and Carlisle Railway, the Whitehaven and Furness Railway, the Furness Junction Railway, and the Cockermouth and Workington Railway were completed or under construction.

Elaborate gardens, with topiary works: see p. 50 ('specimens ... petty art') and note.

the relish for choice and picturesque ... recent origin: see note to p. 52 ('within the last sixty years').

the Sacra Telluris Theoria of the other Burnet: Thomas Burnet's *Telluris Theoria Sacra* (1681; in English translation, *The Theory of the Earth*, 1684) (*PrW* iii. 360).

133 *'Let us not speak ... pass on'*: from *Inferno*, iii. 51 (*PrW* iii. 360).

In my youth ... Keswick: in April 1794 W and DW lodged at Windy Brow at the base of Latrigg, a cottage belonging to William Calvert (*LEY* 113–17).

The first house that was built in the Lake district ... purchase: cf. pp. 30, 53–4, 107.

Rocks and mountains ... degree habitual: an article in *Land We Live In* (1847) rebukes this claim, arguing that 'we have a confiding belief that the second-class railway travellers, who purchase with hard earnings a long summer-day's holiday at Windermere, will bring to the "bright scene from Orrest-head" a reverential love which will be in perfect harmony with the "peace" that here reigns; for they will be the comparatively few in whom the great Poet himself has developed the taste for "rocks and mountains, torrents and wide-spread waters, and all those features of nature which go to the composition of such scenes as this part of England is distinguished for"' ('Windermere', *Land We Live In*, i. 66).

134 *If I had to do ... care of nature*: W worried what would happen to his garden after his death: 'will the old walls & steps remain in front of the house & about the grounds, or will they be swept away with all the beautiful mosses & Ferns & Wild Geraniums & other flowers which their rude construction suffered & encouraged to grow among them?' (*IF* 75). Cf. p. 48 ('These lanes, where ... stone-fern').

135 *He lived many years in Nithsdale ... that mountain*: cf. 'At the Grave of Burns', 39–42: 'Huge Criffel's hoary top ascends | By Skiddaw seen,— | Neighbours we were, and loving friends | We might have been'.

a lamentation from Burns ... of his country: see Burns's poems, 'To a Mountain Daisy' and 'Answer to Verses addressed to the Poet by the Guidwife of Wauchope-House', 21–4 ('The rough bur-thistle, spreading wide | Amang the bearded bear, | I turn'd the weeder-clips aside, | An' spar'd the symbol dear'). (*PrW* iii. 361)

a two hours' walk ... the beautiful country: W describes this walk in *Pr1850*, iv. 1–11. See note to p. 10 ('crossing the Lake by the Ferry').

Go to a pantomime ... noisy pleasure: a Manchester labourer protested to W: 'when there is some talk of our seeing these things which he has taught us to yearn for and to wish to understand, what does our Poet do, but turn us over for relaxation to "pantomime, farce, and puppet show"?' Announcing himself as a descendant of W's Peter Bell, he questions why 'the Manchester tradesman' should be incapable of appreciating the Lake Country while 'Poor Susan in Wood Street', London, can enjoy a reverie of the mountain scenery (*Kendal Mercury*, 8 Feb. 1845).

136 *'O, Nature ... hae charms!'*: Burns, 'To William Simpson', 79–80.

Would not this be pretty much like ... came from?: Baddeley (1880) would use a similar fable to emphasize the importance of preserving the Lake District: 'in encouraging the indiscriminate sacrifice of their beautiful country to enterprises which at the best only promise temporary gain, they may in the end discover that they have "killed the goose that laid golden eggs"' (pp. xvii–xviii). Cf. note to p. 62 ('a charge of inconsistency').

137 *gambling speculations*: the mid-1840s saw 'railway mania' in Britain. There were many satirical cartoons portraying 'widespread preoccupation with railway speculation' (Michael Freeman, *Railways and the Victorian Imagination*, 101). Although W had contemplated investment in the railways as early as 1825, here he condemns such financial speculation (Yoshikawa, *Wordsworth and Modern Travel*, p. 40). See lines 4–5 of the sonnet, 'Proud were ye, Mountains, when, in times of old' (p. 144).

the staple of the country: cf. the last paragraph of the first letter (p. 137). In the same vein Baddeley (1880) remarks that '[t]he well-being of a large proportion of [the Lake District's] inhabitants depends on its popularity as a tourist district', and emphasizes the importance of preserving as far as possible the natural beauty of the land (p. xvii).

unless there be reason ... the sacrifice: cf. p. 136 ('if the unavoidable consequence ... search of?'). W was not completely opposed to the railways. He argued that it was necessary to strike a balance between convenience and the environmental cost of bringing railways to the Lake District.

138 *Turn we to survey ... rage disarm*: from Goldsmith, *The Traveller*, lines 165–76.

they illustrate their position ... hither?: recommendations for free admission to the British Museum were made by a Select Committee of the House of Commons, 1835–6. The National Gallery, founded by W's friend Sir George Beaumont, was opened to the public in April 1838 (*PrW* iii. 363).

139 *among the affluent and benevolent ... Windermere*: by the mid-nineteenth century, numerous excursion trains to Windermere were arranged by 'benevolent employers', railway companies, and voluntary societies such

as Sunday schools, temperance organizations, and philanthropic bodies. Each of these trains could transport as many as 4,000 passengers at once. Susan Major, *Early Victorian Railway Excursions: The Million Go Forth* (Pen & Sword Books, 2015), pp. 14–49.

139   *a Ten Hours' Bill . . . wages*: agitation for a Ten Hours' Bill began in 1830 and continued through the 1840s. W supported it for humanitarian reasons (*PrW* iii. 363).

140   '*—Vane could . . . a king*': Samuel Johnson, *The Vanity of Human Wishes*, lines 321–2.

a gallant officer now serving on the coast of South America: Sir Thomas S. Pasley, distinguished naval officer, who built a house at Bowness (*PrW* iii. 364).

the fear before me of the line . . . the district: see note to p. 131 ('But as no guarantee . . .').

141   '*Utilitarianism*' *. . . gambling speculations*: see note to p. 137 ('gambling speculations').

Upon good authority . . . deviation might be made: although Furness Abbey was spared, the railway was built very close to it and a station and hotel were built in the grounds. Visiting here, in June 1845, while the railway was under construction, MW felt it painful to see 'the Old Abbey occupied by the "Navys" at their meal, who [were] carrying a rail-way, so near to the East window that from it Persons might shake hands with the Passengers!!' (*LLY* iv. 679).

'*No flaring gentleman's-house . . . peace,*' *&c. &c.*: Gray's words are quoted in full at p. 52.

142   *they do not fly fast enough . . . come to see*: cf. 'The Brothers', 1–4: 'These Tourists, Heaven preserve us! needs must live | A profitable life: some glance along, | Rapid and gay, as if the earth were air, | And they were butterflies to wheel about'.

before the new road . . . constructed: W refers to the new section of road between White Moss and Grasmere, opened in 1826 (*Westmorland Gazette*, 4 Feb. 1826). See note to p. 11 ('the high road'). In his note to 'A narrow girdle of rough stones and crags', W mentions that '[t]he character of the eastern shore of Grasmere Lake is quite changed since these verses were written, by the public road being carried along its side' (*IF* 18–19).

Quanto . . . Herba: quoted from Juvenal, *Satires*, iii. 18–20. Francis Hodgson's 1807 translation runs: 'how much more honour'd had the goddess been, | Were the clear fountain edg'd with living green'.

the new military road: constructed by Napoleon, 1801–5 (*PrW* iii. 365).

Brook and road . . . without end. 1799: 'The Simplon Pass', corresponding to *Pr1850*, vi. 621–40.

Thirty years . . . same Pass: W crossed the Simplon Pass in 1790 with Robert Jones and in 1820 with DW and MW. See *Journals* ii. 255–63; *LEY* 33–4; *LMY* ii. 640.

143 *instead of travellers ... or fast asleep*: for W's criticism of tourists who do not
see or feel, see 'On Seeing Some Tourists of the Lakes Pass by Reading',
and the opening lines of 'The Brothers'.

Similar remarks . . . Wales: visiting Wales in 1829, W was impressed by
Thomas Telford's Menai Suspension Bridge, recently built for the main
road through North Wales to Holyhead (*PrW* iii. 366). See also *LLY* ii. 115.

STEAMBOATS AND RAILWAYS *...sublime*: on his Scottish tour, in July 1833,
W took a steamboat from Whitehaven; and later that summer he visited
the Eden Valley, where he saw the Wetheral and Corby Viaducts nearing
completion for the Newcastle and Carlisle Railway, then under construc-
tion. The sonnet was inspired by these experiences (*LLY* ii. 629–30, 635;
Barker 649, 652).

144 *an eye to perceive ... worthily enjoy*: cf. the closing remark of 'Description
of the Scenery of the Lakes' (p. 68).

GLOSSARY OF SELECTED PERSONS
AND PLACES

Entries in this glossary retain Wordsworth's spellings in the *Guide*. Modern spellings are also given. The page references are given in parentheses.

Applethwaite (pp. 12, 111): a hamlet to the north of Keswick, under Skiddaw. In 1803 Sir George Beaumont presented W with a plot of land here hoping that he would be able to live near STC at Greta Hall (*CMY* 218, 220). W expressed his gratitude in 'At Applethwaite, near Keswick'. Although W never lived here his descendants built a small house, the Ghyll, on the plot in the late nineteenth century.

Ara-force (pp. 14, 15, 116, 117): Aira Force is a series of waterfalls on Aira Beck along the western edge of Gowbarrow Park, flowing down to Ullswater; a popular tourist site since the late eighteenth century, the setting of W's 'The Somnambulist' and 'Airey-force Valley'. The latter was reproduced in full in J. M. Wilson (1859), while from the former some stanzas were extracted in numerous guidebooks, including *Black's* (1841), Mackay (1846), *Sylvan's* (1847), Blanchard (1852), J. M. Wilson (1859), *Murray's* (1866), Matthew (1866), Jenkinson (1872), Jennings (1878), Lydon (1880), *Ward & Lock's* (1884), and Bradley (1901). The first stanza was particularly popular: 'List, ye who pass by Lyulph's Tower | At eve; how softly then | Doth Aira-force, that torrent hoarse, | Speak from the woody glen! | Fit music for a solemn vale! . . .'.

Armathwaite (pp. 12, 113): the site of Thomas West's viewing station to the north of Bassenthwaite Lake. W and DW paid several visits to the Speddings (the family of John Spedding, W's Hawkshead schoolfellow) at Armathwaite Hall (*LEY* 115–16).

Ashness (p. 12): a fell to the east of Derwentwater. From Ashness Bridge there are impressive views of Derwentwater and Bassenthwaite Lake, praised by many artists and writers including Farington, Westall, and Southey.

Aysgarth-force (p. 4): a waterfall in Wensleydale; at Aysgarth the River Ure descends a series of limestone terraces, making a triple waterfall, visited by W, with DW in 1799 and with DW and MW in 1802. '[A]t once formal and wild', W describes the falls to STC, 'such a performance as you might have expected from some giant gardiner employed by one of Queen Elizabeth's Courtiers, if this same giant gardiner had consulted with Spenser and they two had finish'd the work together' (*LEY* 277–8).

Black Comb (pp. **9, 83**): Black Combe, a fell in the south-west Lake District, which gives 'the amplest range | Of unobstructed prospect . . . | That British ground commands', as W says in 'View from the Top of Black Comb' (1815), 3–5. This poem was quoted in *Saturday Magazine* (1837), J. M. Wilson (1859), and *Murray's* (1866). Cf. 'Epistle', 5–9: 'huge Black Comb | Frowns deepening visibly his native gloom, . . . | In his own storms he hides himself from sight'.

Blea Tarn (pp. **8, 110**): a tarn located between Great and Little Langdale. Martineau (1855) introduces the place as the scene relating to the Solitary of *Ex*, pointing to the single house, the tarn, and 'the stone, "like a ship, with keel upturned," which is lodged in a stream near to the tarn' (p. 148). The ship-like stone is still visible.

Brougham Hall (p. **17**): a mansion beside the River Lowther, rebuilt from a pele tower in the early nineteenth century for Henry Brougham, Lord Chancellor (Lindop 112). To the north, where the Lowther joins the River Eamont, is Brougham Castle. For W's recollections of early visits in this neighbourhood, see *Pr1805*, vi. 218–32: 'The gentle banks | Of Eamont, hitherto unnamed in song, | And that monastic castle, on a flat, | Low-standing by the margin of the stream, . . . | Have seen us sit in many a summer hour, | My sister and myself, when, having climbed | In danger through some window's open space, | We looked abroad, or on the turret's head | Lay listening to the wild-flowers and the grass | As they gave out their whispers to the wind'.

Broughton (pp. **10, 105**): Broughton-in-Furness, a small town on the Duddon Estuary. In his youth W often stayed here with his cousin Mary Wordsworth Smith and her husband John, whence he explored the Duddon Valley (*IF* 31, 135).

Brown (pp. **38, 52, 111**): John Brown (1715–66), essayist, playwright, and poet. His ode was first published in Richard Cumberland, *Odes* (1776), and reproduced in full in West's guide (1780 and onwards).

Buchanan (p. **36**): George Buchanan (1506–82), Scottish humanist and reformer. For the relevant lines of the ode, see EdS 181.

Burnet, Bishop (p. **132**): Gilbert Burnet (1643–1715), Bishop of Salisbury and historian (*PrW* iii. 359).

Butterlip How (p. **11**): an eminence at the north edge of Grasmere village; 'one of the most exquisite elevations of moderate height in Grasmere', according to Green (1819). Now covered with trees, the views recommended by W can no longer be seen.

Calder Abbey (pp. **13, 41, 115**): a monastery founded in the twelfth century in West Cumbria, for a colony of monks from Furness Abbey.

Chapel-Holm (p. **30**): an island on Windermere, usually called Lady Holm, formerly the site of a chapel. The medieval shrine is noted in *Pr1850*,

ii. 62–5: 'And now a third small Island, where survived | In solitude the ruins of a shrine | Once to Our Lady dedicate, and served | Daily with chaunted rites'.

Cockermouth (p. 112): a market town in the North Lakes; W's birthplace, April 1770.

Cockermouth Castle (pp. 20, 113): a medieval castle dating from *c.*1220, 'a shattered monument | Of feudal sway', whose towers cast their shadows on the 'smooth breast' of the River Derwent (*Pr1850*, i. 283–5). 'Address from the Spirit of Cockermouth Castle' recounts how the 'soul-appalling darkness' of the castle's dungeon made W's 'young thoughts acquainted with the grave' (6–10). These lines are quoted in J. M. Wilson (1859). Part of the castle is still inhabited.

Conishead Priory (p. 5): originally a twelfth-century Augustinian priory, south of Ulverston, it is now a Buddhist temple.

Curwen (pp. 106, 133): John Christian Curwen (1756–1828), MP and agriculturalist, enthusiastic about commercial forestry, especially larch plantations (Mason, 'Larches'). Born John Christian, he took his wife's surname on his marriage to his cousin, Isabella Curwen of Workington Hall, in 1782.

Curwen (pp. 6, 54): Henry Curwen (1783–1861), son of John Christian Curwen. He inherited Workington Hall, where the Wordsworth family were frequent guests, especially after his daughter Isabella married John Wordsworth, the poet's son, in 1830 (Mason, 'Larches').

Dacre Castle (pp. 15, 117): a mid-fourteenth-century castle, 4 miles south-west of Penrith, built for protection from the Scots (Lindop 112).

Devockwater (p. 30): Devoke Water, the largest tarn in England, on Birker Fell between Eskdale and the Duddon Valley.

Duddon Valley (pp. 9, 10, 19, 25, 84, 104–5): a valley in south Cumbria, the setting for W's 'River Duddon' sonnet sequence.

Dungeon-Ghyll Force, Dungeon Gill Force (pp. 8, 110): a waterfall in Langdale, the setting of W's 'The Idle Shepherd-Boys' and a popular location for Victorian tourists.

Easedale (pp. 11, 24): situated north-west of Grasmere village, Easedale was a favourite haunt of W, DW, STC, and De Quincey. W claimed to have written 'thousands of verses' by the river that flows out of Easedale Tarn, including 'It was an April Morning: fresh and clear', evoking a walk up to Easedale Tarn (McCracken 107–8). Easedale was so popular with Victorian tourists that there was a tea house by the tarn.

Eden, the River (pp. 6, 40): a river flowing along the western edge of the Pennines into the Solway Firth. W made an excursion with MW along the River Eden, Aug. 1833, and marked the occasion in a sonnet, 'The River Eden, Cumberland': 'Eden! till now thy beauty had I viewed | By glimpses only . . .' (1–2). From the sonnet a few lines are quoted in *Black's* (1846) and J. M. Wilson (1859).

Ennerdale (pp. **13, 20, 30, 84, 114**): a valley in the west of the Lake District; the setting for W's poem 'The Brothers', widely quoted in guidebooks, including Fielding (1821), *Black's* (1841), *Onwhyn's* (1841), *Sylvan* (1847), Atkinson (1847), J. M. Wilson (1859), Waugh (1861), *Murray's* (1866), E. L. Linton (1864), Topham (1869), Jenkinson (1872), *Shaw's* (1873), *Ward & Lock's* (1884), and Brabant (1902). Hudson (1853, 1859) extracted lines 359–63, depicting 'Pillar', a fell that 'rises like a column from the vale'. The opening lines portraying hasty tourists (1–10) and those describing the churchyard (12–15) were also much quoted.

Evelyn (p. **132**): John Evelyn (1620–1706), diarist and writer.

Farish (p. **9**): Charles Farish (1766–1824), Fellow of Queens' College, Cambridge, had been W's schoolfellow at Hawkshead (EdS 170).

Fox How (p. **10**): holiday home of Thomas Arnold, headmaster of Rugby School, built in 1833–4 on the lane under Loughrigg between Ambleside and Rydal. W advised on the shape and colour of the chimneys (Rawnsley, 'Reminiscences', p. 93). For W's favourite chimneys, see p. 47.

Fountain's Abbey (p. **4**): a ruined Cistercian monastery dating from 1132, 'Fountains Abbey, glorious in decay' (*The Tuft of Primroses*, 493), was as now a popular tourist site in North Yorkshire.

Frier's Crag (p. **12**): Friar's Crag. On this promontory is a memorial to John Ruskin, who praised the view as 'one of the three most beautiful scenes in Europe' (Lindop 151).

Furness Abbey (pp. **5, 41, 104, 141**): a ruined Cistercian monastery in south Cumbria dating from *c.*1123. W recalls a childhood visit there in *Pr*1850, ii. 94–137. From this passage, *Ward & Lock's* (1884) quotes these lines: 'a circuit made | In wantonness of heart, through rough and smooth | We scampered homewards' (129–31). In 1845–6 the Furness Railway between Dalton and Barrow was built close to the abbey. Lamenting this, W wrote two sonnets titled: 'At Furness Abbey'. These poems were inserted in Mackay (1846), *Sylvan's* (1847), *Murray's* (1866), and Jennings (1878).

Giggleswick Scar (p. **5**): a series of limestone cliffs along the road from Settle to Ingleton. The 'ebbing and flowing well' under the scar, seemingly caused by an underground siphon, was often mentioned by travel writers.

Gowbarrow Park (pp. **14, 15, 78, 93, 94, 116, 117**): an ancient deer park to the north of Ullswater, this is the setting of W's most famous poem,

'I wandered lonely as a cloud', quoted in J. M. Wilson (1859) for the first time, followed by Jenkinson (1872), *Ward & Lock's* (1884), and Palmer (1930).

Grasmire (p. 84): Grasmoor, a mountain overlooking Crummock Water in the north-west of the Lake District.

Grathwaite (p. 6): Graythwaite Hall, the seat of the Sandys family, to the west of Windermere. The woods stretching from here towards Esthwaite Water were the site of W's poem 'Nutting' (*IF* 13). Edwin Sandys (1519?–1588), archbishop of York, was the founder of Hawkshead Grammar School (*DNB*).

Great Gavel (pp. **19, 20, 21, 83, 84, 85, 115–16**): Great Gable, along with Scafell and Scafell Pike, located in the Central Lake District. On its summit is a war memorial for those members of the Fell & Rock Climbing Club who died in the First World War.

Grisdale (pp. **16, 92, 118**): Grisedale, a valley extending south-westward from the southern end of Ullswater. W and DW parted with their brother John here, 29 Sept. 1800; having stayed at Dove Cottage for eight months, he returned to command *The Earl of Abergavenny* and drowned when it was wrecked in Weymouth Bay, 5 Feb. 1805. See 'Elegiac Verses': 'if verse of mine | Have power to make thy virtues known, | Here let a monumental Stone | Stand—sacred as a Shrine; | And to the few who pass this way, | Traveller or Shepherd, let it say, | Long as these mighty rocks endure, | Oh do not Thou too fondly brood, | Although deserving of all good, | On any earthly hope, however pure' (61–70). Responding to these lines, Rawnsley erected a memorial stone near Grisedale Tarn in 1882 (Lindop 82).

Hardknot(t) and Wrynose Passes (pp. **10, 13**): a route used since Roman times to connect Ravenglass and Ambleside via Langdale.

Hardraw Scar and Waterfall (p. **4**): claimed to be England's highest unbroken waterfall, near Hawes in Wensleydale, North Yorkshire. W and DW saw the waterfall on their 1799 journey through Wensleydale; W described the scene in great detail in his letter to STC, Dec. 1799 (*LEY* 279–80). Later W saw Turner's drawing, 'Hardraw Scar', in Thomas D. Whitaker's *History of Richmondshire* (1823).

Hartsop Hall (pp. **16, 88, 118**): a fifteenth-century house at the head of Patterdale, commanding Kirkstone Pass.

Hasell (p. **90**): Edward Hasell (1765–1825), squire of Dalemain, possessed the Martindale chase and was famous for his annual Martindale hunts (*PrW* ii. 427).

Hawkshead (pp. **5, 10, 106**): an old market town in the south central Lake District. Hudson (1842) introduces the Grammar School, founded by Edwin Sandys in 1585, as the school where W was educated (1779–87), commenting that 'Some years ago this school was filled with pupils not only from the neighbourhood but from the surrounding counties, numbering at one period about 120' (p. 22). One year earlier, *Black's* (1841) had mentioned W's association with Hawkshead, quoting from 'There was a Boy' ('The grassy churchyard hangs | Upon a slope above the village school') and *Excursion* (1827), i. 55–6 ('The antique market village, where were passed | My school-days'). *Ward & Lock's* (1884) describes the village thus: 'here our Lake poet was educated, and in his "Prelude" he tells us how, when very young, he loved the contemplation of Nature—"even then | I held unconscious intercourse with beauty | Old as creation" ', quoting from *Pr1850*, i. 561–3.

Helvellyn (pp. 11, 15–16, 20, 77, 83, 85, 86–7, 94, 115, 117–18): the third highest peak (3,117 feet/950 metres) in the Lake District, several miles to the north of Grasmere. Climbed by W and featured in several of his poems, including *Pr1805*, viii. 1–15, 228–44; 'Fidelity', 'Elegiac Verses', 'Musings near Aquapendente', 'To Joanna', and 'To——, on Her first Ascent to the Summit of Helvellyn'.

Hutton John (pp. 15, 117): a medieval pele-tower dating from the fourteenth century with many later additions up to 1860, situated 6 miles west of Penrith (Lindop 113). W transferred a tradition pertaining to the place to Egremont in west Cumberland when he wrote 'The Horn of Egremont Castle' (*IF* 15).

Ivy Cottage (p. 11): a cottage under Rydal Mount; the first wife of Edward Quillinan (Dora Wordsworth's husband) died here. As Hudson (1842) comments, it was renamed Glen Rothay and is now a hotel.

Kilchurn Castle (p. 57): built in the mid-fifteenth century on the shore of Loch Awe in western Scotland, Kilchurn Castle was a ruin when W visited in summer 1803.

Kirkstall Abbey (p. 4): a ruined Cistercian abbey north-west of Leeds dating from *c.*1152, visited by W and DW, July 1807. Comparing the abbeys at Kirkstall and Bolton, DW thought the former more impressive, while the latter had a beautiful natural setting (*LMY* i. 158).

Langdale Pikes (pp. 8, 10, 11, 31, 83, 110): these two fells with conspicuous twin peaks, or 'lofty Brethren', are powerfully described in *Ex*, ii. 721–49 with dramatic changes of the sky; the verse passage was a popular quote in Victorian guidebooks, including Rose (1832), Ford (1839), *Onwhyn's* (1841), *Murray's* (1866), Loftie (1875), and Collingwood (1902).

Latrigg (p. 12): a low summit adjacent to Skiddaw, West's seventh viewing station for Derwentwater. In a note to 'To the River Greta, near Keswick' W remarks: ' "The scenery upon this river," says Mr Southey in his *Colloquies*, "where it passes under the woody side of Latrigg, is of the finest and most remarkable kind" ' (*PW* iv. 400).

Lodore Falls (pp. **12, 112**): waterfalls above the south-east shore of Derwentwater, downstream from Watendlath. Following West's guide, in the late eighteenth and early nineteenth centuries Lodore was often compared to Niagara Falls. Southey's poem 'The cataract of Lodore' (1823) was a popular quote; see Mackay (1846), *Sylvan's* (1847), J. M. Wilson (1859), Jenkinson (1872), and Hudson (1842–59). W mentions 'the cataract of Lodore peal[ing] to [the hermit's] orisons' in 'Inscription for the Spot where the Hermitage stood on St Herbert's Island, Derwentwater', 13–14.

Lorton (pp. **13, 20, 112, 113**): a valley extending southwards from Cockermouth to Crummock Water and Buttermere. W's 'Yew-Trees' praises the yew-tree of Lorton Vale, along with the Borrowdale yews (see note to p. 113). The lines describing the Lorton yew also became a stock quotation in nineteenth-century guidebooks, including *PM (1837)* and Hudson (1842–59): 'There is a Yew-tree, pride of Lorton Vale, | Which to this day stands single, in the midst | Of its own darkness, as it stood of yore, | . . . | This solitary Tree! —a living thing | Produced too slowly ever to decay; | Of form and aspect too magnificent | To be destroyed' (1–13). This Yew was severely damaged by a storm in 1883 but survives to the present, beside Whit Beck at High Lorton.

Loughrigg Tarn (pp. **7, 10, 31, 109, 110**): a tarn to the west of Loughrigg Fell. Cf. 'Epistle', 165–70: 'Diana's Looking-glass! | To Loughrigg-tarn, round clear and bright as heaven, | Such name Italian fancy would have given, | Ere on its banks the few grey cabins rose | That yet disturb not its concealed repose | More than the feeblest wind that idly blows'. In his note to the poem W explains that Loughrigg Tarn 'resembles, though much smaller in compass, the Lake Nemi, or *Speculum Dianæ* as it is often called, not only in its clear waters and circular form, and the beauty immediately surrounding it, but also as being overlooked by the eminence of Langdale Pikes as Lake Nemi is by that of Monte Calvo' (*PW* iv. 151). This note is incorporated in Hudson (1853, 1859).

Lowther Castle (pp. **17, 120**): the seat of the Lowther family, the Earls of Lonsdale, located to the south of Penrith. W's father was the land agent for James Lowther, 1st Earl of Lonsdale. In the time of the Earl's son, W visited here frequently (Lindop 275–6) and dedicated a sonnet to the castle: 'Lowther! in thy majestic Pile are seen | Cathedral pomp and grace, in apt accord | With the baronial castle's sterner mien' (1–3). The sonnet was quoted in *Black's* (1841), Hudson (1842–59), and J. M. Wilson (1859).

Lowther, the River (p. **17**): a small river to the east of the Lake District. In the dedicatory sonnet for *Ex*, W describes how he 'roamed, on youthful pleasures bent; | And mused in rocky cell or sylvan tent, | Beside swift-flowing Lowther's current clear' ('To the Right Honorable William, Earl of Lonsdale', 2–4).

Low-wood Inn (pp. **7, 108**): on their 'first visit together' to the Lake District, Apr. 1794, W and DW walked from Kendal to Keswick via Grasmere and stopped near Low-wood Inn, on the north-east shore of Lake Windermere. W wrote a sonnet 'There is a little unpretending rill' to commemorate this walk (*IF* 19, 118).

Lucerne (p. **18**): a city in central Switzerland. W visited here on his Continental tours, 1790 and 1820 (*LEY* 34–5, *LMY* ii. 640).

Lyulph's Tower (pp. **17, 79–80, 119**): a gothic hunting-lodge and viewpoint, built in the late eighteenth century for the Duke of Norfolk on the western shore of Ullswater, near Aira Force. The tower and its fabled owner feature in Scott's *The Bridal of Triermain*, 1805 (Lindop 267). W's 'The Somnambulist' is based on a young woman living in the Tower, who was in the habit of sleepwalking (*IF* 55).

Mudge (p. **9**): Colonel William Mudge (1762–1820), artillery officer, distinguished mathematician and surveyor, portrayed in 'Written with a Slate-pencil, on a Stone, on the Side of the Mountain of Black Comb': 'on the summit whither thou art bound, | A geographic Labourer pitched his tent, | With books supplied and instruments of art, | To measure height and distance; lonely task, | Week after week pursued!' (13–17).

Muncaster Castle (p. **19**): a red sandstone castle on a spur in the Esk estuary, west Cumbria, belonging to the Pennington family. Originally an early thirteenth-century pele tower, it was enlarged over more than six centuries (Lindop 212).

Nunnery (p. **6**): W was acquainted with the 'Nunnery Walk', a landscaped promenade along the Rivers Eden and Croglin, when as a boy he spent summer holidays in Penrith (*IF* 54). See his sonnet 'Nunnery': 'Down from the Pennine Alps how fiercely sweeps | Croglin, the stately Eden's tributary! | . . . | What change shall happen next to Nunnery Dell? | Canal, and Viaduct, and Railway, tell!' (2–3, 13–14). Once a popular site for walking, the 'Nunnery Walk' is no longer open to the public.

Ormathwaite (p. **12**): a hamlet to the north of Keswick, under Skiddaw. The artist Joseph Wilkinson lived at Ormathwaite from 1794 to 1804 (*PrW* ii. 385).

Orrest-head (pp. **106, 130**): a hill to the east of Windermere, overlooking the Kendal and Windermere Railway line and the station at Birthwaite (the present Windermere station).

Ouze Bridge (p. **113**): Ouse Bridge, over the River Derwent at the foot of Bassenthwaite Lake. Gray visited here in 1769 to take a view of the lake.

Penrith (pp. 4, 6, 14, 92, 104, 116): a market town north-east of the Lake District. W spent time here as a child at his maternal grandparents' home. The 'melancholy beacon' on 'the lonely eminence' (see *Pr1805*, xi. 278–315) stands on the hill overlooking Penrith. W revisited the scene with DW and future wife MW in 1787 or 1788 (see *CEY* 72; *Pr1805*, vi. 242–5; xi. 315–25).

Preston (p. 5): Long Preston, a village in Ribblesdale, North Yorkshire, just south of Settle.

Ray (p. 132): John Ray (1627–1705), naturalist and botanist (*PrW* iii. 359).

Rydal Mount (p. 11): W's home, 1813–50. Hudson (1842) refers to the house as 'Rydal Mount (Wm. Wordsworth, Esq.)'. After Horne (1816) introduced it as 'the residence of the admired author of The Excursion', Rydal Mount became a key tourist attraction. Hudson (1853), published after W's death, gives a detailed description of its gardens, extracting from *Memoirs* by the poet's nephew Christopher Wordsworth, including several poetic quotations.

Rydal Park (pp. 11, 109): a park belonging to the Fleming family, who also owned Rydal Mount.

Rydal(e) Waterfalls (pp. 10, 109): the Higher and Lower Falls at Rydal are located in the grounds of Rydal Hall, ancestral home of the Fleming family. Adjacent to the Lower Fall is a small viewing house or 'Grotto', built in 1669. As Gilpin (1786) describes, tourists in search of the picturesque enjoyed a view of the Lower Fall 'appearing through the window like a picture in a frame'. It became a popular subject for painters, such as George Barrett, Joseph Farington, George Pickering, Francis Towne, William Green, William Banks, and A. F. Lydon. Many writers, including William Mason, Joseph Budworth, and Elizabeth Lynn Linton, left descriptions of it (Lindop 38–9). Here is W's description in *An Evening Walk* (1836): 'a small cascade, | Illumes with sparkling foam the impervious shade; | Beyond, along the vista of the brook, | Where antique roots its bustling course o'erlook, | The eye reposes on a secret bridge | Half grey, half shagged with ivy to its ridge' (63–8). This verse passage (with slight variations) was a familiar quote in Victorian guidebooks, including various versions of *Black's*, Atkinson (1847), Mogridge (1849), Hudson (1853, 1859), and Lydon (1880).

St. Herbert's Island (pp. 30, 53): an island on Derwentwater; named after St Herbert who lived here as a hermit. He was a friend of St Cuthbert of Lindisfarne and the two are said to have died on the same day in 688 (Lindop 149). W wrote 'Inscription for the Spot where the Hermitage Stood on St. Herbert's Island, Derwent-water' in praise of their friendship: 'Though here the Hermit number'd his last day | Far from

St. Cuthbert his beloved friend, | Those holy men both died in the same hour' (19–21). This poem was popular, quoted in Robinson (1819, 1833), *Black's* (1841), Jackson (1847), Hudson (1853, 1859), J. M. Wilson (1859), *Murray's* (1866), Jenkinson (1872), Payn (1870), and Loftie (1875).

Scale Hill (pp. 12, 13, 113, 114): an eminence at the north end of Crummock Water, planted with trees by W's acquaintance John Marshall.

Scaw-fell, Scawfell Head (pp. 19, 20, 21, 83–6): Scafell, the second-highest mountain (3,162 feet/964 metres) in England, is situated at the head of Borrowdale. STC found a 'nice Stone Table' on Scafell summit, 5 Aug. 1802, on which he wrote to Sara Hutchinson 'surely the first Letter ever written from the Top of Sca' Fell' (*CL* ii. 840).

Scawfell-Pike (pp. 84–5): Scafell Pike, formerly called 'The Pikes', is the highest summit in England (3,210 feet/978 metres) and is divided from Scafell by Mickledore Ridge (*PrW* ii. 424).

Skiddaw (pp. 12, 72, 83, 85, 111, 112, 113, 115, 135): a mountain lying north-west of Keswick. Cf. 'Pelion and Ossa', 10–12: 'What was the great Parnassus' self to thee, | Mount Skiddaw! in his natural sovereignty | Our British hill is fairer far'. The sonnet is quoted in Robinson (1819, 1833), Fielding (1821), Rose (1832), *Black's* (1841), *Sylvan's* (1847), J. M. Wilson (1859), Topham (1869), Jenkinson (1872), and Collingwood (1902).

Stockgill-force (pp. 10, 109): Stockghyll-force, a waterfall situated a little to the east of Ambleside. Consisting of four falls, 70 feet (21 metres) in height, it was a popular site for Victorian tourists. Keats visited here in June 1818.

Storr's Hall (p. 6): Storrs Hall, a mansion house built on the east shore of Windermere by Yorkshire landowner Sir John Legard in the mid-1790s, then purchased and remodelled by John Bolton of Liverpool, 1808–9. W, Walter Scott, Southey, and John Wilson were visitors during the Regatta of August 1824, 'one of the most splendid regattas that ever enlivened Windermere' ('The Life of Sir Walter Scott', quoted in *Black's*, 1841).

Styebarrow Crag (pp. 15, 19, 94, 117): a precipitous cliff adjacent to the Glenridding road on the south-west shore of Ullswater; the 'huge cliff' that suddenly 'upreared its head' and 'strode after' the boy in the boat-stealing episode (*Pr1805*, i. 372–426) is identified by Lindop with this crag (pp. 261–2). Baines (1830) records a similar experience: 'whilst [the boatman] directed us all to keep our eyes on the crag, we shot out towards the middle of the lake. The effect was magical. The naked peak of a mountain, before concealed, seemed to rise up swiftly out of the woody eminence from which we were receding' (p. 194). Compare this passage with *Pr1805*, i. 405–12.

Thirlmere, Wyth(e)burn(e) Lake (pp. 11, 12, 111): the present Thirlmere is a reservoir, completed in 1894 for supplying water to Manchester. The original lake was shaped like an hourglass and could be crossed at the narrowest point by bridges (Lindop 90–1).

Tickel (p. 38): Thomas Tickell (1685–1740), poet, born at Bridekirk, two miles north-west of Cockermouth (*PrW* ii. 401).

Ulpha Kirk (pp. 9, 10, 105): St John's Church at Ulpha in the Duddon Valley. Cf. 'The Kirk of Ulpha to the Pilgrim's eye | Is welcome as a Star, that doth present | Its shining forehead through the peaceful rent | Of a dark cloud' (*The River Duddon*, XXX, 1–4). These lines were a popular quote in Victorian guidebooks, including Thorne (1844), Mackay (1846), *Sylvan's* (1847), J. M. Wilson (1859), E. L. Linton (1864), *Murray's* (1866), *Ward & Lock's* (1884), and *Pearson's* (1902).

Urswick (p. 5): W seems to refer to Great Urswick Hillfort, an iron-age fort, located to the south of Ulverston. Known also as Skelmore Heads, from this low flat-topped hill there are extensive views in all directions.

Watenlath (pp. 12, 112): Watendlath, a long valley high above the east shore of Derwentwater. At its head is a hamlet and a tarn of the same name, from which Watendlath Beck flows down to Lodore Falls.

Weathercote Cave (p. 5): a cave at Chapel-le-Dale, popularized by John Hutton's 'A Tour to the Caves in the West-Riding of Yorkshire' (1781; included also in West's *Guide to the Lakes*, 2nd edn, 1780). Weathercote Cave was a popular subject for painters, including Westall and Turner. See W's sonnet, 'Pure element of waters! wheresoe'er'. Now overgrown, with collapsing slippery stone steps, it is difficult to access.

Wilson, Professor (p. 140): poet, critic, and writer, John Wilson (1785–1854) wrote many articles on the Lake District using the pen-name Christopher North. He bought the Elleray property on the western slope of Orrest Head and built a house that attracted literary tourists in the Victorian era. If the Kendal and Windermere Railway had been extended to Ambleside it would have gone through Wilson's property.

Wythburn Chapel (p. 11): a simple rectangular church dating from at least the sixteenth century, situated on the south-east shore of Thirlmere. Cf. *Waggoner*, ii. 276–7: 'Wytheburn's modest House of Prayer, | As lowly as the lowliest Dwelling'. These lines were referenced in E. L. Linton (1864), Jenkinson (1872), *Ward & Lock's* (1884), and Brabant (1902). W's friend Joseph Sympson was vicar here, the model for the priest in *Ex*, vii. 39–310 (*IF* 87–8, 191). Wythburn village, at the south of the lake, was submerged when Thirlmere reservoir was constructed (Lindop 92).

Yewdale and Tilberthwaite (pp. 9, 105): valleys lying to the north of Coniston. Cf. 'Epistle', 225–8: 'Descend and reach, in Yewdale's depths, a plain | With haycocks studded, striped with yellowing grain— | An area level as a Lake and spread | Under a rock too steep for man to tread'. W's 'Unpublished Tour' gives several pages to these vales (*PrW* ii. 310–21).

INDEX

People